SRA

A

Connecting Math Concepts

SRA

Columbus, Ohio

The **McGraw·Hill** Companies

Acknowledgments

The authors are grateful to the following people for their input in the field-testing and preparation of *Connecting Math Concepts, Level A:*

Linda Achterhof
Jill Andrews
Karen Davis
Jane Dougall
Frank Falco
Susie Hanner
Debbi Kleppen
Amy Patrice Lindquist
Lori McGinty
Mary Rosenbaum
Vicky Santos
Nancy Stuckey
Linda Van Hook
Mary Webster
Roberta Weisberg
Tina Wells
Bryan Wickman

www.sra4kids.com

SRA
McGraw-Hill

Send all inquiries to:
The McGraw-Hill Learning Group
4400 Easton Commons, 2nd Floor
Columbus, OH 43219

Printed in the United States of America.

ISBN 0-02-684683-7

6 7 8 9 10 11 12 12 11 10 09 08

Contents

Program Summary

Facts about *Connecting Math Concepts, Level A*

Children who are appropriately placed in Level A	Children who can count to 10 and count 9 objects
Placement criteria	Pass qualifying items (1 & 2) on placement test (See page 10)
Format of lessons	Scripted presentations for all activities Program designed for presentation to entire class
Number of lessons	120 total (plus 12 test lessons)
Options for using Level A	For lower performers: lessons 1–120 For high performers: lessons 11–120
Scheduled time for math periods	20–35 minutes per period for teacher–directed activities Additional 10–20 minutes for independent work
Weekly schedule	5 periods per week
Teacher's material	*Teacher's Guide* *Presentation Book 1* (lessons 1–Test 6) *Presentation Book 2* (lessons 61–end of program) *Answer Key*
Children's material	Program material: *Workbook 1* (lessons 1–Test 6) *Workbook 2* (lessons 61–end of program) Additional materials: ruler dice counters pennies scissors
In-program tests	Test lessons 1–12 Following every 10th regular Lesson (10, 20, 30, etc.)
Remedies	Specified in each Test Lesson script

Scope and Sequence for

Connecting Math Concepts, Level A

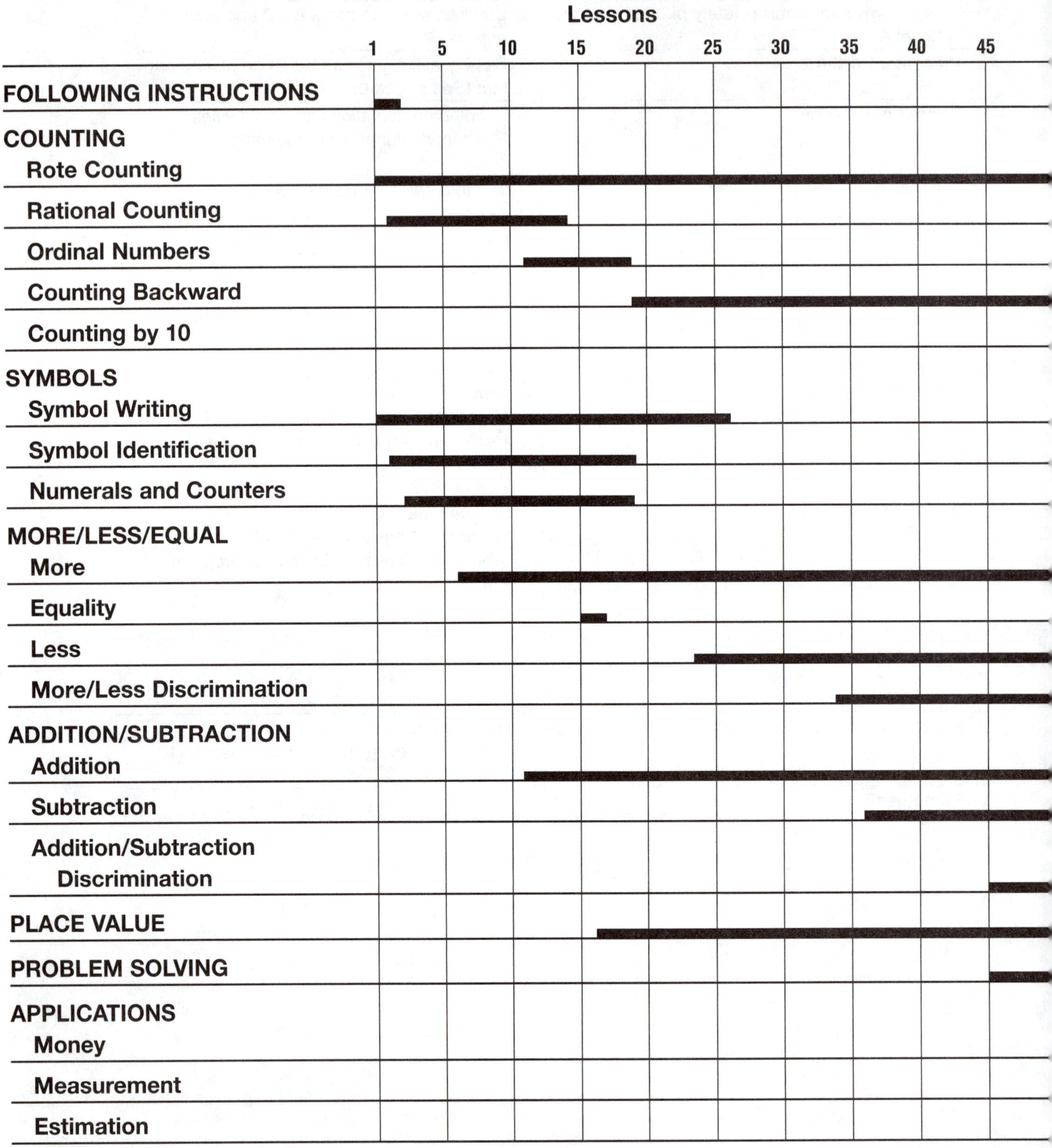

The Scope and Sequence Chart shows where each track or major topic begins and where it ends. The chart does not show various lessons on which activities are presented. For more details on the lessons in which particular skills are taught, see pages 107–112.

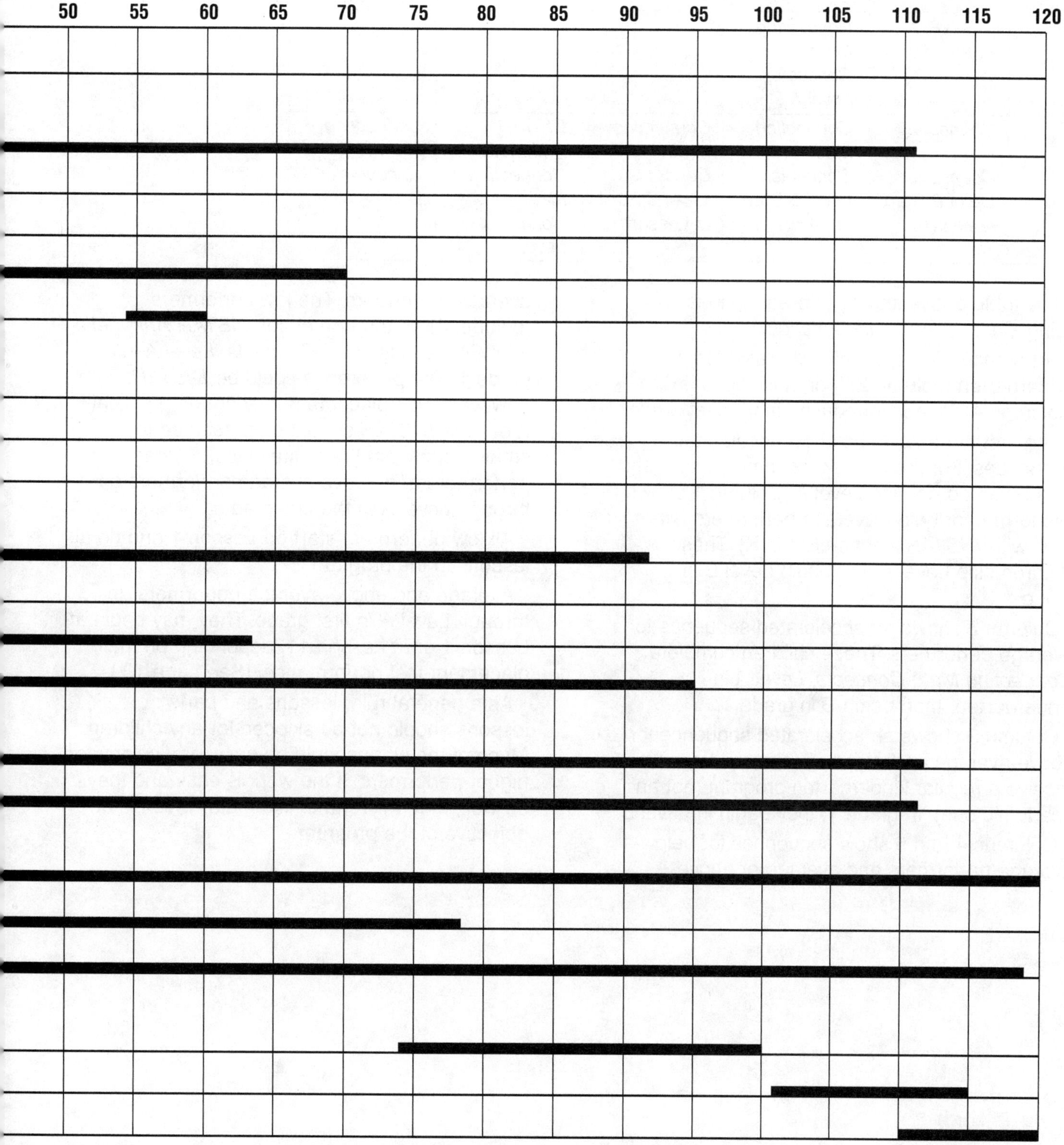

Options for Using Level A

Grade	Accelerated Sequences			Regular Sequences	
	1. Low performers	2. Average performers	3. High performers	4. Low performers	5. Average to high performers
K	*DISTAR® Arithmetic 1*	*Connecting Math Concepts, Level A*			
1	*Connecting Math Concepts, Level* ***B*** Start at Lesson 1	*Connecting Math Concepts, Level* ***B*** Start at Lesson 1	*Connecting Math Concepts, Level* ***B*** Start at Lesson 1	*DISTAR Arithmetic* 1 or *Connecting Math Concepts, Level A*	*Connecting Math Concepts, Level A*

The table above shows different options for using *Connecting Math Concepts.*

For some options, Level A is presented in kindergarten (column 2). For other options (columns 4–5), A is introduced in the first grade.

The first three columns show accelerated sequences. For the sequences in columns 1 and 3, children do not use Level A. Column 1 shows this format for below-average performers (who start with *DISTAR Arithmetic 1* in K). These children skip Level A and begin Level B in grade 1.

Column 2 shows an accelerated sequence for average performers. These children complete *Connecting Math Concepts, Level A* in kindergarten, then begin *B* in grade 1.

Column 3 shows an accelerated sequence for above-average performers. These children receive a regular kindergarten program (not an academic one). In grade 1, they begin in Level B.

Columns 4 and 5 show sequences for below-average performers and average or above-average performers. The low performers (column 4) go through either *DISTAR Arithmetic 1* or *Connecting Math Concepts, Level A* in grade 1. The preference could be *DISTAR;* however, such placement may not be practical (because *DISTAR* should be presented to small groups, not the entire class). Average performers and above-average performers go through Level A in the first grade.

All low performers start on Lesson 1 and do all lessons in the program.

Average and above-average performers go through Level A in first grade. They may begin at Lesson 1 or at Lesson 11, depending on their placement-test performance. (See page 10.)

As a general rule, lessons and parts of lessons should not be skipped for any children. Much of the work should be easy, particularly for higher performers. If the work is easy and they do well, they will tend to like math, which is an objective of the program.

How the Program Is Different

Connecting Math Concepts differs from traditional approaches in the following ways:

Field Tested

Connecting Math Concepts has been shaped through extensive field-testing and revising based on problems children and teachers encountered. This work was completed before the program was published. The development philosophy of *Connecting Math Concepts* is that, if teachers or children have trouble with material presented, the program is at fault. Revisions are made to correct the problems.

Organization

The organization of how skills are introduced, developed, and reviewed is unique. In traditional programs, the curriculum is called a spiral. The children work exclusively on a particular topic for a few lessons. Then a new topic (often unrelated to the preceding topic) is presented. *Connecting Math Concepts* does not follow this format for the following reasons:

a) During a period, it is not productive to work only on a single topic. If new information is being presented, it is very easy for children to become overwhelmed with the information. A more sensible procedure, and one that has been demonstrated to be superior in studies of learning and memory, is to distribute the practice, so that, instead of working 30 minutes on a single topic, children work each day for possibly 7 minutes on each of four topics.

b) When full-period topics are presented, it becomes very difficult for the teacher to provide practice on the latest skills that had been taught. Unless the skills that had been taught are used and reviewed, children's performance will deteriorate, and the skills will have to be re-taught when they again appear. A more sensible organization is to present work on skills continuously (not discontinuously), so that children work on a particular topic (such as column addition) for part of 70 or 80 lessons, not for 5 or 6 entire lessons at a time. In this context of continuous development of skills, review becomes automatic, and reteaching becomes unnecessary because children use the skills on every lesson.

c) When skills are not developed continuously, children must learn a lot of new concepts during a short period and are also expected to become "automatic" in applying the new concepts and skills. For most children, adequate learning will not occur. A better method is to develop skills and concepts in small steps, so that children are not required to learn as much new material at a time so they receive a sufficient amount of practice to become facile or automatic in applying it.

d) When skills are not developed continuously, children and teachers may develop very negative attitudes about mastery. Children may think that they are not expected to "learn" the new material, because it will go away in a few days. Teachers become frustrated because they often understand that children need much more practice, but they are unable to provide it and at the same time move through the program at a reasonable rate. Again, the continuous development of skills solves this problem, because children learn very quickly that what is presented is used, in this lesson, the next lesson, and in many subsequent lessons. When the practice is sufficient, children develop the mind-set needed for learning to mastery because the skill is something they will need in the immediate future.

e) When lessons are not clearly related to "periods" of time, the teacher has no precise way to gauge the performance of the children or to judge how long to spend on a particular "lesson." A more reasonable procedure is to organize material into lessons, each requiring so much time to teach. The teacher then knows that the lesson has the potential of teaching children within a class period of 30–35 minutes.

In *Connecting Math Concepts*, skills are organized in tracks. A track is an ongoing development of a particular topic. Within each lesson, work from 3 to 5 tracks is presented. The teaching presentations are designed so it is possible to present the entire lesson in 30–35 minutes (although some lessons may run longer and some shorter, and more time may be needed for lower performers).

From lesson to lesson, the work on new skills develops a small step at a time, so that children are not overwhelmed with new information and receive enough practice both to master skills and to become facile with them. Children, therefore, learn quickly about *learning new concepts* and realize that what they will use what they have learned.

From Skills to Problem Solving

Connecting Math Concepts develops learning from component skills to applications and problem solving, not from applications to skills (which is a currently popular approach).

The problem-solving-to-skills approach is rejected because it is fraught with difficulties. The issue, however, is not whether problem-solving is a goal or whether it is legitimate for children to engage in problem-solving activities, but whether teaching should start with problem solving and then proceed to skills.

a) There is no evidence to suggest that starting children with problem solving works very well. That method is predicated on the philosophy that problem solving is an end in itself. However, there is no compelling data to suggest that it works very well.

b) The problem-solving approach is not time-efficient. Some problem-solving activities may require more than an hour if children do not have the component skills and knowledge they need to analyze and work the given problem. The same problem, when presented after the teaching of component skills and discriminations, may require only two minutes.

c) If activities are viewed in terms of how "noisy" they are (distractors, ease of identifying relevant information, and steps in solving the problem), problems can be arranged from simple to more complex. Here's a rough sequence:

1. $4 + 2 = \square$
2. Jane has 4. Then she gets 2 more. She ends up with how many?
3. Real-life applications involving somebody having 4 and then getting 2 more.

Starting with the real-life application and working backward presents the danger of children learning solution strategies that will not work for 1 and 2 above. If the skill development proceeds from the least noisy application to the real-life applications (from 1 to 3), the learning will occur in a way that relates the real-life application to what children know about statements of math and to simple word problems.

Connecting Math Concepts proceeds from the least noisy type of problems to increasingly complex types. This progression assures that children learn the basic facts and relationships of math and learn how these facts and relationships apply to the full range of problem-solving situations. The procedure assures that children master all the concepts and discriminations needed for complex applications and that learning the complex applications is not overwhelming. The procedure also permits the teaching to occur in far less time.

Connections

Connecting Math Concepts does what the title implies—makes connections between related topics and extensions of what the children learn. The goal of the program is not necessarily to teach a variety of ways to solve different problems, but to apply the same solution strategies in a variety of applications. Also, part of the goal is to provide strategies that are efficient. Connections occur with everything that is taught in Level A. The rule is that if something is taught, a) it is used extensively and b) it is related to other relevant topics the children learn.

Connecting Math Concepts presents skills in applications in a way that permits children to connect concepts. This feature of the program is particularly important because much of what the beginning learner must learn about arithmetic involves mechanical information as well as conceptual links.

A strong program develops both the mechanical skills as well as conceptual understanding. Children learn the relationships between numbers like 30 and numbers that are more (34) and those that are less (29). Children would understand more and less in other contexts—such as the word-problem context. "You have four and you get two more...." The program connects familiar counting to concepts like more and less, and connects both more and less and counting to spatial representations of numbers. Finally, the program relates knowledge of numbers and counting to statements of arithmetic, such as:

$4 + 2 = \square$

If the program did an effective job of articulating connections between the various concepts, the child who completes the first level would have a strong conceptual foundation on which to build—the foundation relationships between counting, more-less, representations with counters, and statements of arithmetic.

How does *Connecting Math Concepts* forge these basic connections?

The principal vehicle is the number line. The number line is potentially dangerous for teaching number facts because it provides children with a method of figuring out the answer without ever attending to relationship. To figure out 4 plus 3, the children simply go to 4 on the number line and then move 3 places further. Although children learn the right answer, they don't easily learn the relationship between 4 + 2 and 4 + 3 because they have never been required to do anything that focuses on the relationship. They just follow the number line as a "rote" procedure.

A similar problem exists with any method that permits children to count and figure out the answer to problems like 4 plus 2. Finger operations are logical. (Hold up 4 fingers; hold up 2 more; count all.) However, these operations don't prompt systematic learning of relationships because children are not required to attend to relationships. Line-making operations suffer from the same problem. They provide children with a reliable method for figuring out answers to problems; however, they do not induce fact knowledge or knowledge of relationships. Furthermore, they often militate against systematic learning of facts because so long as the child is able to use a finger-counting operation or a number line, what motivation is there for learning facts?

Connecting Math Concepts solves this problem by using a number line with numbers covered up. The card that covers them has an arrow to show the direction. For addition, the arrow faces right:

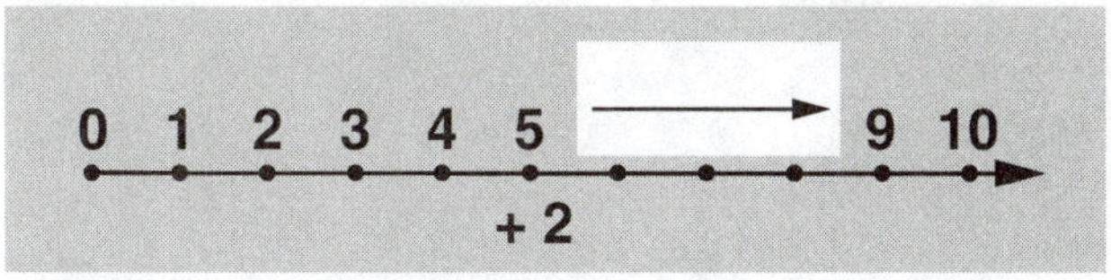

This problem shows 5 (the number in front of the arrow card) plus 2.

For subtraction, the arrow faces left:

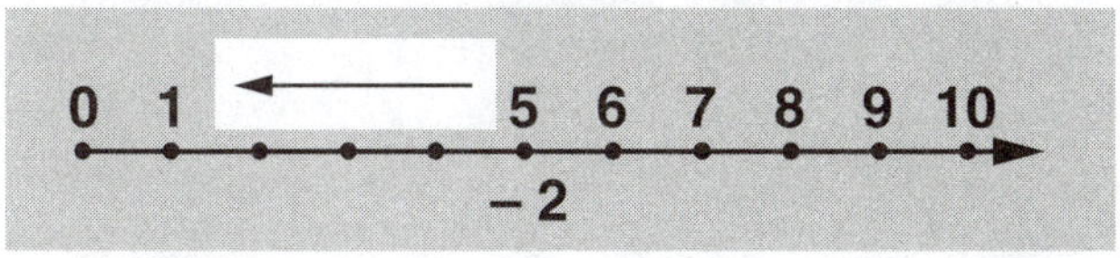

This problem shows 5 minus 2. The number next to the card is 5. The arrow points in the direction of smaller numbers.

This setup permits the teacher to ask addition or subtraction questions and permits children to answer them.

For the first example, the teacher can ask:

"What's the last number showing?"
"How many are you going to plus?"
"So 5 plus 2 equals what number?"

The confirmation involves uncovering the two numbers after 5.

The procedure assures that children internalize the number line and the notion that to progress to the right is to go to bigger numbers (those that occur later in the counting order). To go left is to go to smaller numbers.

The basic number-line setup can be used to show the more fundamental relationships between counting and addition.

For instance, the teacher can present this example and ask the children:

"What's the last number showing?"
"So what's the next number?"

The teacher can then uncover 6 and confirm that the children were correct.

Later in the program, the teacher can use the setup to teach 1 more:

"What's the last number showing?"
"What number is 1 more than 5?"

The teacher uncovers the next number and confirms that it is 6.

The same setup can be used to show the relationship between 1 more and plus 1. Using the same setup as above, the teacher can ask:

"What's the last number showing?"
"What's 1 more than 5?"
"So what's 5 plus 1?"

Throughout this development, children must predict the answer. They can't answer questions by simply looking at the numbers shown on the number line. They must know which numbers are covered. Therefore, they understand the number line primarily as a source for confirming answers, not as a method for figuring out answers.

To teach some of the relationships between facts, Level A presents number-line problems that involve a bug.

For some of these activities, the display shows where the bug starts and where the bug goes. Children write two facts. The first shows what the bug did in the picture; the second shows what the bug does to get back to the starting place.

Here's an example:

Children write these facts:

$5 + 2 = 7$
$7 - 2 = 5$

Another variation involves the bug that always wants to go to zero. Children complete this type of statement:

______________________ $= 0$

Children indicate the starting number and the number of places the bug must minus to reach zero:

$6 - 6 = 0$

This relationship is particularly important for work on later levels. Often children have trouble working column subtraction problems involving regrouping because they don't understand that you can't count past zero. (You can't simply subtract the smaller digit from the larger one.)

$$\begin{array}{r} 56 \\ \underline{-27} \end{array}$$

The number line and the bug on the number line form the bridge for teaching word problems. The initial word problems present verbal representations of problems that children have worked. Here's an early word problem:

A bug starts at 4 on a number line.
Then the bug plusses 2 places.
The bug ends up at what number?

Children write the problem using a box for "what number?":

$4 + 2 = \square$

Then children write the answer:

$4 + 2 = 6$

The entire process is internalized, with no reference to a physical number line.

Once children understand how to internalize simple problems, other variations are presented:

"A bug starts at 6 on a number line. Then the bug goes to the number that is 2 more. The bug ends up at what number?"
"Six bugs met 2 more bugs. How many bugs were there?"
"A bug met 6 bugs. Then 1 more bug joined them. How many bugs were there?"
"A girl walked to school with 6 other girls. Then 2 more girls joined them. How many girls walked to school?"

Each problem type (including types that are not illustrated here) are introduced carefully so that children receive lots of examples and work with the new type until it becomes familiar.

The type of connections that are made between counting, more and less, plussing, statements of arithmetic, the number line, and verbal representations are developed for all the basic skills that children learn in Level A. A goal of the program is to teach facts, but facts are not taught at the expense of conceptual understanding. Facts become an extension of concepts.

Placement Testing

Level A is appropriate for children who meet the placement criteria. A placement test is used to measure children's abilities to:

- count to 10 (part 1)
- count objects (part 2)
- identify numbers that are one more (part 3)
- write numerals from dictation (part 4)

A reproducible copy of the placement test for Level A appears on pages 10 and 11. ***Note:*** The test consists of teacher's instructions and child's sheet.

The test is administered to children individually, not to groups of children.

Administration takes 3–5 minutes per child.

Administering the Placement Test

Arrange to test children in a place that is reasonably quiet. Make sure that each child has a pencil.

The test may be administered by parents or volunteers.

The administrator is to:

- fill out the information at the top of the Teacher's Instructions.
- present parts 1 and 2 as specified.
- circle + or – to indicate pass or fail.

If the child does not pass parts 1 and 2, do not present any more parts of the test. The child should not be placed in Level A.

If the child passes both items 3 and 4, the child should start at Lesson 11 of Level A.

If the child does not pass both parts 3 and 4, the child should start at Lesson 1 of Level A.

Circle the appropriate placement for the child in the placement box at the bottom of the Teacher's Instructions.

Placement Test for *Connecting Math Concepts, Level A*

Teacher's Instructions

Child's Name: ______________________ Teacher's Name: ______________________

Date: ______________________

Note: Test is administered **individually**. Not to groups of children.

1. COUNTING
   "Count to 10." (Cross out missed or omitted numbers. Saying 11 is an error.)

   1 2 3 4 5 6 7 8 9 10 11

   Passing Criteria: No mistakes.

2. OBJECT COUNTING
   a. (Touch stars.) "Count the stars." (Child counts.) "How many stars?" + −
   b. (Touch lines.) "Count these lines." (Child counts.) "How many lines?" + −

   Passing Criteria: No mistakes.

   Placement Instructions for parts 1 and 2:
   a. Present parts 3 and 4 to children who passed both parts 1 and 2.
   b. Do not place children who fail either parts 1 or 2 in Level A.
   A possible placement is *DISTAR Arithmetic 1.*

3. ONE MORE
   "My turn: What number comes after 7? 8."
   a. "Your turn: What number comes after 4?" + −
   b. "What number comes after 9?" + −
   c. "What number comes after 5?" + −

   Passing Criteria: No mistakes.

4. NUMERAL DICTATION
   (Point to blanks on child test sheet.) "You're going to write some numerals."
   a. (Touch the first blank.) "Write a 7." + −
   b. (Touch the next blank.) "Write a 4." + −
   c. (Touch the next blank.) "Write a 5." + −
   d. (Touch the last blank.) "Write an 8." + −

   Passing Criteria: No mistakes. (Count correct numbers written backwards as correct.)

   Placement Instructions for parts 3 and 4:
   a. Children who do **not** pass both parts 3 and 4 begin *Connecting Math Concepts, Level A* on **Lesson 1**.
   b. Children who pass both parts 3 and 4 begin **Lesson 11**.

   Note: Children who pass both parts 3 and 4 and who know answers to simple addition problems such as **5 + 1** and **6 + 2** could be given the placement test for *Connecting Math Concepts Level B.*

PLACEMENT:

DISTAR 1	***CONNECTING MATH CONCEPTS, LEVEL A***	
Lesson 1	Lesson 1	Lesson 11

Name: ____

Placement Test for *Connecting Math Concepts, Level A:* Child Test Sheet

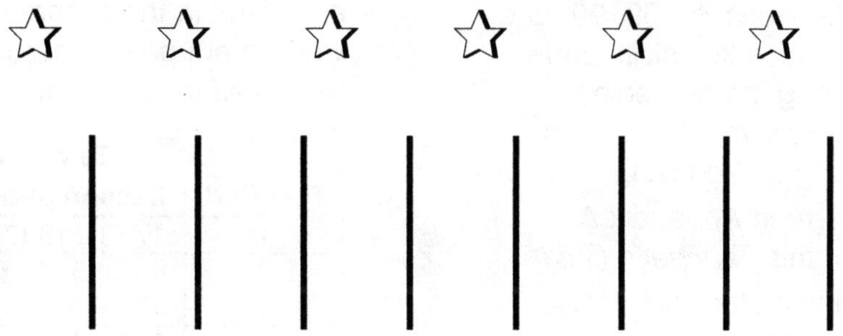

____

________ ________ ________ ________

____

Cumulative Tests

In *Connecting Math Concepts, Level A,* cumulative tests follow Lessons 30, 60, 90, and 120. The tests sample various key skills and discrimination taught during the preceding 30–lesson period, as well as important skills taught since the beginning of the level.

The Cumulative Tests are in Appendix A, beginning on page 85 of this *Teacher's Guide.*

- The teacher presentation for each test appears first, followed by the reproducible blackline masters. Each test contains between 30 and 50 items and requires about thirty minutes to complete.
- The answer key, Scoring Chart, Percent Summary chart, and Test Remedy chart for each cumulative test appear immediately after the section of Cumulative Test blackline masters.
- The reproducible Group Summary form is at the end of Appendix A.

Scoring

Here is the Scoring Chart for Cumulative Test 1, which follows Test Lesson 3.

TEST 1 SCORING CHART

PART	SCORING	POSSIBLE	PASSING
1	1 for each number	6	5
2, 3	2 for each item	10	8
4	1 for each group of lines	5	5
5, 6	2 for each item	16	14
7	3 for each item: [Number of Lines 2] [Number written 1]	9	8
8	1 for each object	5	5
9	1 for each number	8	8
10	2 for each item	8	6
11	1 for each group of items	5	5
	Total	**72**	

The Scoring Chart shows how to score each item, the possible score for each part, and the passing score for each part. Test 1, for example, has eleven parts and a total possible score of 72.

Remedies

Remedies are provided for each part that is not passed. The Remedies table tells you what exercises in the program to present to students who do not pass a particular part. Here are the remedies for Cumulative Test 1.

Test 1 Remedies	
Test Part	**Lesson and (Exercise)**
1	17 (3), 18 (7), 19 (8)
2	4 (5), 5 (4), 6 (5), 7 (5), 8 (4), 9 (3), 10 (4)
3	3 (3), 4 (3), 5 (5), 6 (6), 7 (6), 9 (4)
4	18 (2), 19 (9), 20 (4)
5	17 (3), 18 (3), 19 (6), 20 (5), 21 (4), 22 (4), 23 (6)
6	15 (2), 16 (3), 24 (3), 25 (2), 26 (4), 27 (5), 28 (6), 29 (7)
7	2 (1), 5 (3), 6 (4), 7 (4), 8 (3), 9 (2), 12 (5), 13 (4), 14 (4)
8	11 (3), 12 (2), 13 (2), 14 (2), 17 (2), 18 (6), 19 (7)
9	17 (7), 18 (7), 19 (8), 25 (3), 26 (2), 27 (2), 28 (3), 29 (2)
10	24 (4), 25 (1), 26 (1), 27 (4), 28 (5), 29 (4), 30 (5), 31 (2)
11	28 (2), 29 (6), 30 (4), 31 (5)

For each part of the test that some students don't pass, you should present some or all of the exercises listed. (Present the exercises in the order they are listed. Present them only to the students who did not pass the part. Try to present the remedies at a time other than the regularly scheduled math period.)

The goal of each remedy is to teach students well enough that they can work items of that type in the context presented in the *Connecting Math Concepts* program.

PLACING STUDENTS WHO FAIL THREE OR MORE PARTS OF THE TEST

As a rule of thumb, if a student fails three or more parts of the test, the student is not placed properly in the program, which means that the student will continue to have problems with the material. The ideal remedy would be to place students at a lesson in which they could be successful on about 90 percent of the tasks in each exercise.

PLACING MID-YEAR STUDENTS

The tests may be used to place student who come in after the school term has started. Here are the steps:

(1) Present the Level A Cumulative Post Test.

(2) Use the scoring chart to determine which of the parts the students passed.

(3) Determine placement or need for further testing.

- If the student passed no more than three parts, place the student at the beginning of Level A, or test the student for placement in *Distar Arithmetic I.*
- If the student passed four to eleven parts, give the student another cumulative test:
  Cumulative Test 1, if the student passed four, five, or six parts.
  Cumulative Test 2, if the student passed seven or eight parts.
  Cumulative Test 3, if the student passed nine or ten parts.
- If the student passed eleven, twelve, or thirteen parts of the Level A Cumulative Post Test, place the student in Connecting Math Concepts Level B.

(4) If you give the student another cumulative test, use the scoring chart for that test to determine which of the parts the student passed and which parts the student failed.

(5) Place student so they need remedies for no more than two skills.

Here's an example:

(Step 1): A teacher gave a student Level A Cumulative Post Test.

(Step 2): The test was graded and the student passed only six parts of it.

(Step 3): The teacher determined that the student should be tested further.

(Step 4): Then, the teacher gave the student Level A Cumulative Test 1. According to the scoring chart for Cumulative Test 1, the student failed parts 4, 6, 9, 10, and 11.

(Step 5): The appropriate remedies for Part A begin in Lesson 18; those for Part 6 begin in Lesson 15; those for Part 9 begin in Lesson 17; Part 10 in Lesson 24; and Part 11 in Lesson 28. If the student is placed in or before Lesson 18, the student would need remediation for only Parts 6 and 9. The remaining remedies would be covered in the subsequent lessons. Placing the student beyond Lesson 18 wouldn't be acceptable because the student would need remedies for at least three parts—Parts 4, 6, and 9.

Test Preparation Materials

Level A contains 15 test-preparation lessons that acquaint children with some of the formats and contents of standardized achievement test. The material appears at the end of *Presentation Book 1.* It is placed there as a reminder that the time for test-preparation work might be near.

Reproducible blackline masters for all 15 test-preparation lessons follow the teacher presentation for the lessons. Here is the teacher presentation for Lesson 10 of *Connecting Math Concepts, Level A* Test Preparation, followed by the blackline master.

Lesson 10

EXERCISE 1 TELLING TIME

a. Look at the worksheet for Lesson 10 and touch Part 1. √

b. Some of the clocks show an hour beginning and some show an hour that is half over.
- **Circle** the letter of each clock that shows an hour that is **beginning.**
- Raise your hand when you're finished.
- (Observe children and give feedback.)
- You should have circled the letters of clock D, clock F, and clock G.

c. Make a **box** around the letter of each clock that shows an hour that is **half over.**
- Raise your hand when you're finished.
- (Observe children and give feedback.)
- You should have made a box around the letters of clock B, clock E, and clock H.

d. Listen: One of the clocks shows the beginning of the third hour. Write the number **3** on the line below the clock that shows three o'clock.
- (Observe children and give feedback.)
- You should have written 3 below clock D.

e. Listen: One of the clocks shows half past the third hour. Write the number **3** on the line below the clock that shows half past three.
- (Observe children and give feedback.)
- You should have written 3 below clock B.

f. Listen: One of the clocks shows half past the eleventh hour. Write the number **11** on the line below the clock that shows half past eleven.
- (Observe children and give feedback.)
- You should have written 11 below clock H.

g. Listen: One of the clocks shows the beginning of the eleventh hour. Write the number **11** on the line below the clock that shows eleven o'clock.
- (Observe children and give feedback.)
- You should have written 11 below clock F.

Lesson 10

EXERCISE 2 CHARTING

a. Find Part 2.
- You're going to make a graph and then answer questions.

b. Touch the top row of boxes. √
- Make a **T** in each white box in the top row.
- Everybody, what are you going to make in each white box on the top row? (Signal.) *T.*
- Make your Ts.
- (Observe children and give feedback.)

c. Touch the next row of boxes. √
- Make the number **1** in each white box in that row.
- What are you going to make in each white box in that row? (Signal.) *1.*
- Make your 1s.

d. Touch the next row of boxes. √
- You're going to make the number **2** in each box that is white.
- What are you going to make in each white box in that row? (Signal.) *2.*
- Make your 2s.
- (Observe children and give feedback.)

e. Touch the next row of boxes. √
- You're going to make the letter **B** in each box that is white.
- What are you going to make in each white box in that row? (Signal.) *B.*
- Make your **Bs.**
- (Observe children and give feedback.)

f. Two rows have letters. Touch the row that has the most letters. √
- Everybody, what letter is in that row? (Signal.) *T.*
- Raise your hand when you know how many letters are in that row. √
- How many letters are in that row? (Signal.) *Ten.*

g. Touch the row that has the fewest letters.
- That's the shortest row. √
- What letter is in that row? (Signal.) *B.*
- Raise your hand when you know how many letters are in that row. √
- How many letters are in that row? (Signal.) *Two.*

h. Two rows have numbers. Touch the row that has the most numbers. √
- Everybody, what number is in that row? (Signal.) *1.*
- Raise your hand when you know how many numbers are in that row. √
- How many numbers are in that row? (Signal.) *Seven.*

i. Touch the other row that has numbers. √

- Everybody, what number is in that row? (Signal.) *2.*
- Raise your hand when you know how many numbers are in that row. √
- How many numbers are in that row? (Signal.) *Six.*

j. Find question number 1. √
- You're going to **circle** answers to questions. Don't say the answer, circle it. Touch the space where you'll circle the answer to question 1. √

k. Question 1: Are there more **Ts** or more **Bs** on the graph? Circle the answer. √
- (Observe children and give feedback.)

l. Question 2: How many letters are there all together? You'll have to count all the letters—all the **Ts** and all the **Bs.**
- Circle the number that shows how many letters are on the whole graph. √

m. Question 3: Are there more number **1s** or more number **2s**? Circle 1 or 2. √

n. Question 4: How many numbers are there all together. Circle the number that shows how many numbers there are on the whole graph. √

o. Question 5: Are their fewer **Bs** or fewer **2s.** Circle the answer. √

p. Question 6: Are there more letters on this graph or more numbers on this graph? Circle the word letters or the word numbers. √

q. Check your work.
- Question 1: Are there more **Ts** or more **Bs** on the graph? Everybody, what's the answer? (Signal.) *Ts.* You should have circled **T.**
- Question 2: How many letters all together? Everybody, what's the answer? (Signal.) *12.* You should have circled **12.**
- Question 3: Are there more number 1s or number 2s? Everybody, what's the answer? (Signal.) *1s.* You should have circled **1.**
- Question 4: How many numbers are there all together? Everybody, what's the answer? (Signal.) *13.* You should have circled **13.**
- Question 5: Are there fewer **Bs** or fewer **2s**? Everybody, what's the answer? (Signal.) *Bs.* You should have circled **B.**
- Question 6: Are there more letters on this graph or more numbers on this graph? Everybody, what's the answer? (Signal.) *Numbers.* You should have circled **Numbers.**

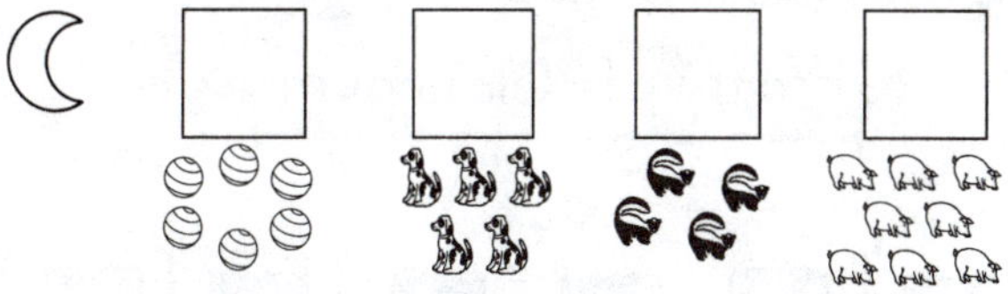

Teaching the Program

Level A is designed to be presented to the entire class. You should generally be able to teach one lesson during a 20–35 minute period. Children's independent work requires 10–20 minutes. The independent work can be scheduled at another time during the day.

Organization

The program will run far more smoothly if you follow these steps after giving the placement test and deciding the lesson on which the children will start the program.

- Arrange seating so you can quickly receive information on high performers and lower performers. A good plan is to organize the children something like this:

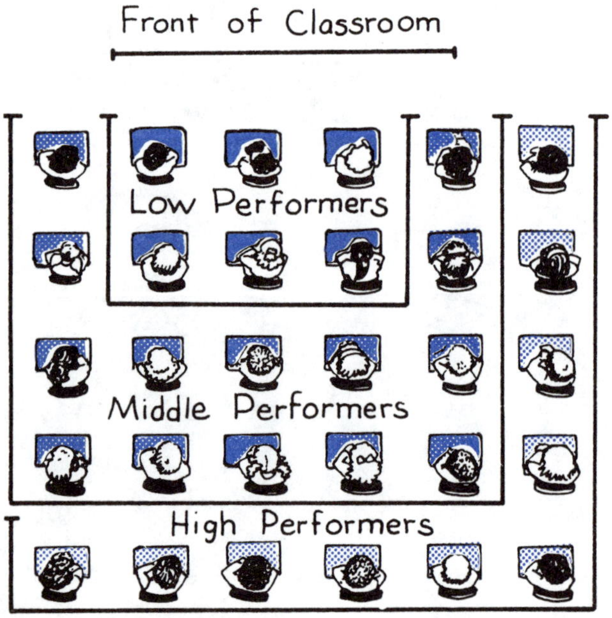

The lowest performers are closest to the front of the classroom. Middle performers are arranged around the lowest performers. Highest performers are arranged around the periphery. With this arrangement, you can position yourself so that, by taking a few steps during the time that children are working problems, you can sample low, average, and high performers.

While different variations of this arrangement are possible, be careful not to seat low performers far from the front-center of the room. The highest performers, understandably, can be farthest from the center because they attend better, learn faster, and need less observation and feedback.

- Arrange permanent pairs of children to work together in the team games. The pairings should be based on performance. Each low performer should be paired either with an average performer or a high performer.

Teaching

When you teach the program, a basic rule is that you shouldn't present from the front of the room unless you're showing something on the board.

For most of the activities, you direct children to work specified problems. For these activities, you should present from somewhere in the middle of the room (in no set place), and as children work the problem you should observe a good sample of children. Although you won't be able to observe every child working every problem, you can observe at least half a dozen children in possibly 15 seconds.

Rehearse the lesson before presenting it to the class. Don't simply read the text, but act it out. When you are to write something on the board, look at the shaded cells that show what's going to happen, how you'll change the display. If you keep the changes in mind, you'll be much more fluent in presenting the activity.

Watch your wording. With the non-board activities, it's much easier than it is with board activities. The board formats are usually designed so they are manageable if you have an idea of the steps you'll take. If you rehearse each of the early lessons before presenting them, you'll soon learn how to present efficiently from the script. In later lessons, you should scan the list of skills at the beginning of each lesson. New skills are in boldface type. If a new skill is introduced on that lesson, rehearse it. Most of what occurs on the lesson will not be new, but a variation of what you've presented earlier, so you may not need to rehearse these activities.

Using the Teacher Presentation Scripts

The script for each lesson indicates precisely how to present each structured activity. The lesson is a script that shows what you say, what you do, and what the children's responses are.

What you say appears in blue type:
You say this.
What you do appears in parentheses:
(You do this.)
The responses of the children are in italics.
Children say this.

Follow the specified wording in the script. While wording variations from the specified script are not always dangerous, you will be assured of communicating clearly with the children if you follow the script exactly. The reason is that the wording is controlled, and the tasks are arranged so they provide succinct wording and focus clearly on important aspects of what the children are to do. Although you may feel uncomfortable "reading" from a script (and you may feel that the children will not pay attention), follow the scripts very closely; try to present them as if you're saying something important to the children. If you do, you'll find after a while that working from a script is not difficult and that children indeed respond well to what you say.

A sample appears on page 19.

The arrows show the five different things you'll do that are not spelled out in the script. You'll signal to make sure that group responses involve all the children. You'll "firm" critical parts of the exercises. You'll also use information based on what the children are doing to judge whether you'll proceed quickly or wait a few more seconds before moving on with the presentation. For some exercises, you'll write things on the board, and you'll often change the board display.

ARROW 1: GROUP RESPONSES

Some of the tasks call for group responses. If children respond together with brisk unison responses, you receive good information about whether "most" of the children are performing correctly. The simplest way to signal children to respond together is to adopt a timing practice—just like the timing in a musical piece.

A signal follows a question (as shown by arrow 1) or the words, "Get ready."

You can signal by nodding, clapping one time, snapping your fingers, or tapping your foot. After initially establishing the timing for signals, you can signal through voice inflection only.

Children will not be able to initiate responses together at the appropriate rate unless you follow these rules:

a) Talk first. Pause a standard length of time (possibly 1 second), then signal. Never signal when you talk. Don't change the timing for your signal. Children are to respond on your signal—not after it or before it.

b) Model responses that are paced reasonably. Don't permit children to produce slow, droning responses. These are dangerous because they rob you of the information that can be derived from appropriate group responses. When children respond in a droning way, many of them are copying responses of others. If children are required to respond at a reasonable speaking rate, all children must initiate responses; therefore, it's relatively easy to determine which children are not responding and which are saying the wrong response.

Also, don't permit children to respond at a very fast rate or to "jump" your signal.

To correct mistakes, show the children exactly what you want them to do.

- "I'm good at answering the right way."
- "Watch: What does 1 plus 5 equal? 6."
- "Wasn't that great?"
- "Let's see who can do it just that way: What does 1 plus 5 equal?" (Signal.) *6.*

c) Do not respond with the children unless you are trying to work with them on a difficult response. You present only what's in blue. You do not say the answers with the children, and you should not move your lips or give other spurious clues about what the answer is.

Think of signals this way: If you use them correctly, they provide you with much diagnostic information. A weak response suggests that you should repeat a task and provides information about which children may need more help. Signals are, therefore, important early in the program. After children have learned the routine, the children will be able to respond on cue with no signal. That will happen, however, only if you always give your signals at the end of a constant time interval after you complete what you say.

ARROW 2: FIRMING

When children make mistakes, you correct them. A correction may occur during any part of the teacher presentation that calls for the children to respond. It may also occur in connection with what the children are writing. Here are the rules for corrections:

- You correct a mistake as soon as you hear it.
- A mistake on oral responses is saying the wrong thing or not responding.

To correct: Say the correct answer. Repeat the task the children missed.

For example: "Four plus two equals what number?"

(Signal.)

If some children do not respond, respond late, or say anything but 6, there's a mistake.

As soon as you hear the mistake, you correct it. Say the correct answer. "It's 6."

(Repeat the task.)

"Listen again: Four plus two equals what number?"

(Signal.)

Remember, wherever there's a signal, there's a place where children may make mistakes. You correct mistakes as soon as you hear them.

A special correction is needed when correcting mistakes on tasks that teach a relationship. This type of correction is marked with the note:

(Repeat step __ until firm.)

The note (Repeat step until firm.) occurs when children must produce a series of responses (as in counting) and where they may not understand a relationship that is structured so it involves answering more than one question (as in step B).

When you "repeat until firm," you follow these steps:

1) Correct the mistake. (Tell the answer and repeat the task that was missed.)

2) Return to the beginning of the specified step and present the entire step.

In step B, you present two different problems. For each problem, you ask, "Is the box in the middle or at the end of that problem?"

If the children are confused, if some don't answer either question, or if the answers to both questions are wrong, you repeat step B after you have corrected.

When you hear a mistake, you say the correct answer and repeat the question or task. However, you make sure that children are firm in both the problems you present in step B. You can't be sure that children are firm unless you repeat the step.

Here's a summary of the steps you follow when repeating a part of the exercise until firm.

Correct the mistake:

(Tell the correct answer.) "It's in the middle."

Repeat the task:

"Listen again. A bug starts at 6 on the number line. Then the bug plusses some. The bug ends up at 8. Is the box in the middle or at the end of the problem?"

Repeat the step:

"Let's see who remembers how those problems work."

(Start at the beginning of step B and present the entire step.)

"Repeating until firm" is based on the information you need about the children. When the children made the mistake, you told the answer. Did they remember the answer? Would they now be able to perform the step correctly? The repeat-until-firm procedure provides you with answers to these questions. You present the context in which the mistake occurred, and the children can show you through their responses whether or not the correction worked, whether or not they are firm.

The repeat-until-firm direction appears only on the most critical parts of new-teaching exercises. It usually focuses on knowledge that is very important for later work.

As a general procedure, follow the repeat-until-firm directions.

However, if you're quite sure that the mistake was a "glitch" and does not mean that the children lack understanding, don't follow the repeat-until-firm direction.

a. Some bug problems end with the box. Some bug problems have the box in the middle.

b. Listen: A bug starts at 5 on the number line. Then the bug plusses 2. The bug ends up at what number? Is the box in the middle or at the end of that problem? (Signal.) *At the end.*

1 How you secure group responses

- Listen: A bug starts at 6 on the number line. Then the bug plusses some. The bug ends up at 8. Is the box in the middle or at the end of that problem? (Signal.) *In the middle.*

(Repeat step b until firm.)

2 What you firm

Workbook Practice

c. Find part 4. I'm going to tell you bug problems. Some of these problems tell how many places the bug plusses or minuses. Some don't. Remember, if the problem says plus some, you write plus box. If it says that the bug plusses 2 or plusses 5, you write plus 2 or plus 5. I'll read each problem two times. Then you'll write the whole problem.

d. Problem A: A bug starts at 2 on the number line. Then the bug plusses 4 places. The bug ends up at what number?

- Listen again: A bug starts at 2. Then the bug plusses 4. The bug ends up at what number? Write the question for problem A. Don't write the answer, just the problem. Raise your hand when you're finished.

3 How you pace your presentation

(Observe children and give feedback.)

- (Write on the board:)

A. 2 + 4 = ☐

4 What you write

- Here's the problem you should have.

e. Problem B: A bug starts at 2 on the number line. Then the bug plusses some places. The bug ends up at 4.

- Listen again: A bug starts at 2. Then the bug plusses some. The bug ends up at 4. Write the problem for B. Just the problem. Raise your hand when you're finished. √

3 How you pace your presentation

- (Write on the board:)

A. 2 + 4 = ☐
B. 2 + ☐ = 4

5 What you change

- Here's what you should have for problem B.

ARROW 3: PACING YOUR PRESENTATION

You should pace your verbal presentation at a normal speaking rate—as if you were telling somebody something important.

> ***Note:*** The presentation works much better and the inflections are far more appropriate if you pretend that you're talking to an adult, not a young child. But make your message sound important.

The most typical mistakes teachers make is going too slowly or talking as if to preschoolers.

The arrows for number 3 on the diagram show two ways to pace your presentation for activities where children write or get involved in touching or finding parts of their workbook page. The first is a note to (Observe children and give feedback.) The second is a √ mark.

A √ is a note to check what the children are doing. It requires only a second or two. If you are positioned close to several "average performing" children, check whether they are performing. If they are, proceed with the presentation.

The (Observe children and give feedback) direction implies a more elaborate response. You sample more children and you give feedback, not only to individual children, but to the group. Here are the basic rules for what to do and not to do when you observe and give feedback.

a) Make sure that you are not at the front of the class when you present the directions for the tasks that involve observing children's performance. For the workbook-practice activity, you assign problems for the children to work (step C). When presenting the workbook activity, move from the front of the room to a place where you can quickly sample the performance of low, middle, and high performers.

b) As soon as children start to work, start observing. As you observe, make comments to the whole class. Focus these comments on children who are (1) following directions, (2) working quickly, and (3) working accurately. "Wow, a couple of children are almost finished. I haven't seen one mistake so far."

c) When children raise their hand to indicate that they are finished, acknowledge them. (They are to raise their hand. When you acknowledge that they are finished, they put their hand down.)

d) If you observe mistakes, do not provide a great deal of individual help. Point out any mistakes, but do not work the problems for the children. For instance, if a child gets one of the problems wrong, point to it and say, "I think you made a mistake." If children don't line their numerals up correctly, say, "You'd better erase that and try again. Your numerals are not lined up." If children are not following instructions that you gave, tell them, "You're supposed to write the answer under the other two numbers. You have to listen very carefully to the instructions."

e) Do not wait for the slowest children to complete the problems before presenting the work check during which children correct their work and fix up any mistakes. A good rule early in the program is to allow a reasonable amount of time. You can usually use the middle performers as a gauge for what is reasonable. As you observe that they are completing their work, announce, "Okay, you have about 10 seconds more to finish up." At the end of that time, continue in the exercise. "Here's the problem you should have."

f) During the workcheck, continue to circulate among the children and make sure that they are checking their work. They should fix up any mistakes. Praise children who are following the procedure. Allow a reasonable amount of time for them to check each problem. Do not wait for the slowest children to finish their check. Try to keep the workcheck moving as quickly as possible.

g) If you observe a serious problem that is not unique to only the lowest performers, tell the class, "Stop. We seem to have a serious problem." Repeat the part of the exercise that gives them information about what they are to do.

> ***Note:*** Do not provide new teaching, or new problems. Simply repeat the part of the exercise that gives them the information they need and reassign the work. "Let's see who can get it this time. . . ."

h) When higher-performing children do their independent work, you may want to go over any parts of the lesson with the children who had trouble with the structured work (made mistakes or didn't finish). Make sure that you check all the problems worked by the lower performers and give them feedback. Show them what they did wrong. Keep your explanations simple. The more you talk, the more likely you'll confuse them. If there are serious problems, repeat the exercise that presented difficulties for the lower performers.

If you follow these procedures very closely, your children will work faster and more accurately. They will also become facile at following your directions.

If you don't follow these rules, you may think that you are helping children, but you will actually be reinforcing them for behaviors that you are trying to change.

If you wait far beyond a reasonable time period before presenting the workcheck, you punish the higher performers and the others who worked quickly and accurately. Soon, they will learn that there is no payoff for doing well—no praise, no recognition—but instead a long wait while you give attention to lower performers.

If you don't make announcements about children who are doing well and working quickly, the class will not understand what's expected. Children will probably not improve much.

If you provide extensive individual help on independent work, you will actually reinforce children for not listening to your directions, for being dependent on your help. Furthermore, this dependency becomes contagious. If you provide extensive individual guidance, it doesn't take other children in the class long to discover that they don't have to listen to your directions, that they can raise their hand and receive help, and that children who have the most serious problems receive the most teacher attention. These expectations are the opposite of the ones you want to induce. You want children to be self-reliant and to have a reason for learning and remembering what you say when you instruct them. The simplest reason is that they will use what they have just been shown and that those who remember will receive reinforcement.

If you provide wordy explanations and extensive reteaching to correct any problems you observe, you run the serious risk of further confusing the children. Their problem is that they didn't attend to or couldn't perform on some detail that you covered in your initial presentation. So tell them what they didn't attend to and repeat the activity (or the step) that gives them the information they need. This approach shows them how to process the information you already presented. A different demonstration or explanation, however, may not show them how to link what you said originally with the new demonstration. So go light on showing children another way.

Because Level A is carefully designed, it is possible to teach all the children the desired behaviors of self-reliance, following instructions, and working fast and accurately. If you follow the management rules just outlined, by the time the children have reached Lesson 40, all children should be able to complete assigned work within a reasonable period of time and have reasons to feel good about their ability to do math.

As they improve, you should tell them about it. "What's this? Everybody's finished with that problem already? That's impressive...." That's what you want to happen. Follow the rules, and it will happen.

ARROWS 4 AND 5: BOARD WORK

What you write and how you change what you've written is indicated with display boxes. In the sample exercise, you first write a problem (Arrow 4). Then you write a second problem (Arrow 5). The convention used in the display boxes is that what you initially present is shown in a gray box. Any changes in that display (additions or alterations) are shown with parts that are in white. Scanning the boxes shows both what you'll write and how you'll change the display.

Unacceptable Error Rates

During structured activities, you should firm the children and make sure that children can run each activity quickly and accurately (if not on the first trial, after the firming has been provided).

Children's independent work should also be monitored. Specifically, no more than 30 percent of the children should make mistakes on any independent activity. On the first lesson that a recently-taught skill is perfectly "independent," error rates may exceed the ideal (more than 30 percent of the children making mistakes). However, if an excessive error rate continues, there is a problem that should be corrected.

Consider whether the preceding steps you've taken are adequate. High error rates on independent practice may be the result of the following problems:

1) The children may not be appropriately placed in the program.

2) The initial presentation may not have provided adequate firming. (The children made mistakes that were not corrected. The parts of the teacher presentation in which errors occurred were not repeated until firm.)

3) Children may have received inappropriate help. (When they worked structured problems earlier, they received too much help and became dependent on the help.)

4) Children may not have been required to follow directions carefully. (If children do not learn early in the program to follow directions precisely, serious problems may result later.)

Consider these possibilities if children tend to have many problems with the materials. If you look at their work as possible feedback about the way you are presenting material, the mistakes can be a source of information that is useful to you in showing you how to teach more effectively. Also make sure that you do not permit high error rates to continue. The simplest procedure is to show the children the types of mistakes they are making and tell them what they should be doing. Then award bonus points (or some other form of reward) for doing well in independent parts of the worksheet.

Test Lessons

Following every tenth lesson, beginning with Lesson 10, are test lessons. Sometimes a test lesson includes some teaching activities followed by the 10-lesson test. Sometimes a test lesson consists of only a test.

The test is designed to assess the most important skills taught in the 10-lesson period. Those skills will be elaborated on during the next 10 lessons. The 10-lesson test, therefore, provides you with information about how well prepared children are to proceed in the program.

Sometimes, children copy from their neighbors. A good method of discovering who is copying is to spread children out during the test if it's physically possible to do so. Discrepancies in the test performance and daily performance of some children pinpoints which children may be copying.

If copying is occurring, reassign seating so that the children who tend to copy are either separated from those who know the answers, or seated near the front-center of the room where it is easier for you to monitor them.

Here's the test Lesson 60.

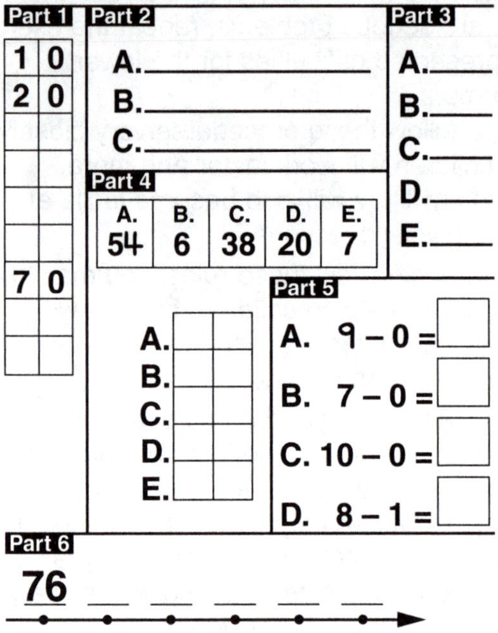

Test 6

Note: Present Test 6 after Lesson 60, but before Lesson 61.

EXERCISE 1 NUMBER LINE
Tens

a. Open your workbook to test 6 and find part 1. √

b. Your turn: Write all the missing numerals. Raise your hand when you're finished.

EXERCISE 2 PROBLEM SOLVING
Word Problems

a. Find part 2. You're going to write number problems the fast way. I'll read each story problem twice. Then you'll write the whole number problem.

b. Touch line A. Here's the problem. Listen carefully: A bug starts at **5** on the number line. Then the bug plusses some places. The bug ends up at **7** on the number line.
- Listen again: A bug starts at **5.** Then the bug plusses some. The bug ends up at **7.**
- Your turn: Write the problem. Then write the answer. Raise your hand when you're finished.

c. Touch line B. Here's the problem. Listen carefully. A bug starts at **9** on the number line. Then the bug plusses some places. The bug ends up at **10** on the number line.
- Listen again: A bug starts at **9.** Then the bug plusses some. The bug ends up at **10.**
- Your turn: Write the problem. Then write the answer. Raise your hand when you're finished.

d. Touch line C. Here's the problem. Listen carefully: A bug starts at **10** on the number line. Then the bug minuses some places. The bug ends up at **9**.
- Listen again: A bug starts at **10.** Then the bug minuses some places. The bug ends up at **9.**
- Your turn: Write the problem. Then write the answer. Raise your hand when you're finished.

EXERCISE 3 MENTAL ARITHMETIC
Plus Zero, 1, or 2

a. Find part 3.

b. Touch space A. Write the answer to this question: What's 29 plus 1? Raise your hand when you're finished.
- Touch space B. Write the answer to this question: What's 79 plus 1? Raise your hand when you're finished.
- Touch space C. Write the answer to this question: What's 40 plus 2? Raise your hand when you're finished.
- Touch space D. Write the answer to this question: What's 60 plus 0? Raise your hand when you're finished.
- Touch space E. Write the answer to this question: What's 70 plus 2? Raise your hand when you're finished.

EXERCISE 4 PLACE VALUE
Alignment

a. Find part 4. Your turn. Write the numerals in columns. Raise your hand when you're finished.

EXERCISE 5 SUBTRACTION
Minus Zero and 1

a. Find part 5.

b. Your turn: Write the answers. Raise your hand when you're finished.

EXERCISE 6 COUNTING

a. Find part 6.

b. Your turn: Fill in the missing numerals. Raise your hand when you're finished.

EXERCISE 7 MARKING THE TEST

- (Use the **Workbook Answer Key** to check the tests and award points.)

Test Answer Key

The teacher's *Answer Key* provides the correct answer for each lesson and 10-lesson test. The answer key for each test shows the correct work for each item, and a table for assigning percent grades based on the number of points earned.

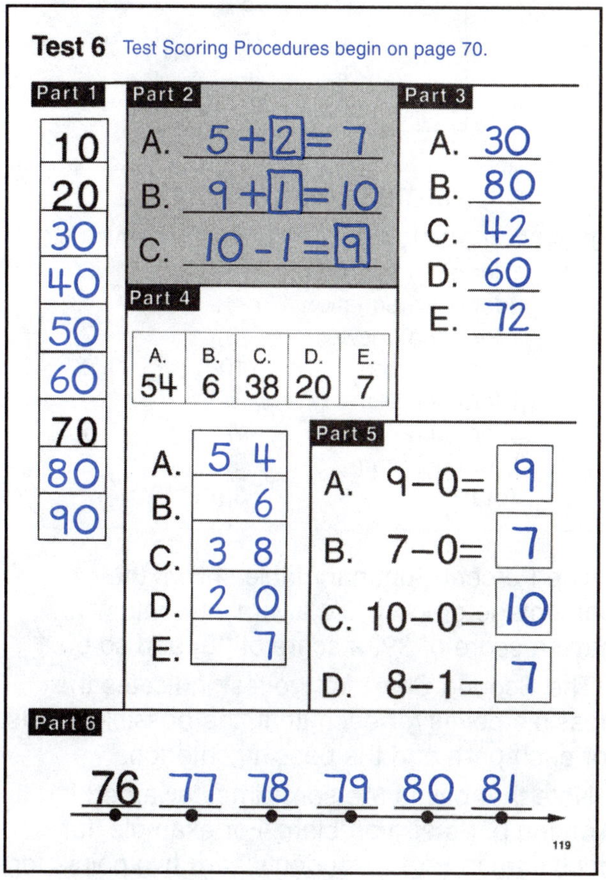

Test 6 Test Scoring Procedures begin on page 70.

Part 1

10
20
30
40
50
60
70
80
90

Part 2

A. 5 + [2] = 7
B. 9 + [1] = 10
C. 10 − 1 = [9]

Part 3

A. 30
B. 80
C. 42
D. 60
E. 72

Part 4

A.	B.	C.	D.	E.
54	6	38	20	7

A. 5 4
B. 6
C. 3 8
D. 2 0
E. 7

Part 5

A. 9−0= [9]
B. 7−0= [7]
C. 10−0= [10]
D. 8−1= [7]

Part 6

76 77 78 79 80 81

119

PERCENT SUMMARY	
Score	%
39	100
38	97
37	95
36	92
35	90
34	87
33	85
32	82
31	79
30	77
29	74
28	72

TEST 6 SCORING CHART

PART	SCORING	POSSIBLE	PASSING
1	1 for each numeral	6	6
2	2 for each equation	6	
	1 for each answer	3	7
3	2 for each item	10	8
4	1 for each item	5	
	1 for each item	4	4
5	1 for each numeral	5	5
	Total	**39**	

The Percent Summary table shows the percentage grade you'd award students who have a score of 39, a score of 38, and so on.

The Scoring Chart for the test indicates the possible points for each item, the possible points for each part, and the passing criterion.

Note that points are sometimes awarded for working parts of a problem. For example, for each item in Part 2, students earn two points for writing the problem correctly and one point for the correct answer.

Marking 10-Lesson Tests

Use the criteria in the *Answer Key* for marking each student's test. Record the results on the Group Summary of Test Performance Charts, found on pages 118–123 of this *Teacher's Guide.*

Here's an example of a Group Summary as it might look after Test 6.

Name	Test 6: Check parts not passed. 1	2	3	4	5	6	Total %
1. Amanda Adams		√					84%
2. William Alberts		√			√		72%
3. Henry Bowman							98%
4. Phillip Caswell				√			87%
5. Zoe Collier			√				83%

The Summary provides you with a cumulative record of each student's performance on the 10-Lesson Tests.

- Make a checkmark in the appropriate columns to indicate any part of the test that was failed.
- At the bottom of each column, write the total number of failures for that part and the total number of students in the class. Then divide the number of failures by the number of students to determine the failure rate for each part.
- Provide a remedy for each part that has a failure rate of 25 percent (.25) or more.

Test Remedies

The Presentation Book specifies remedies for each test. Any necessary remedies should be presented before the next lesson (Lesson 61). Extra-practice pages are provided in the student Workbook immediately following the test.

Here are the remedies for Test 6:

TEST 6 REMEDIES			
PART	LESSON	EXERCISE	EXTRA PRACTICE TEST 6 WORKBOOK PART
1	55	6	1
2	42	4	2
3	48	2	3
4	48	3	4
5	45	4	5
6	57	1	6
	Then tell the students to find part 6 and fill in the numbers.		

If the same group of students predictably fail parts of the test, it might be possible to provide remedies for those students as the others do an independent extension activity. The program is designed so that students use everything that has been taught. So, if students are weak on a particular skill, they will have trouble later in the program when that skill becomes a component of a larger operation of more complex application.

Additional Information

LESSON OBJECTIVES

The lessons begin with objectives that show the various skills that are being taught and the order of activities in the structured-teaching part of the lesson.

Here are the objectives for Lesson 42 (the lesson with the board demonstration for writing problems in columns.)

Objectives

- Count from 27 to 36, then say the number that comes after a specified number. (Exercise 1)
- Write "turn around" addition problems (the commutative property). (Exercise 2) *Note:* Children have answered plus-1 questions and now are shown that plus-1 questions have the same answer (for example: $4 + 1 = 5$ and $1 + 4 = 5$).
- Write teen and twenties numerals from T's and lines. (Exercise 3)
- Write answers to plus-1 questions that start with twenties and thirties numbers. (Exercise 4)
- Write answers to orally presented plus-1 problems that "turn the corner." (Exercise 5)
- Write teen, twenties, and thirties numerals from dictation. (Exercise 6)

Some of the objectives are in regular type:

- Count from 27 to 36, then say the number that comes after a specified number.

These are objectives for exercises that are just like exercises from the preceding lesson, except that the instances or examples are changed.

Some of the objectives are in bold type:

- **Write "turn around" addition problems (the commutative property). (Exercise 2)** *Note:* Children have answered plus-1 questions and now are shown that plus-1 questions have the same answer (for example: $4 + 1 = 5$ and $1 + 4 = 5$).

These objectives signal a new activity or variation that is more difficult than what the children have done earlier.

The note explains what is new about the exercise. Children are learning that familiar questions like $4 + 1 = \square$ have the same answer as questions like $1 + 4 = \square$.

The bold objectives give you information for activities that are new. It's a good idea to rehearse these activities before presenting to the children.

EXTENSION ACTIVITIES

At the end of each lesson are optional activities that provide extensions or applications to every major topic or track presented in Level A. A complete list of the activities and the lessons in which they appear are on pages 81, 82, and 83.

One possible procedure is to select those activities that target specific areas of knowledge that you feel should be strengthened. Some of the activities require more time than you might judge reasonable because of problems students have with manipulatives. The measurement activities, for instance, are very good because they provide additional practice in manipulating a ruler and measuring; however, children often need a great deal of feedback before they become facile at measuring things.

An important point is that the main parts of the lessons are critical to developing necessary skills. None of these activities should be slighted or eliminated in favor of presenting extension activities. Also, the rate at which children progress through the program is important. Ideally, they should complete the entire level during the school year. Sometimes, you'll have to provide remedies following test lessons. In some cases, the remedies may require an entire period. With the 120 regular lessons, the 12 test lessons, possible lessons needed for providing remedies, and lessons that may not be completed during a period, the program will require about 150 periods if children start on Lesson 1. Completing it should be your major priority. Any extension activities you present should not interfere with this schedule.

Tracks

Following Instructions

At the beginning of the program are activities on following instructions. These activities are important because they introduce children to the type of activities they will be doing throughout the program:

a) They will follow your directions precisely.

b) They will sometimes wait for other children to finish.

c) They will do activities in different parts of their workbook lesson.

In the early parts of the program (through Lesson 30), the items in each workbook part are designated by pictures that always occur in the same order. The parts are: star, moon, tree, and dog.

In Lessons 1 and 2, children follow specific directions involving rows of these symbols. Here's the first part of the activity from Lesson 1:

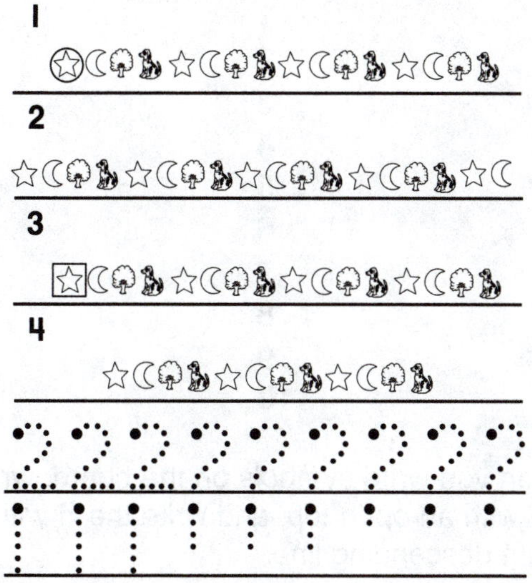

a. (Write on the board:)

Lesson 1

- Everybody, this says **Lesson 1.** Open your workbook and find the page that says **Lesson 1** right at the top. Raise your hand when you've found it. (Observe children and give feedback.)

b. You're going to follow a lot of instructions. When you follow instructions, you listen big and do just what the instructions say.

- Here's an instruction: Touch the words that say **Lesson 1** on your page. Do it. Raise your hand when you're touching it. After I see that your hand is raised, you can put it down. (Quickly acknowledge children who raise their hand.)
- Here's another instruction: Find the big number **3** on the page and touch it. Raise your hand when you're touching it. √
- Here's another instruction: Find the big number **4** on the page and touch it. Raise your hand when you're touching it. √
- Here's another instruction: Find the big number **1** on the shaded part of the page. Raise your hand when you're touching it. √

c. There are little pictures of a star, moon, tree, and dog below the number **1.**

- The first picture is a star. It has a circle around it. Touch that star. √
- Listen: Touch the picture next to the star. Everybody, what is the picture you're touching? (Signal.) *A moon.*
- It's a moon.
- (Draw on the board:)

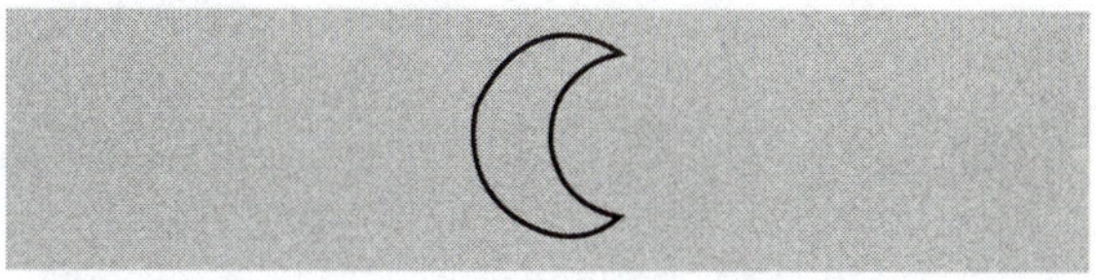

- This is what you should be touching. Make sure you're touching the moon.
- Listen: Touch the next picture. Everybody, what are you touching? (Signal.) *A tree.*
- Listen: Touch the next picture. Everybody, what are you touching? (Signal.) *A dog.*

d. Everybody, go back and touch the first picture in the row. The first picture. √

- Everybody, what's that picture? (Signal.) *A star.*
- Keep touching the star. Let's see if you can follow the instructions really fast. You're touching the star.
- Everybody, touch the next picture. What's that picture? (Signal.) *A moon.*
- Everybody, touch the next picture. What's that picture? (Signal.) *A tree.*
- Everybody, touch the next picture. What's that picture? (Signal.) *A dog.*
  (Repeat step d until firm.)

e. Let's play a new game. Touch the big number **3.** Raise your hand when you're touching it.

- There are pictures below the number **3.** Touch the first picture below the number **3.** Everybody, what's the first picture? (Signal.) *A star.*
- Does that picture have a circle around it? (Signal.) *No.*
- What does it have around it? (Signal.) *A box.*
- Yes, it has a box around it.

f. Listen: Touch the big number **2.** Raise your hand when you're touching it.

- There are pictures below the number **2.** Everybody, what's the first picture? (Signal.) *A star.*
- Does that star have a circle around it? (Signal.) *No.*
- Does that star have a box around it? (Signal.) *No.*
- What does that star have around it? (Signal.) *Nothing.*
- Right, it doesn't have anything around it.

g. Listen: Touch the big number **4.** Raise your hand when you're touching it.

- There are pictures below the number **4.** Everybody, what's the first picture? (Signal.) *A star.*
- Does that star have anything around it? (Signal.) *No.*
- Now it's your turn to think big.

h. Touch the big number **3.** Raise your hand when you're touching it. Here's a rule about the pictures below the number **3.** Listen big: Every star should be crossed out. Once more: Every star should be crossed out. Everything else is fine in that row. But the stars should be crossed out.

- (Draw on the board:)

- Here's a star. And here's how you cross it out. (Make a slash mark through the star:)

- Cross out the first star below the number **3.** Remember, that star has a box around it. Raise your hand when you've crossed it out.
- (Observe children and give feedback.)
- You've crossed out 1 star below the number **3.** Touch that crossed-out star.
- There are other stars in the row. Find the other stars. Find all of them. And cross out every star. Raise your hand when you're finished. (Observe children and give feedback.)
- Everybody, count all the stars you crossed out and raise your hand when you know how many stars you crossed out. But don't say anything until I tell you.
- Everybody, how many stars did you cross out? (Signal.) *4.*
- Yes, you should have crossed out 4 stars.

The children first touch specified symbols. Next, they follow instructions involving the next step (step D). Children then follow rules about crossing out and boxing specified symbols.

This exercise and similar ones prepare children for operating on symbols in different ways.

When presenting this exercise, you'll write on the board in step A, step C, and step H.

For the other steps, circulate among the children. Keep the activity moving rapidly, and praise children who are responding correctly to your instructions.

Numerals

For many activities in Level A, you'll write numerals on the board. The directions in the teacher-presentation script specify what to write. For example:

(Write on board: 1 2 3 4 5)

The symbols that are shown in the script do not correspond precisely to the symbols as the children write them. Here are the symbols as the children are taught to write them:

1
2
3
4
5
6
7
8
9
10

When you write symbols on the board, write the 4 with an open top, and write the 9 with a straight descending line.

Counting

Counting relationships are fundamental to beginning arithmetic; however, there are many subtle differences in counting activities. Children who are proficient in all basic counting operations are well prepared for the inferences and questions of basic arithmetic. Some children pick up many of these relationships through informal exposure; however, many don't. For this reason, *Connecting Math Concepts, Level A* provides careful instruction in the following types of counting:

a) Rote counting. Children are often not practiced in counting in the 30s through 90s. They may also be unpracticed with hundreds numbers.

b) From __ to __. Counting from a number to a number (from 30 to 36, for example) sets the stage for working with problems that involve counters and number-line work. (A bug starts at 4 on the number line and ends up at 6. How many places did the bug plus?)

c) Counting objects. Objects are not "ordered." They can be counted by starting with any object and proceeding in any order. The trick in arriving at the correct ending number is to count each object once and only once.

d) Counting events. Events (such as claps) are different from objects. They are ordered in time. To "count" events, you must represent and count each occurrence.

e) Counting backward. This is a rote-counting operation implied by subtraction.

f) Responding to counting operations that are signalled by instructions involving "more" and "less." "What number is 2 more than 6?" suggests starting with 6, then counting two places in the regular counting direction—7, 8. "What number is 2 less than 6?" implies counting to smaller numbers. A variation calls for the identification of the "next" number. Both of these activities present implied counting operations.

g) Counting ordinals. An altered number vocabulary is used for the same event as regular (cardinal) counting. For example, to cross out the third object, the child counts, "first, second, third." These designations are parallel to 1, 2, 3.

h) Counting like groups of more than one involves a "double take." Three groups of 10, for example, is 3 groups. The total number within the set is 30. Different procedures may be used in arriving at the total, such as counting by 10 or counting members of the groups one at a time.

ROTE COUNTING FROM __ TO __

Children are presented with rote-counting tasks in most lessons. The typical exercise presents the number span the children are to count. Then the children count. Here's a typical exercise from Lesson 41:

- Listen: Say **29.** Then count all the way to 39. Get ready. (Signal.) *29, 30, 31, 32, 33, 34, 35, 36, 37, 38, 39.*

(Repeat step until firm.)

The counting activity is normally the first in the lesson. It is not intended to be particularly difficult; however, it is important. It establishes the recursive nature of the number system, sets the stage for place value, and establishes conventions for following instructions and working as a group.

The activity can be fun. To make it fun, follow these steps:

a) Act as if you're having a good time.

b) Establish a good rhythm—not one that drags.

c) Praise children for doing a good job. Do not praise them if they are sloppy. Follow the note about repeating until firm. After children repeat the task and do well, however, praise them. "What good counters we have."

Here's a schedule for the various segments of rote counting that children practice as they move through the program:

Children Count to:	Starting in Lesson:
15	12
25	28
30	34
35	38
40	43
45	46
50	49
60	51
70	53
80	55
90	57
100	59
110	95
120	96
130	97
150	98

NUMERALS AND COUNTERS

Children receive a lot of practice in making lines for numerals and numerals for lines. The first activities start in Lesson 3. They continue through Lesson 19.

Making counters for numerals implies an understanding of the "number value" that a symbol like 5 indicates. To show that value, 5 lines are drawn. Writing the number of lines in a group requires the opposite process. The children count the lines, and then make the symbol that indicates that number.

The work on making a given number of lines parallels the work on symbol identification. Line-making activities are not introduced before children learn to identify the numerals involved in specific line-making activities. Preceding the initial activities with numerals, children practice counting to specified numbers and review symbol identification.

Here are the activities from Lesson 3. In the first exercise, the teacher makes lines. Children count and say when to stop.

In the second activity, the teacher first models what the children will do, then directs workbook practice.

EXERCISE 2 MAKING LINES

a. I'm going to make lines on the board. You're going to count and tell me when to stop.

b. Listen: I want to make 4 lines. How many lines? (Signal.) *4.*

- So I count **1, 2, 3, 4** as I make the lines. Then you tell me to stop, or I'll just keep making lines.

c. Here we go: Making 4 lines. Count and tell me when to stop. Get ready.
(Make 4 lines as children say:) *1, 2, 3, 4, stop.*

||||

(To correct:)
(If the children don't say **stop**, make 1 or 2 more lines. Then say:) You have to remember when to tell me to stop.

d. New game. I want to make 6 lines. How many lines? (Signal.) *6.*

- Count and tell me when to stop. Get ready. (Make 6 lines as children say:) *1, 2, 3, 4, 5, 6, stop.*

e. New game. I want to make 3 lines. How many lines? (Signal.) *3.*

- Count and tell me when to stop. Get ready. (Make 3 lines as children say:) *1, 2, 3, stop.*

f. You're pretty good at that game.

EXERCISE 3 LINES FOR NUMERALS

a. (Write on the board:)

4 2 5

- You're going to tell me these numerals.

b. (Touch **4.**) Everybody, what numeral? (Signal.) *4.*
- (Touch **2.**) What numeral? (Signal.) *2.*
- (Touch **5.**) What numeral? (Signal.) *5.*
(Repeat step b until firm.)

c. The numerals tell you how many lines to make.
- (Touch **4.**) This is 4. So I make 4 lines for this numeral. Listen: What's this numeral? (Signal.) *4.*
- So how many lines do I make? (Signal.) *4.*
- (Touch **2.**) What's this numeral? (Signal.) *2.*
- So how many lines do I make? (Signal.) *2.*
- (Touch **5.**) What's this numeral? (Signal.) *5.*
- So how many lines do I make? (Signal.) *5.*

d. (Touch **4** again.) My turn to make the lines. This numeral is 4. So I'll make 4 lines. Count and tell me when to stop. Get ready.
(Make 4 lines under **4** as children say:)
1, 2, 3, 4, stop.

4
||||

e. (Touch **2.**) This is 2. So how many lines do I make? (Signal.) *2.*
- I'll make the lines. You count and tell me when to stop. Get ready.
  (Make 2 lines under **2** as children say:)
  1, 2, stop.

f. (Touch **5.**) This is 5. So how many lines do I make? (Signal.) *5.*
- I'll make the lines. You count and tell me when to stop. Get ready.
  (Make 5 lines under **5** as children say:)
  1, 2, 3, 4, 5, stop.

g. (Do not erase the board.)

Workbook Practice

a. Now it's your turn: Open your workbook and find the page that says **Lesson 3** at the top. √
- Touch the big star on the page. The big star. √
- There's a row of numerals below the big star.

b. The first numeral is **4.** Touch it.
- Everybody, touch the next numeral after **4.** Everybody, what numeral are you touching? (Signal.) *2.*
- Touch the next numeral after 2.
- Everybody, what numeral are you touching? (Signal.) *5.*
- Touch the numeral after **5.** Everybody, what numeral are you touching? (Signal.) *3.*
- Touch the numeral after **3.** Everybody, what numeral are you touching? (Signal.) *1.*
  (Repeat step b until firm.)

c. Each numeral should have lines under it. Some of the numerals don't have any lines under them.
- Touch the **4** at the beginning of the row. Does the **4** have lines under it? (Signal.) *Yes.*
- Touch the next numeral after that **4.** That numeral is **2.** Does that numeral have lines under it? (Signal.) *No.*
- You'll fix it up. The numeral is **2.** That tells you how many lines to make. Everybody, how many? (Signal.) *2.*
- Your turn: Make the lines for **2.** Don't do any of the other numerals. Just the **2**. Raise your hand when you're finished.
  (Observe children and give feedback.)
- (Point to the **2** on the board.) Here's what your lines for the **2** should look like. Raise your hand if you did it the right way.

d. Now touch the next numeral after **2.** That numeral is **5.** So how many lines do you make? (Signal.) *5.*
- Your turn: Make the lines for **5**. Raise your hand when you're finished.
  (Observe children and give feedback.)
- (Point to the **5** on the board.) Here's what your lines for the **5** should look like. Raise your hand if you did it the right way.

e. Your turn to fix up the rest of the numerals in the top row. Remember, read the numeral. Then make the right number of lines. Raise your hand when you're finished.
  (Observe children and give feedback.)

f. (Write on the board:)

3	**1**
III	**I**

- Here's what you should have for **3** and **1.** Raise your hand if you got them right.

Note: If some children have trouble making the correct number of lines, use the shaded segment of the workbook page at a later time. Give the children directed practice in which you have them identify the numeral and indicate the number of lines to make. Give feedback as they make the lines.

For some of these activities, you write on the chalkboard. During the bulk of the workbook practice, however, you should circulate among the children.

EXERCISE 2

Make the lines at about 1-second intervals. Keep a very steady pace.

The correction is specified for step C. Follow the rule that if the children don't tell you to stop or don't tell you in time, make one or two more lines, then say: "You have to tell me when to stop." Make it a game. Praise children who do tell you when to stop. Always repeat a task that children fail, particularly early in the program so they learn exactly what good performance is.

EXERCISE 3

Children first identify symbols that you write on the board. These symbols will be used in the workbook practice, so make sure that children are firm in identifying the numerals.

Follow the same rules for making lines. If children don't tell you to stop, don't stop. Correct the mistake. Erase the lines and start over.

At the end of the board exercise, do not erase the board. The reason is that children are doing the workbook activity for the first time. The first examples they work are the same examples you just worked on the board. The coordination of board exercises and workbook practice assures that children will perform well on the initial workbook items. In later lessons, children will work in their workbook without any board demonstration to prompt them.

Be very careful to praise children who are following your directions. Although most children would be able to do the workbook activity without waiting for your directions, it's important to establish a good working relationship with the children. In many later exercises, children will not be able to complete the workbook exercise following a simple inspection of the material.

If children get ahead of you, direct them to erase any part that you haven't directed. Try to keep the pacing "reasonable" for the average student. Do not go so slowly that most of the children are waiting for a few children. If some children have trouble keeping pace or making the appropriate number of lines, you can use the shaded part of the workbook to provide additional practice. First, make sure that the children are performing appropriately on the set of numerals that is used in the regular exercise. Then present the shaded part.

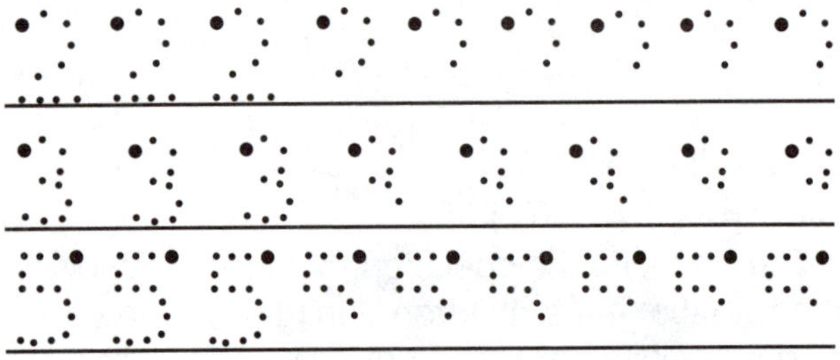

a. You're going to complete the rows of numerals. Remember, if the numeral doesn't have all its dots, you have to finish the numeral so it goes all the way to the bottom line, just like the dotted numerals.
b. Touch the top row of dotted numerals. √
- Everybody, what numeral do you make for that row? (Signal.) *2.*
- Touch the next row of dotted numerals.

The additional-practice section appears in only one lesson—Lesson 3. However, you can use the same procedure if some children continue to have trouble with the line-making activity. Present a sheet of paper that displays the numbers they tend to miss and provide additional practice. In fact, very few children who are appropriately placed in Level A should need this additional practice; however, some children may need it in Lesson 3.

NUMERALS FOR LINES

Starting in Lesson 4, children do exercises making numerals for lines. Here's the exercise from Lesson 4:

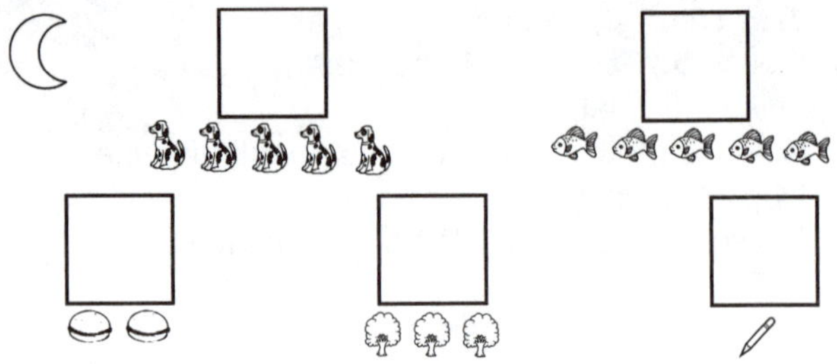

a. Now you're going to write numerals to tell how many.
b. Touch the moon on your workbook page. √
- There's a row of dogs near the moon. Touch that row.
- There's a row of fish near the moon. Touch that row.
- There's a row of hamburgers near the moon. Touch that row.
- Find the row of trees and touch that row.
- Find the pencil and touch that pencil.

c. Here's what you're going to do. You're going to write the numeral in the box just above each row.
- Touch the row of dogs. Listen: Count the dogs to yourself. Then write the numeral in the box just above the row of dogs. Write the numeral that shows how many dogs are in the row. You can look at the numerals on the board to make sure you don't write your numeral backward. Raise your hand when you've written the numeral for the dogs. (Observe children and give feedback.)
- Everybody, how many dogs are in the row? (Signal.) *5.*
- So what numeral did you write just above the dogs? (Signal.) *5.*
- (Point to **5** on the board.) Here's the numeral you should have. Raise your hand if you wrote it the right way.

d. Touch the row of fish. Listen: Count the fish and write the numeral in the box just above the fish. Raise your hand when you're finished. (Observe children and give feedback.)
- Everybody, how many fish are in the row? (Signal.) *5.*
- So what numeral did you write just above the fish? (Signal.) *5.*
- (Point to **5** on the board.) Here's the numeral you should have. Raise your hand if you wrote it the right way.

e. Touch the row of hamburgers. Listen: Count the hamburgers and write the numeral in the box just above the hamburgers. Raise your hand when you're finished. (Observe children and give feedback.)

- Everybody, how many hamburgers are in the row? (Signal.) *2.*
- So what numeral did you write just above the hamburgers? (Signal.) *2.*
- (Point to **2** on the board.) Here's the numeral you should have. Raise your hand if you wrote it the right way.

f. Touch the row of trees. Listen: Count the trees and write the numeral in the box just above the trees. Raise your hand when you're finished.
(Observe children and give feedback.)

- Everybody, how many trees are in the row? (Signal.) *3.*
- So what numeral did you write just above the trees? (Signal.) *3.*
- (Point to **3** on the board.) Here's the numeral you should have. Raise your hand if you wrote it the right way.

g. Touch the pencil. Listen: Write the numeral in the box just above the pencil.
Raise your hand when you've finished.
(Observe children and give feedback.)

- So what numeral did you write just above the pencil? (Signal.) *1.*
- (Point to **1** on the board.) Here's the numeral you should have. Raise your hand if you wrote it the right way.

Earlier in Lesson 4, children made lines for familiar numerals. The numerals are on the board so that children are able to refer to them. In exercise 5, children work in their workbooks. Position yourself so that you can observe the children as they work. Do not remain at the front of the room.

When children count the objects, some may count out loud. Remind them to whisper, but do not require them to count without any verbalization. Some children can't do it.

Again, praise children who follow your directions and who work quickly and accurately. "Wow, we have some good, fast workers in this class. I'm impressed with Donna and James, and all the people in this row. Good work."

Children will work faster and more accurately if they receive such praise.

COUNTING BACKWARD

Counting backward is introduced in Lesson 18. The concept of zero is included as part of the introduction to counting backward.

Here's the exercise from Lesson 18:

a. (Write on the board:)

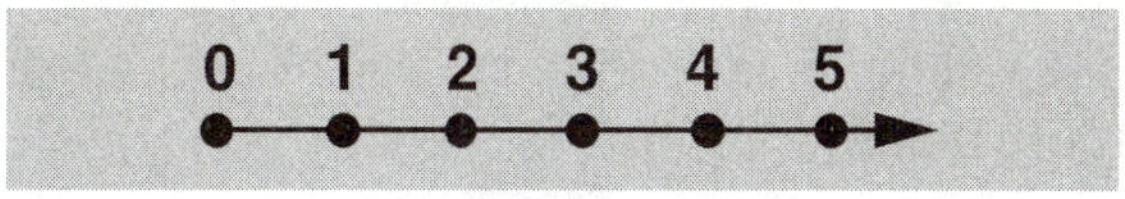

- This number line begins with zero. Listen: If you had zero dollars, how many dollars would you have? (Signal.) *None.*

b. Everybody, hold up 2 fingers. (Signal.)
(Observe children and give feedback.)

- Hold up zero fingers. (Signal.)
(Observe children and give feedback.)
- You should be holding up no fingers because zero fingers are no fingers.

c. (Point to zero.) You've learned to count forward. You just start with zero and say the numbers. Do it. Get ready. (Signal.) *Zero, 1, 2, 3, 4, 5.*

d. That's counting **forward.** I'm going to show you how to count **backward.** You start with 5 and count **back toward** zero.

- My turn.
(Touch the dot for each numeral as you say;) 5, 4, 3, 2, 1, zero.

e. (Point to **5.**) Your turn: Start with **5** and count backward. Get ready. (Touch the dot for each numeral as children say:) *5, 4, 3, 2, 1, zero.*
(Repeat step e until firm.)

f. (Erase **4** and **3,** leaving the dots:)

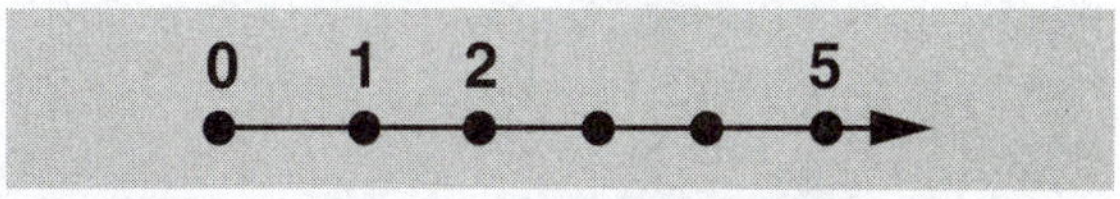

- This is hard. I've erased a couple of the numbers. Let's see if you can do it now. Get ready. (Touch the dot for each numeral as children say:) *5, 4, 3, 2, 1, zero.*

g. (Erase **2, 1,** and **0,** leaving the dots:)

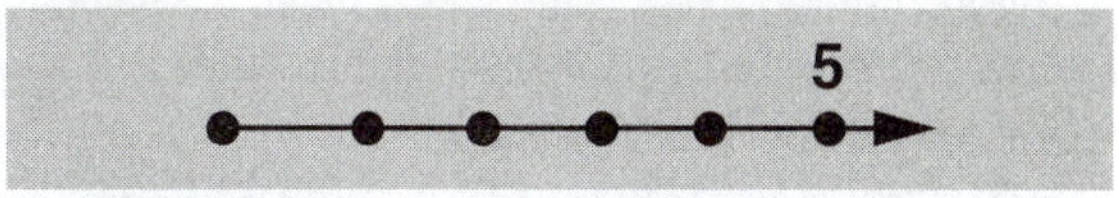

- Now it's really tough. Let's see who can do it.

h. I'll touch. You count backward. Get ready. (Touch the dot for each numeral as children say:) *5, 4, 3, 2, 1, zero.*
(Repeat step h until firm.)

i. Good counting backward.

j. (Erase the board.)

The rule for counting backward is that you count back toward zero. You go backward along the number line. This relationship is fundamental. Children use it as the basis for subtraction and for representing values that are presented in word problems.

Although most of the children will be able to do the counting in step H, make sure they are very firm. In later lessons, the counting-backward tasks will be expanded to include counting from larger values.

ORDINAL COUNTING

Ordinal counting is introduced in Lesson 11. The most difficult part of the ordinal-counting sequence is the first three entries. The word "first" is not closely related to "one," and the word "second" is not closely related to "two." The word "third" is closer to "three." After the fifth ordinal entry, the correspondence between the cardinal numbers (6, 7, 8) and the ordinals (sixth, seventh, eighth) is very close. The ordinal name is the cardinal name with "th" at the end.

The introduction to ordinal counting provides children with a demonstration of the relationship between ordinals and the counting numbers (which many of the children already understand). Following your demonstration of three actions, children show the action you did first, second, and third. Here's the introduction:

a. We're going to play the great memory game. I'm going to do three things. Then you'll see how well you remember them.
- Here's the first thing. (Clap.)
- Here's the second thing. (Touch your head.)
- Here's the third thing. (Smile big.)

b. I'll do those three things again. Watch carefully.
(Clap.)
(Touch your head.)
(Smile big.)
- You're going to show me the things I did.

c. Listen: show me the **first** thing I did. (Signal.)
(Children clap.)
- Show me the **second** thing I did. (Signal.)
(Children touch their heads.)
- Show me the **third** thing I did. (Signal.) (Children smile big.)
(Repeat step c until firm.)

d. Pretty good. But now I'm going to make it harder. I'm going to mix them up.
- Listen: Show me the **third** thing I did. (Signal.)
(Children smile big.)
- Show me the **first** thing I did. (Signal.) (Children clap.)
- Show me the **second** thing I did. (Signal.)
(Children touch their heads.)
- Show me the **first** thing I did. (Signal.) (Children clap.)
- Show me the **third** thing I did. (Signal.) (Children smile big.)
- Show me the **second** thing I did. (Signal.)
(Children touch their heads.)

e. Raise your hand if you remembered all of them.
- Good for you.

When you present the events in step A, use good pacing. Say your lines. Then perform the action. Then move to the next item.

"Here's the first thing (clap). Here's the second thing (touch your head)."

In step C, make sure that children are performing together. Do not permit some children to lead and others to follow. If children get into the pattern of having some children lead, a lot of children may not learn but may simply listen to what the leaders say. So repeat step C until firm. Make sure you give children feedback about why you're repeating the step:

"I have to hear everybody. Let's try that again. Show me the first thing I did....Good. Show me the second thing I did....That's it. Show me the third thing I did....Now that's the way to do it."

If some children persist in lagging or not responding, provide a treat for those children who do perform. Also make sure that the non-performers are able to perform.

Starting in Lesson 17, children are introduced to groups of static objects. The teacher demonstrates which is "first," "second," and so forth. The children then identify objects according to their ordinal number. This activity is different from counting events because the events occur in time, one after the other. The order of the static objects, however, is imposed by operating on the objects.

Here's the exercise from Lesson 17:

a. (Write on the board:)

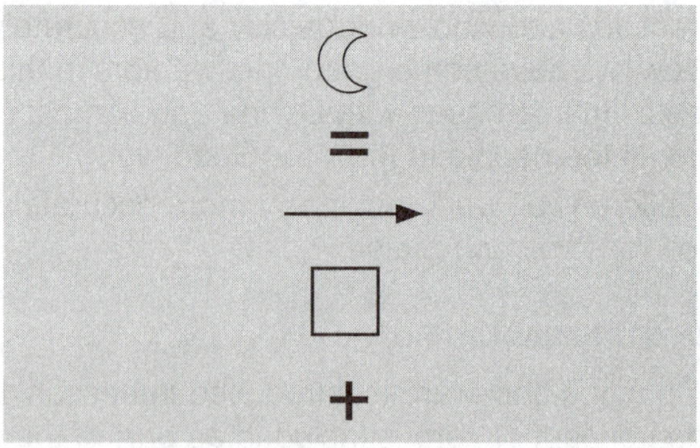

- Here are some things in a column. That means they go up and down. When you read things in a column, you start at the top.

b. (Touch the moon.) Here's the first thing.
- (Touch the equal sign.) Here's the second thing.
- (Touch the arrow.) Here's the third thing.
- (Touch the box.) Here's the fourth thing. Fourth thing.
- (Touch the plus sign.) Here's the fifth thing. Fifth thing.

c. Your turn to tell me the name of each thing. I'm not going to point.

d. Everybody, what's the first thing? (Signal.) *Moon.*
- What's the second thing? (Signal.) *Equals.*
- What's the third thing? (Signal.) *Arrow.*
- What's the fourth thing? (Signal.) *Box.*
- What's the fifth thing? (Signal.) *Plus.*
  (Repeat step d until firm.)

e. This time, I'll touch each thing. You'll tell me **first thing, second thing,** and so forth.

f. (Touch the moon.) Tell me. (Signal.) *First thing.*
- (Touch the equal sign.) Tell me. (Signal.) *Second thing.*
- (Touch the arrow.) Tell me. (Signal.) *Third thing.*
- (Touch the box.) Tell me. (Signal.) *Fourth thing.*
- (Touch the plus sign.) Tell me. (Signal.) *Fifth thing.*
  (Repeat step f until firm.)

g. Now comes the toughest game of all. You're going to name the objects.

h. Listen: Count to yourself and find the fourth thing. The fourth thing.
- Everybody, what is the fourth thing? (Signal.) *Box.*
- Listen: Find the third thing. The third thing.
- Everybody, what's the third thing? (Signal.) *Arrow.*
- Listen: Find the fifth thing. The fifth thing.
- Everybody, what's the fifth thing? (Signal.) *Plus.*
- Listen: Find the second thing. The second thing.
- Everybody, what's the second thing? (Signal.) *Equals.*
  (Repeat step h until firm.)

i. Raise your hand if you got all of them right.
- Wow, such smart people.

Children should have no trouble with this activity if they are firm on preceding activities.

COUNTING BY 10

In Lesson 54, children are introduced to the number line for tens. This number line is shown as going down (not to the right). The introduction presents the tens numbers as a transformation of the ones numbers. By adding a zero to the ones numbers, tens are created.

By the time the tens are introduced, children have practiced rote counting through 70. Children have also written 2-digit numerals through 87.

Here's the introduction to tens from Lesson 54:

a. (Draw on the board:)

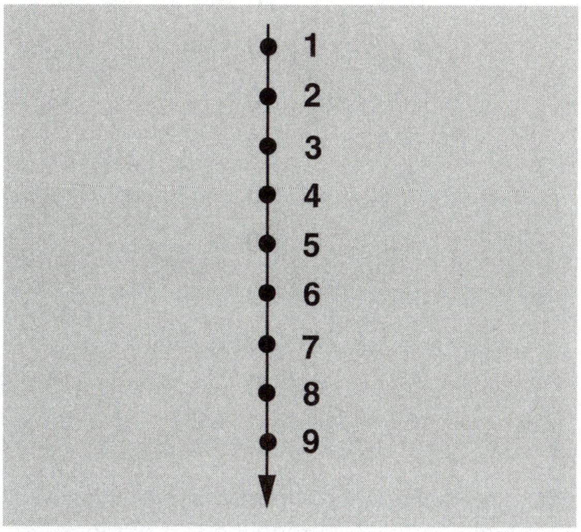

- Here's a number line that goes down. I'll touch the numbers. You read them.

b. (Point to **1.**) Get ready.
  (Touch the dot for each numeral as children say:) *1, 2, 3, 4, 5, 6, 7, 8, 9.*
- We're going to play the cover-up game. You'll tell me the number that comes next. Close your eyes.

c. (Cover the numerals below **6,** using the arrow card. Arrow must point down.)

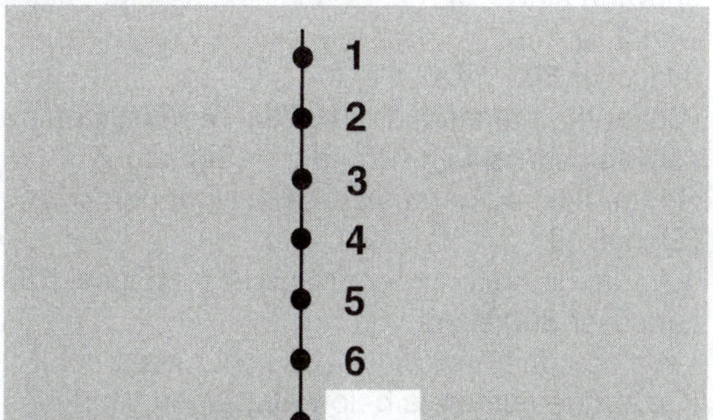

- Open your eyes. What's the last number showing? (Signal.) *6.*
- What's the next number? (Signal.) *7.*
- (Uncover 7.) You're right.

d. I'll show you something very interesting. The numbers that end in zero work the same way.

- (Write **0** after each numeral:)

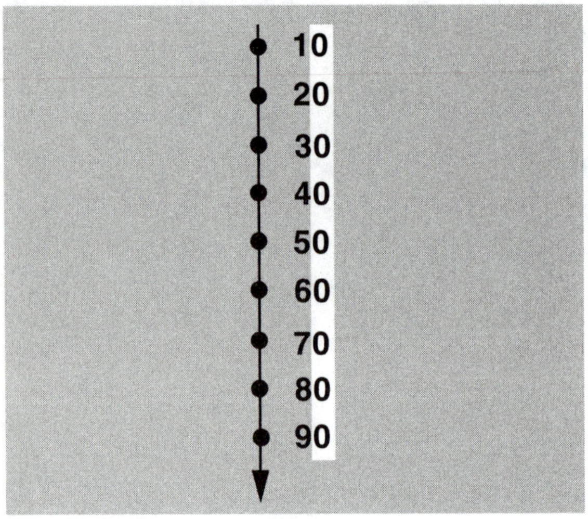

- You already know how to read some of these numerals. It's easy to read the rest of them. My turn: (Touch the dot for each numeral as you say:) 10, 20, 30, 40, 50, 60, 70, 80, 90.

e. (Point to **10.**) Your turn: I'll touch. You read. (Touch the dot for each numeral as children say:) *10, 20, 30, 40, 50, 60, 70, 80, 90.*
(Repeat step e until firm.)

f. The cover-up game for these numbers works just like the cover-up game with the smaller numbers.
- (Cover the numerals below **20.**) The last numeral showing starts with **2**. So the next numeral starts with **3.**
- (Uncover **30.**) See? It's 30.

g. (Cover the numerals below **70.**) The last numeral showing starts with what digit? (Signal.) *7.*
- So the next numeral starts with what digit? (Signal.) *8.*
- Tell me the next numeral. Get ready. (Signal.) *80.*
- (Uncover **80.**) Were you right?

h. Let's do it the hard way. Close your eyes.
- (Cover the numerals below **40.**) Open your eyes. The last numeral showing starts with what digit? (Signal.) *4.*
- So the next numeral starts with what digit? (Signal.) *5.*
- Tell me the next numeral. Get ready. (Signal.) *50.*
- (Uncover **50.**) Were you right?

i. Close your eyes again.
- (Cover the numerals below **70.**) Open your eyes. Look at the last numeral showing and raise your hand when you know the next numeral.
- Everybody, what's the next numeral? (Signal.) *80.*
- (Uncover **80.**) Were you right?

j. Close your eyes again.
- (Cover the numerals below **10.**) Open your eyes. Look at the last numeral showing and raise your hand when you know the next numeral.
- Everybody, what's the next numeral? (Signal.) *20.*
- (Uncover **20.**) Were you right?
- Close your eyes again.
- (Cover the numeral below **80.**) Open your eyes. Look at the last numeral showing and raise your hand when you know the next numeral.
- Everybody, what's the next numeral? (Signal.) *90.*
- (Uncover **90.**) Were you right?
(Repeat step j until firm.)

k. You're learning all about 2-digit numerals that end with zero.

For this activity, you use the same arrow card that is used in other activities. The number line is shown going down so that it won't be confused with the number line for ones. Therefore, when presenting various tasks, you will have to remain at the board and hold the arrow card in place. (This is one of the few exercises in the program that require you to operate on the card as you present.)

A good way to prepare for presenting this activity is to think of the main things you'll do. You will start with a number line that has ones. You do one cover-up. Then you change the numbers into tens. You demonstrate how to read them and have children read them (step E). Then you cover up different numbers and ask questions about the next number. After children predict the next number, you move the arrow card down to uncover the next number. Make sure the arrow card is pointing down and that the number just above the arrow card is the number you ask about.

Practice going through this exercise before presenting it to the class.

Symbol Writing

A large percentage of children require substantial practice in symbol writing. Symbols are unusual "objects" to many children because symbols must be positioned a particular way. Often, children write them backward. The problem is magnified with 2-digit numerals, in which the digits may be transposed (41 for 14). *Connecting Math Concepts, Level A* provides a lot of practice on writing the numerals through 19. Three types of exercises are included: symbol identification tasks, symbol writing tasks, and editing tasks, which involve identifying backward numerals. Here's the order of introduction of the symbols in the first 15 lessons of Level A: 1, 2, 3, 4, 5, 6, 10, 7, 9, 8, +, =.

The introduction involves reading, writing, writing from dictation, and following-instructions applications. Note that symbols like = and + are introduced in isolation before they are presented in statements such as 4 + 2 = 6.

The first symbol-writing activities occur in Lesson 1 immediately after the work on following instructions. Children trace numerals that have varying parts dotted.

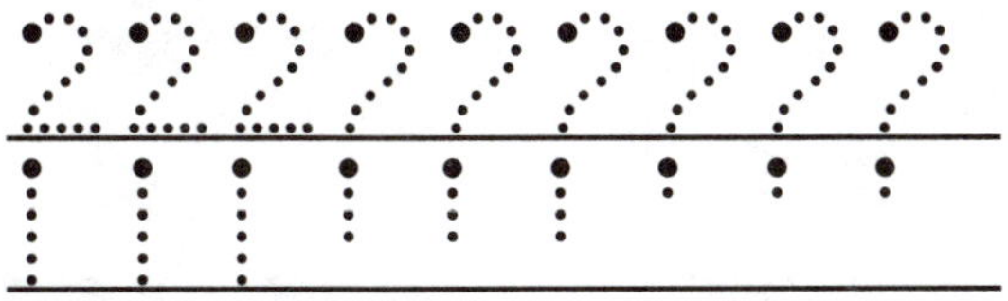

a. (Write on the board:)

- You're going to write some numerals. I'll show you how to do it.

b. Everybody, what numeral is this? (Signal.) *2.*

- When you write the **2,** you put your pencil on the big dot and follow the dots very carefully. Watch how I do it.
  (Place chalk on the big dot and trace the numeral.)

c. Your turn: Find the row of dotted twos near the bottom of your workbook page. A whole row of twos.

- Listen: Trace the first **2.** Remember, put your pencil on the big dot and follow the dots. Raise your hand when you're finished.
  (Observe children and give feedback.)

d. Now go to the very last **2** in the row.
(Write on the board:)

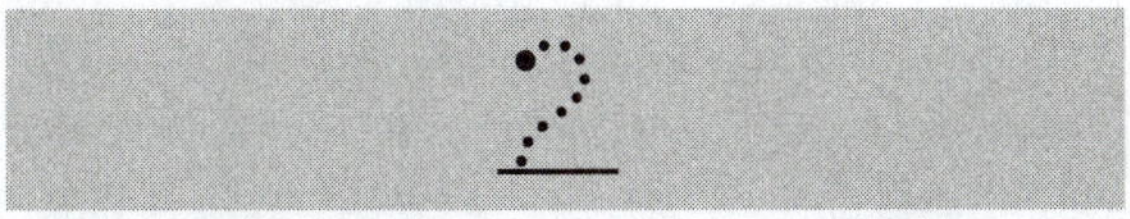

- Somebody forgot to put all the dots on that **2** and some of the others. So here's what you'll do to write that **2.** You'll follow the dots. Then you'll make a straight line to complete the **2.** Watch.
- (Complete the 2:)

e. Your turn: Complete all the twos in the row. Start with the twos that have all the dots. Then do the harder twos. Raise your hand when you're finished with all the twos.
(Observe children and give feedback.)

f. (Write on the board:)

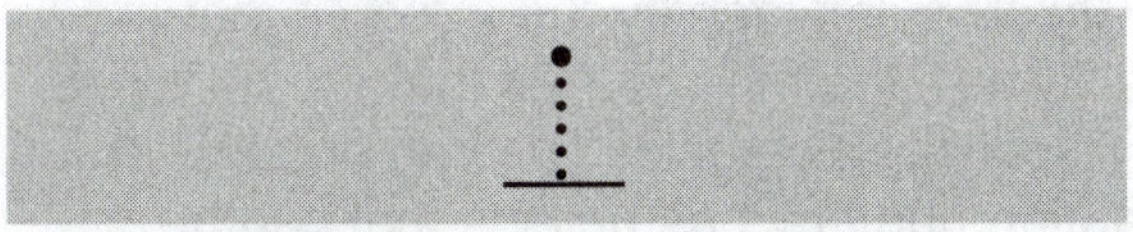

- The next row has the number **1** in it. You complete the ones by putting your pencil on the big dot and following the dots. Watch.
- (Complete the **1.**)

g. Your turn: Complete all the ones. But be careful. Somebody forgot dots on some of those ones. Remember, the ones have to go all the way to that bottom line. Raise your hand when you're finished.
(Observe children and give feedback. Praise children who complete the numerals appropriately.)

When observing children and providing feedback (as in step C), praise children who start at the big dot and stay reasonably close to the dots. "Some folks are really hitting all those dots. It's tough, but they're doing it."

Beginning in Lesson 2, children work on symbol-identification exercises. The general pattern is for children first to identify symbols, then write them.

For the symbol-identification activity in Lesson 2, you write the numerals 1–5 in order on the board. Children identify them. Then you write them so they do not occur in counting order. Children again identify them. This activity, like most of the symbol-identification exercises, requires only about a minute or two.

a. (Write on the board:)

1 2 3 4 5

- Here are the numerals 1 through 5. I'll touch them and say them.
  (Touch each numeral as you say:) 1, 2, 3, 4, 5.
- Your turn: Tell me the numerals.

b. (Touch **1.**)

- Everybody, what is it? (Signal.) *1.*
- (Touch **2.**) Everybody, what is it? (Signal.) *2.*
- (Touch **3.**) Everybody, what is it? (Signal.) *3.*
- (Touch **4.**) Everybody, what is it? (Signal.) *4.*
- (Touch **5.**) Everybody, what is it? (Signal.) *5.*
  (Repeat step b until firm.)

c. Now I'm going to skip around. (Touch **3.**) Raise your hand when you know it.

- Everybody, what is it? (Signal.) *3.*
- (Touch **5.**) Everybody, what is it? (Signal.) *5.*
- (Touch **2.**) Everybody, what is it? (Signal.) *2.*
- (Touch **4.**) Everybody, what is it? (Signal.) *4.*

d. Now I'm going to make it really tough. Watch.

- (Erase the numerals and write:)

3 5 4 1 2

- They're all mixed up now. Let's see who knows them.

e. (Touch **3.**) Raise your hand when you know it.

- Everybody, what is it? (Signal.) *3.*
- (Touch **5.**) Everybody, what is it? (Signal.) *5.*
- (Touch **4.**) Everybody, what is it? (Signal.) *4.*

- (Touch **1.**) Everybody, what is it? (Signal.) *1.*
- (Touch **2.**) Everybody, what is it? (Signal.) *2.*
(Repeat step e until firm.)

f. We have some people who really know their numerals.

In later lessons, children write series of three or more numerals. These activities help shape children's understanding of how to write the numbers of the series, because children write one numeral, then another, then another. Because they are not simply writing the same numeral over and over, they are forced to remember the details of the individual numerals. The numbers that are presented in series are presented in counting order, so knowledge of counting order is associated with the specific symbols the children make.

Here's the first series activity from Lesson 11:

a. Find part 3. √
You're going to write the numerals **1, 2,** and **3.**

b. The numerals in the first boxes are dotted. When you write each numeral, you start with the big dot. Then you trace along the dotted lines.
- Your turn: Trace **1, 2, 3** in the first box—just the first box. Raise your hand when you're finished.
(Observe children and give feedback.)

c. Now trace **1, 2, 3** in the next box. Raise your hand when you're finished.
(Observe children and give feedback.)

d. Now trace **1, 2, 3** in the next box. Raise your hand when you're finished.
(Observe children and give feedback.)

e. Now you'll write **1, 2, 3** in the last box. Remember, your numerals should go all the way to the bottom line of the box. Write the numerals **1, 2, 3** so they look just like the numerals you traced. Raise your hand when you're finished.
(Observe children and give feedback.)

f. We have some pretty good numeral writers.

Children have repeatedly written the component numerals (1, 2, 3) in various lessons. In step E, children write the numerals in the last box. The only prompts are the starting dots for the numerals. When observing and giving feedback, make a great fuss over children who perform well—writing numerals that start at the dot, have the correct form, and go all the way to the baseline. Don't be shy about letting the children know that this job is difficult. "I'm going to hold up some of the better writing papers so you can see what stars we have in this class. Very good writers."

The final symbol-writing activity involves crossing out backward numerals. This activity begins in Lesson 2 and continues through Lesson 15. Here's the introductory activity from Lesson 2.

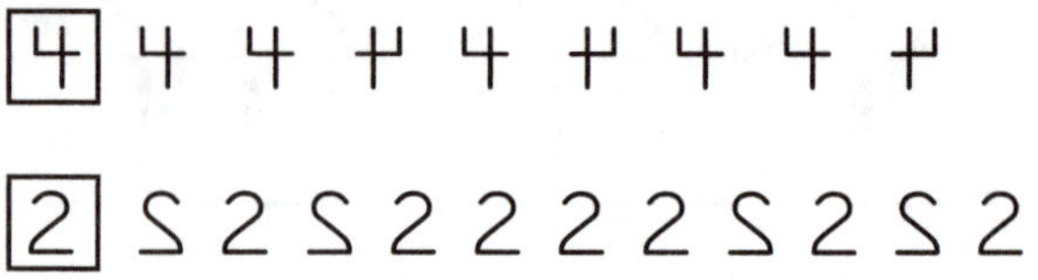

a. (Write on the board:)

- You're going to play the great mix-up game. It's called the great mix-up game because somebody got all mixed up and wrote some numerals backward.

b. There's a **4** in a box just below the row of dotted twos you made. Touch the **4** in the box. √
- That **4** is written the right way. But there are other fours in that row and not all of them are written the right way. Somebody wrote some of them backward. In fact, there are 3 of them that are wrong.
- Look at the **4** in the box very carefully. Then find all the fours that are written backward and cross them out. They're wrong. Raise your hand when you've crossed out all the backward fours.
(Observe children and give feedback.)
- Count the fours you crossed out and make sure you found all 3 of them. Raise your hand if you crossed out all 3 of them.
(Praise children who raise their hand.)

c. Touch the boxed **2** at the bottom of your worksheet.
- That **2** is written the right way. But some of the twos in the row are written backward.
- Look at the **2** in the box very carefully. Then find all the twos that are written backward and cross them out. They're wrong. Raise your hand when you've crossed out all the backward twos.
(Observe children and give feedback.)
- There are 4 twos that are backward. Count the twos you crossed out and make sure you found all 4 of them. Raise your hand if you crossed out all 4 of them.
(Praise children who raise their hand.)

Children first identify the three 4s that are backward, then the four 2s that are backward. This activity also gives children practice in treating numerals as objects that can be counted, as they count the numerals they crossed out.

In Lesson 12 children start working with 2-digit numerals. First, they see them on the number line and read them. Later, starting at Lesson 14, they write them. The work with 2-digit numerals ties in with place value and addition.

Place Value

Level A conveys the following concepts about place value in 2-digit numerals:

- Numerals have digits.
- The first digit represents tens.
- The second digit represents ones.
- When 2-digit numerals are written in a column, the digits should be aligned.
- Two-digit numbers can be modeled using counters (tens counters for the first digit and individual counters for the second digit, or ones).
- For models made with tens counters and individual counters, it is possible to write 2-digit numerals using symbols for the corresponding values.

Because place value assumes column alignment, many place-value activities require children to write numerals from dictation. The first dictation exercise is presented in Lesson 14. The introduction presents the terminology "first digit" and "second digit." It shows conventions for aligning digits, and it presents the connection between the teen numerals and the familiar 1-digit numerals.

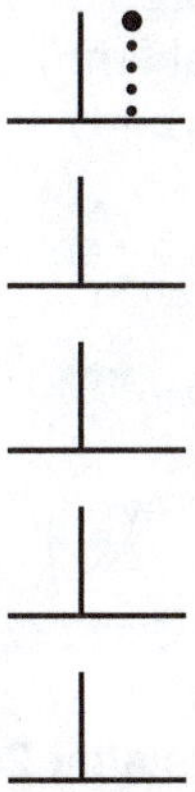

a. (Write on the board:)

1
1
1
1
1

- I'll show you how to write the numerals for 11, 12, 13, 14, and 15.

b. Here's the rule about all those numerals: They start with a **1**. That's called the **first digit.** The second digits are the numbers you say when you count—1, 2, 3, 4, 5.

- I've written the first digit on the board. So I'll complete each numeral with the numbers you say when you count. Watch.
- (Write the second digits as you say:) 1, 2, 3, 4, 5.
- Now I have the numerals **11, 12, 13, 14, 15.** Pretty slick. Remember, the first digit is **1**; the second digit is **1** for 11, **2** for 12, **3** for 13, **4** for 14 and **5** for 15.

c. (Point to **12.**) Here's 12. Listen: What's the first digit of this numeral. (Signal.) *1.*

- What's the second digit? (Signal.) *2.*
- (Point to **14.**) Listen: What's the first digit of this numeral? (Signal.) *1.*
- What's the second digit? (Signal.) *4.*
- (Point to **15.**) Listen: What's the first digit of this numeral? (Signal.) *1.*
- What's the second digit? (Signal.) *5.*
(Repeat step c until firm.)

d. Are you going to remember how these numerals work?

- (Erase the board.)

Workbook Practice

a. Find part 3. You're going to complete the numerals so you have 11, 12, 13, 14, and 15.

b. Touch the top numeral. That's going to be **11.** So the second digit is **1**. It's dotted.

- Touch the next numeral. That's going to be **12.** So the second digit won't be **1.** What will it be? (Signal.) *2.*
- Touch the next numeral. That's going to be **13.** So the second digit won't be **1** or **2.** What will it be? (Signal.) *3.*

c. Your turn: Trace the dotted **1** for 11. Then write the second digit for 12, 13, 14 and 15. Raise your hand when you're finished.

d. (Write on the board:)

11
12
13
14
15

- Here's what you should have for your numerals. Check them over.

e. Raise your hand if you got all of these numerals right. Make sure none of your digits are backwards.

For the workbook practice, the first digit of all the numerals is shown. Children complete the numerals, which requires simply writing the familiar numerals for 1 through 5.

In later lessons, the first digit is not shown. Here's the exercise from Lesson 16.

a. Find part 7. You're going to write numerals that have two digits.
b. Touch the space for the first numeral. That's the first space.
- The first numeral is going to be 13. Listen: What's the first digit of 13? (Signal.) *1.*
- What's the second digit of 13? (Signal.) *3.*
- Write **13.** Trace the **1** and write the **3**. Raise your hand when you're finished.
  (Observe children and give feedback.)
- (Write on the board:)

13

- Here's what you should have for the first numeral.

c. Touch the space for the next numeral. That numeral is going to be 14. What numeral? (Signal.) *14.*
- Write the first digit right under the first digit of 13. Write **14.** Raise your hand when you're finished.
  (Observe children and give feedback.)
- (Write **14**:)

13
14

- Here's what you should have.

d. Touch the space for the next numeral. That numeral is going to be 12. What numeral? (Signal.) *12.*
- Write **12.** Raise your hand when you're finished.
  (Observe children and give feedback.)
- (Write **12**:)

14
12

- Here's what you should have.

e. Touch the space for the last numeral. That numeral is going to be 15. What numeral? (Signal.) *15.*
- Write **15.** Raise your hand when you're finished.
  (Observe children and give feedback.)
- (Write **15**:)

12
15

- Here's what you should have.

f. Raise your hand if you got all of them right.

The position for the first digit is shown for the first numeral. In step C, after children have written 13, you identify the next numeral as 14. Then you tell the children, "Write the first digit right under the first digit of 13. Write 14." Often, children have trouble with this notion. They sometimes crowd the digits or fail to align them. When you observe and give feedback, praise children who are following your instructions about digit alignment.

As part of the work on 2-digit numerals, children are taught to read 2-digit numerals. For instance, in Lesson 30, children read 2-digit numerals in the teens and twenties. The teacher uses the arrow card to cover numerals, then uncover them as children answer the questions, "What's 1 more than 20? What's 1 more than 21?" and so forth. Here's the exercise:

a. (Write on the board:)

- You're going to count to some really big numbers.

b. (Touch **18.**) Everybody, what numeral is this? (Signal.) *18.*
- My turn to read all the numbers on this number line. (Touch the dot for each numeral as you say:) 18, 19, 20, 21, 22, 23.

c. (Point to **18.**) Your turn: Start with **18** and say all the numbers. Get ready.
- (Touch the dot for each numeral as children say:) *18,19, 20, 21, 22, 23.*
  (Repeat step c until firm.)

d. (Point to **20.**) Everybody, what numeral is this? (Signal.) *20.*
- 20 has two digits. The first digit is **2**. The second digit is **zero.**
- (Point to **21.**) Everybody, what numeral is this? (Signal.) *21.*
- 21 is a two-digit numeral. What's the first digit? (Signal.) *2.*
- What's the second digit? (Signal.) *1.*

e. Let's play the great cover-up game.
  (Cover the numerals after **20,** using the arrow card:)

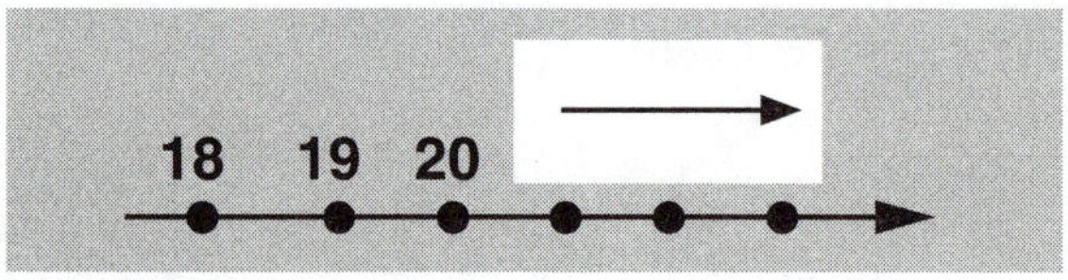

- Everybody, what's the last number showing? (Signal.) *20.*
- What's 1 more than 20? (Signal.) *21.* (Uncover **21.**)
- It's 21. What's 1 more than 21? (Signal.) *22.* (Uncover **22.**)

- It's 22. What's 1 more than 22? (Signal.) *23.* (Uncover **23.**)
- It's 23.

f. (Cover the numerals after **19.**) New game. Everybody, what's the last number showing? (Signal.) *19.*

- What's 1 more than 19? (Signal.) *20.* (Uncover **20.**)
- It's 20. What's 1 more than 20? (Signal.) *21.* (Uncover **21.**)
- It's 21.

g. (Do **not** erase the board:)

In Lesson 30, children are also introduced to the notion that the digits in 2-digit numerals have different values. Children are shown that the first digit is ten and can be represented with a T. Then they write appropriate numerals from displays that show a single T and a group of lines.

Here's the introduction from Lesson 30:

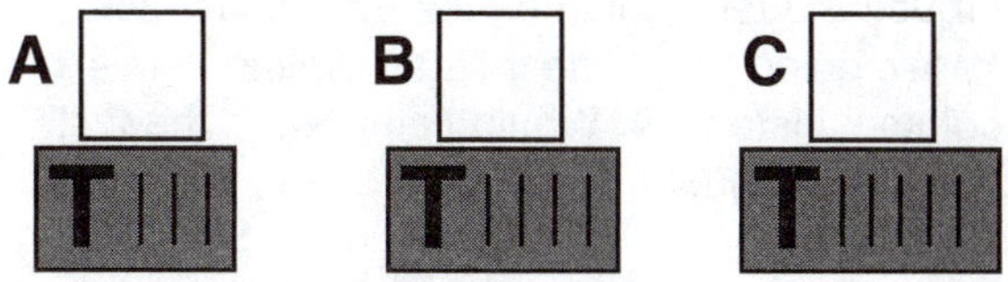

a. (Write on the board:)

Ten

- (Point to **Ten.**) This word is **ten**. Everybody, what's the first letter in **ten**? (Signal.) *T.*
- Watch this. (Erase **en.**)
- We'll use the letter **T** to stand for **ten**. What does the **T** stand for? (Signal.) *Ten.*

b. (Write on the board:)

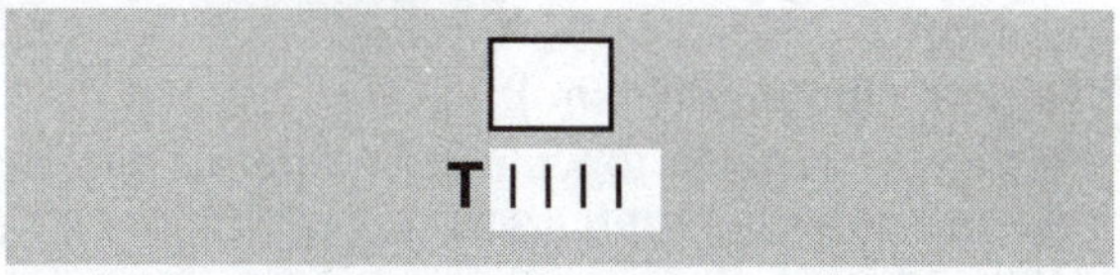

- Here's **10** and some lines. When I touch the **T**, I'll say **10.** Then I'll count the lines. Watch. (Touch the **T** and then each line as you say:) 10, 11, 12, 13, 14.
- Your turn: Remember to say **10** for the **T**.

c. (Point to **T.**) Get ready. (Touch the **T** and then each line as children say:) *10, 11, 12, 13, 14.* (Repeat step c until firm.)

d. There are **14** in this group. So I write 14 in the box. (Write **14**:)

e. (Write on the board:)

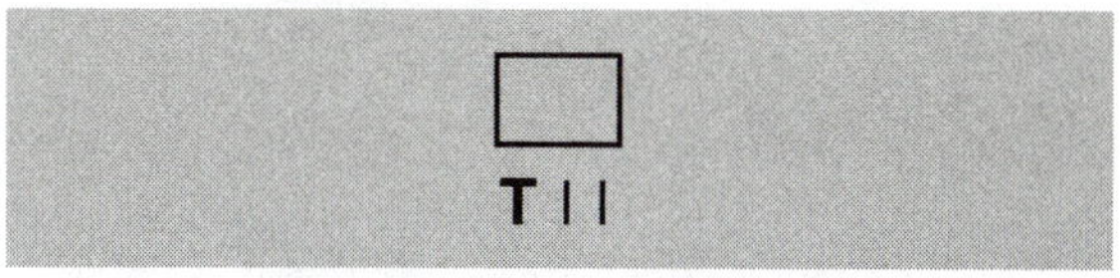

- New problem. What are you going to say for the **T**? (Signal.) *Ten.*
- Get ready. (Touch the **T** and then each line as children say:) *10, 11, 12.*
- There are **12** in this group. So I write 12 in the box. (Write **12**:)

f. (Write on the board:)

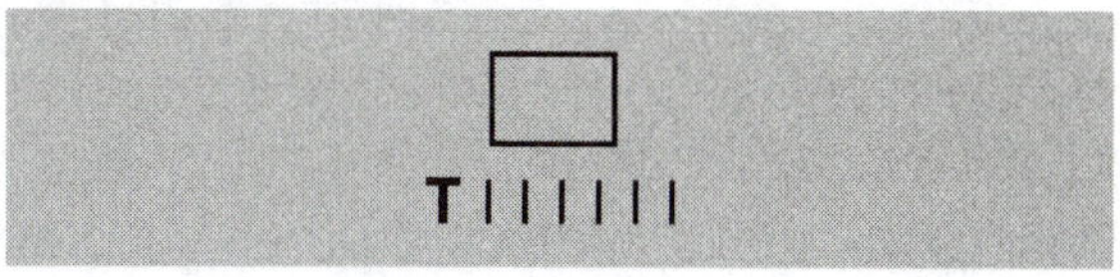

- New problem. What are you going to say for the **T**? (Signal.) *Ten.*
- Get ready. (Touch the **T** and then each line as children say:) *10, 11, 12, 13, 14, 15, 16.*
- How many are in this group? (Signal.) *16.*
- So what do I write in the box? (Signal.) *16.* (Write **16**:)

Workbook Practice

a. Open your workbook to Lesson 30 and find part 1. √

b. Touch group A. What are you going to say for the **T** in the group? (Signal.) *Ten.*

- Start with 10 and count group A. Raise your hand when you know how many are in group A.
- Everybody, how many in group A? (Signal.) *13.* Yes, 13. Write **13** in the box for group A. √
- (Write on the board:)

A. **13**

- Here's what you should have for group A. Raise your hand if you got it right.

c. Touch group B. Start with 10 and count group B. Raise your hand when you know how many are in group B.

- Everybody, how many in group B? (Signal.) *14.*
- Yes, 14. Write **14** in the box for group B. √

- (Write **14**:)

B. 14

- Here's what you should have for group B. Raise your hand if you got it right.

d. Touch group C. Start with the number for **T** and count group C. Raise your hand when you know how many are in group C.

- Everybody, how many in group C? (Signal.) *15.*
- Yes, 15. Write **15** in the box for group C. √
- (Write on the board:)

C. 15

- Here's what you should have for group C. Raise your hand if you got it right.

For the board demonstration, you present examples of a group composed of a T and some lines. Children say 10 for the T and then count for the lines: 10, 11, 12....

During the structured work, children generally do not have any trouble with T's and lines; however, good performance in this activity does not suggest that children have learned the fundamental assumptions of place value. They have practiced only the first step.

Starting in Lesson 52, children write numerals in columns. The ones column is shaded. Children discriminate between 1-digit and 2-digit numerals and indicate whether each numeral begins in the first column or in the second column. The idea that single-digit numerals do not begin in the first column is difficult for some children. If you follow the exercise as specified, however, they'll get it. Here's the exercise from Lesson 52:

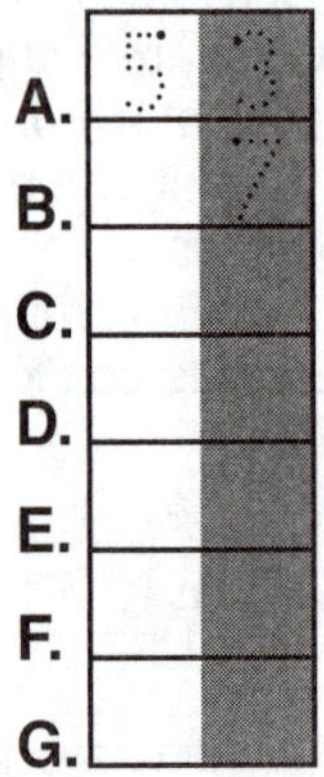

a. (Draw columns on the board:)

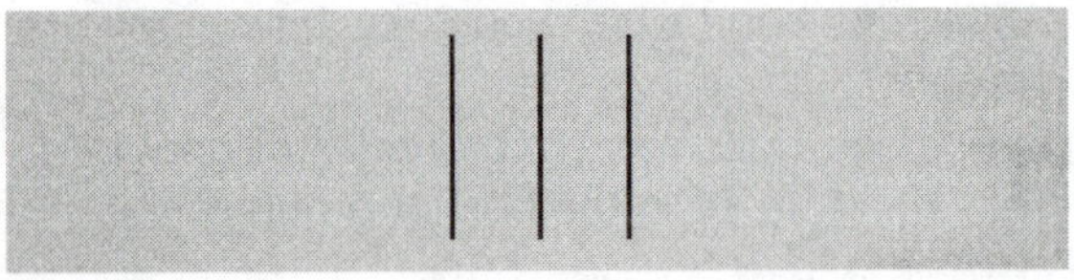

- I'm going to write numerals. You'll tell me whether to write a 1-digit numeral or a 2-digit numeral. Let's practice.

b. Listen: **17.** How many digits? (Signal.) *2.*

- Listen: **4.** How many digits? (Signal.) *1.*
- Listen: **34.** How many digits? (Signal.) *2.*
- Listen: **9.** How many digits? (Signal.) *1.*
- Listen: **29.** How many digits? (Signal.) *2.*
- Listen: **30.** How many digits? (Signal.) *2.*
- Listen: **10.** How many digits? (Signal.) *2.*
  (Repeat step b until firm.)

c. (Point to the columns on the board.) I'm going to write the numerals in these columns. Writing numerals in columns is very tricky, because you don't always start in the **first** column. Here's the rule: You start in the first column if it's a 2-digit numeral. You don't start in the first column if it's a 1-digit numeral. Remember, you don't start in the first column unless the numeral has **two digits**.

d. (Touch the tens column.) Here's the first column. You're going to tell me if I start writing in this column. Listen: **14.** Would I start **14** in the first column? (Signal.) *Yes.*

- My turn: Why would I start 14 in the first column? Because it's a 2-digit numeral. Your turn: Why would I start 14 in the first column? (Signal.) *Because it's a 2-digit numeral.*

e. Listen: **29.** Everybody, would I start **29** in the first column? (Signal.) *Yes.*

- Why? (Signal.) *Because it's a 2-digit numeral.*
- Listen: **4.** Everybody, would I start **4** in the first column? (Signal.) *No.*
- Right. **4** is not a 2-digit numeral.
- Listen: **1.** Everybody, would I start **1** in the first column? (Signal.) *No.*
- Why not? (Signal.) *Because it's not a 2-digit numeral.*
  (Repeat step e until firm.)

f. This time I'm going to write the numerals. Listen: **36.** Do I start **36** in the first column? (Signal.) *Yes.*

- (Write **36**:)

g. Listen: **5.** Do I start **5** in the first column? (Signal.) *No.*

- (Write **5**:)

h. Listen: **2.** Do I start **2** in the first column? (Signal.) *No.*

- (Write **2**:)

3	6
	5
	2

i. Listen: **12.** Do I start **12** in the first column? (Signal.) *Yes.*
- (Write **12**:)

	5
	2
1	2

j. Listen: **22.** Do I start **22** in the first column? (Signal.) *Yes.*
- (Write **22**:)

	2
1	2
2	2

k. Listen: **17.** Do I start **17** in the first column? (Signal.) *Yes.*
- (Write **17**:)

1	2
2	2
1	7

l. Listen: **3.** Do I start **3** in the first column? (Signal.) *No.*
- (Write **3**:)

2	2
1	7
	3

Workbook Practice

a. Open your workbook to Lesson 52 and find part 1.√
- Now it's your turn. The first column in part 1 is not shaded. The second column is shaded.

b. Numeral A is **53.** It's already written with dotted lines. Do you start **53** in the first column? (Signal.) *Yes.*
- Why? (Signal.) *Because it's a 2-digit numeral.*
- Your turn: Trace **53**. Raise your hand when you're finished.√

c. Touch numeral B. That numeral is **7.** It doesn't have two digits, so it doesn't start in the first column. Your turn: Trace **7.** Raise your hand when you're finished.√

d. Touch the space for numeral C. Listen: Numeral C is **17.** What numeral? (Signal.) *17.*
- Do you start **17** in the first column? (Signal.) *Yes.*
- Write **17.** Raise your hand when you're finished. (Observe children and give feedback.)
- (Write on the board:)

C.	1	7

- Here's what you should have for numeral C.

e. Touch the space for numeral D. Listen: Numeral D is **9.** What numeral? (Signal.) *9.*
- Do you start **9** in the first column? (Signal.) *No.*
- Write **9.** Raise your hand when you're finished.√
- (Write on the board:)

C.	1	7
D.		9

- Here's what you should have for numeral D.

f. Touch the space for numeral E. Listen: Numeral E is **50.** What numeral? (Signal.) *50.*
- Do you start **50** in the first column? (Signal.) *Yes.*
- Write **50.** Raise your hand when you're finished.√
- (Write on the board:)

C.	1	7
D.		9
E.	5	0

- Here's what you should have for numeral E.

g. Touch the space for numeral F. Listen: Numeral F is **51.** What numeral? (Signal.) *51.*
- Do you start **51** in the first column? (Signal.) *Yes.*
- Write **51.** Raise your hand when you're finished.√
- (Write on the board:)

D.		9
E.	5	0
F.	5	1

- Here's what you should have for numeral F.

h. Touch the space for numeral G. Listen: Numeral G is **1.** What numeral? (Signal.) *1.*
- Do you start **1** in the first column? (Signal.) *No.*
- Write **1.** Raise your hand when you're finished.√
- (Write on the board:)

E.	5	0
F.	5	1
G.		1

- Here's what you should have for numeral G.

i. Raise your hand if you wrote all the numerals correctly.

Do not present the workbook practice until the children are quite firm in responding to the board activity (steps F through L). Even so, expect some children to have trouble with 1-digit numerals.

The workbook practice is set up so that children receive prompts for a 2-digit numeral (53) and a 1-digit numeral (7). After children trace these numerals, they write a 2-digit numeral (17) and then a 1-digit numeral (9). Children may write these numerals in the appropriate columns but still have trouble with the last numeral, 1. "It's hard to remember that numerals like 1 do not start in the first column." Make sure that children perform well on this activity. If they are having trouble, give them additional practice.

An ongoing activity that first appears in Lesson 58 presents numerals in a row. Children write them in columns. Here's the introduction from Lesson 58:

A.

A.	B.	C.	D.	E.	F.	G.
23	8	80	18	81	1	21

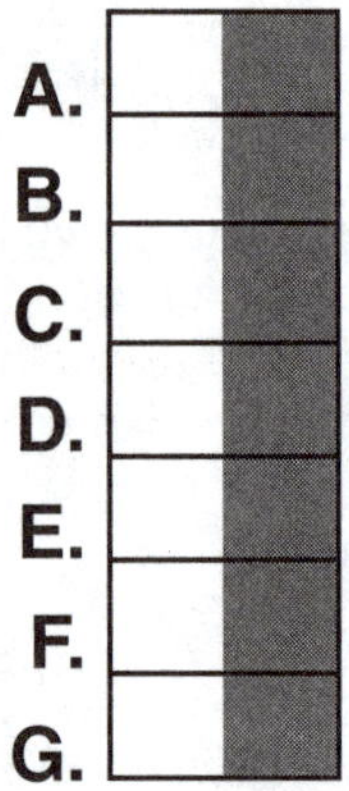

a. Find part 2. There's a row of numerals. You're going to write them in columns.
b. Touch numeral A. Everybody, what numeral? (Signal.) *23.*
- Touch numeral B. What numeral? (Signal.) *8.*
- Touch numeral C. What numeral? (Signal.) *80.*
- Touch numeral D. What numeral? (Signal.) *18.*
- Touch numeral E. What numeral? (Signal.) *81.*
- Touch numeral F. What numeral? (Signal.) *1.*
- Touch numeral G. What numeral? (Signal.) *21.*

c. Touch the space in the columns for numeral A. That's where you'll write numeral A. Everybody, what's numeral A? (Signal.) *23.*
- Touch the space in the columns for numeral B. What numeral goes in that space? (Signal.) *8.*
- Touch the space in the columns for numeral C. What numeral goes in that space? (Signal.) *80.*

d. Your turn: Write the numerals in columns. Write numeral A in space A; write numeral B in space B; and so forth. Remember the rule about 2-digit numerals. Don't get fooled. Raise your hand when you're finished.
(Observe children and give feedback.)
e. (Write on the board:)

A.	**2**	**3**
B.		**8**
C.	**8**	**0**
D.	**1**	**8**
E.	**8**	**1**
F.		**1**
G.	**2**	**1**

- Check your work. Here's what you should have for the numerals. Check your numerals carefully. Make sure all of the 2-digit numerals start in the first column and none of the 1-digit numerals start in the first column.

f. Raise your hand if you wrote all the numerals correctly.

The set of numerals presented in this (and similar) activities includes those that give children the greatest difficulty. The problem is not as much with the children as it is with the numeral names. For example, the name for 80 is not "eighty-zero," it's "eighty." Children sometimes write the 8 in the first column and forget the zero. The name for 18 is not "tenty-eight." Furthermore, the name "eighteen" suggests that the first numeral is 8. The name "eighty-one" is perfectly regular. The set of examples presented to the children gives them practice in writing these and other potentially confusing numerals in a context that all but eliminates errors. Children do not have to concern themselves as much with how to compose the numeral as with how to write it and which column to start in.

The independent work with 2-digits follows copying and writing. For instance, as children learn to read and write 40s and 50s numerals, they do independent numeral-writing activities that involve different parts of a number line. Here's an independent activity from Lesson 47.

c. Find part 7. These are number lines that show only the first number. You'll write the missing numbers for each number line.

Both number lines require children to "turn the corner" (going from 19 to 20 and from 39 to 40). Variations of both number lines have been practiced many times in earlier lessons. The practice assures that children learn the recursive nature of the counting system (which goes from 39 to 40, not from 39 to "thirty-ten") and the parallel between the numbers and the way they are written.

Once this relationship has been practiced with various 2-digit values, children are introduced to writing T's and lines from numerals.

The first activity is presented in Lesson 70.

A. **3 4**

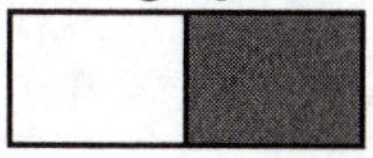

a. You've learned to make numerals from **T's** and lines. Now you're going to make **T's** and lines for 2-digit numerals.

b. Listen: 10. How many **T's** do you make for 10? (Signal.) *1.*

- Listen: 50. How many **T's** do you make for 50? (Signal.) *5.*
- Listen: 70. How many **T's** do you make for 70? (Signal.) *7.*
- Listen: 30. How many **T's** do you make for 30? (Signal.) *3.*

c. Listen: 32. That's 30 plus 2. How many **T's** do you make for 30? (Signal.) *3.*

- How many **lines** do you make for 2? (Signal.) *2.*
- Listen: 53. That's 50 plus 3. How many **T's** do you make for 50? (Signal.) *5.*
- How many **lines** do you make for 3? (Signal.) *3.*
- Listen: 86. That's 80 plus 6. How many **T's** do you make for 80? (Signal.) *8.*
- How many **lines** do you make for 6? (Signal.) *6.*

(Repeat step c until firm.)

Workbook Practice

a. Find part 2. You're going to write **T's** and lines for numerals.

b. Touch numeral A. Everybody, read the numeral. (Signal.) *34.*

- That's 30 plus 4. How many **T's** do you make for 30? (Signal.) *3.*
- How many **lines** do you make for 4? (Signal.) *4.*
- Your turn: Make the **T's** and lines for 34. Make the **T's** under the digit for 30. Make the lines under the **4.** Raise your hand when you're finished. (Observe children and give feedback.)
- (Write on the board:)

A.	**3**	**4**
	T T T	**I I I I**

- Check your work. Here's what you should have for numeral A. 34 has 3 **T's** plus 4 leftover lines. Raise your hand if you got it right.

When you describe the numerals, you use the expanded form. "That's 30 plus 4." Children are to make the T's under the first digit of the number and the lines under the second digit. When you observe and give feedback, make sure that children are following this convention. Even if some children miss the first item, they'll do well on subsequent items if they receive feedback.

More/Less

The concepts of more and less are related to amounts. They are also related to the order of the counting numbers. The numbers that come after a number are more than the number. The number that comes immediately after a number is 1 more than the number. The next is 2 more than the number, and so forth. The values can be represented on a number line. The concept of more is directional. Getting more involves moving to the right. Less works in the opposite way. Less involves moving to smaller numbers. On the number line, getting less involves moving to the left.

The concepts of more and less are fundamental for addition and subtraction. Starting at a number and moving to a number that is 1 more is to plus 1. Starting at the same number and moving to a number that is 1 less is to minus 1.

Level A teaches the concepts of more and less and relates them to quantities to the number line, and to statements of addition and subtraction.

Here's the general progression of activities for more:

Children identify various numbers that are more. "Say some numbers that are more than 5."

Children identify numbers that are 1 more than specified numbers.

Children identify numbers that are 2 more than specified numbers.

As children become proficient at identifying these values, children work from statements of addition. They also construct statements from problems presented on number lines. For instance, the bug on the number line starts at 5. Arrows show that the bug plusses 2 places. Children write the statement: 5 + 2 = 7.

Finally, children work with word problems that describe more and less. Two variations are:

Henry weighs 54 pounds. John weighs 2 pounds more than Henry. How many pounds does John weigh?

John had 7 books. Then he buys 2 more books. How many books does he end up with?

The concept of less follows roughly the same progression; however, less starts later in the program. (More starts in Lesson 8. Less starts in Lesson 23.)

Children identify 1 less and 2 less. They relate these values to bug problems on a number line and word problems. Beginning in Lesson 91, students learn how to construct the greater-than/less-than sign. (The rule is the big end of the sign is next to the bigger number.)

The primary function of more and less is to form the link between common counting phenomena and the operations of plussing and minusing.

Starting in Lesson 1, children identify the next counting number.

Here's what the children say after counting to 10:

c. Good counting! Listen: I'll count. Then I'll stop and ask you the next number I should say. So listen big.
d. 1, 2, 3, 4. Everybody, what's the next number? (Signal.) *5.*
- Listen: 1, 2, 3, 4, 5, 6. What's the next number? (Signal.) *7.*
- Listen: 1. What's the next number? (Signal.) *2.*
- Listen: 1, 2, 3, 4, 5, 6, 7, 8. What's the next number? (Signal.) *9.*
(Repeat step d until firm.)

In Lesson 3, children play a variation of the next-number game—the cover-up game. For this game, you'll use the arrow card and a number line.

A good plan is to make the number line close to the chalkboard rail. Here's the note from the beginning of Lesson 3 and the cover-up activity:

Note: For this exercise, you'll draw a number line on the board. If possible, make the line near the bottom of the board, just above the chalk rail. The numerals should be close enough together that the 8 1/2″ x 11″ arrow card covers three numerals.

When covering the numerals, place the arrow card on the rail. Make sure the arrow points to the right:

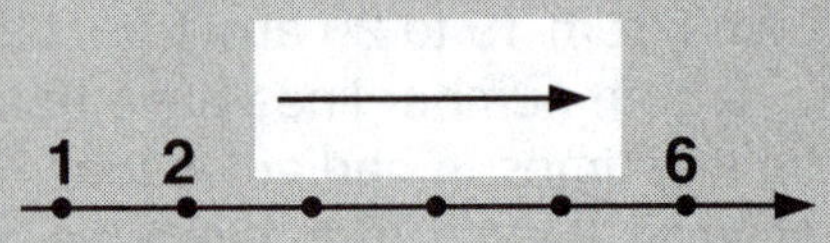

Also, make sure that all children can see the number line.

a. Everybody, count to 10. Get ready. (Signal.) *1, 2, 3, 4, 5, 6, 7, 8, 9, 10.*
b. Let's see if anybody can do that all alone. Raise your hand if you're good at counting to 10. (Call on several children:) *Count to 10.*
- That was good counting.

c. (Write on the board:)

- Here's a number line for counting. It has the numbers up through 6.

d. I'll touch the numbers and say them. Watch. (Touch the dot for each symbol as you say:) 1, 2, 3, 4, 5, 6.
- Let's see if you can say those numbers as I touch them. Don't say a number until I touch it. (Point to **1.**) Get ready. (Touch the dot for each symbol as children say:) *1, 2, 3, 4, 5, 6.*

e. Now let's see if you can tell me the numbers I touch. Raise your hand when you know, but don't say anything until I tell you to.
f. (Point to **2.**) Raise your hand if you know it. Everybody, what is it? (Signal.) *2.*
- (Point to **4.**) Raise your hand if you know it. Everybody, what is it? (Signal.) *4.*
- (Point to **6.**) Raise your hand if you know it. Everybody, what is it? (Signal.) *6.*
- (Point to **5.**) Raise your hand if you know it. Everybody, what is it? (Signal.) *5.*
- (Point to **3.**) Raise your hand if you know it. Everybody, what is it? (Signal.) *3.*
(Repeat step f until firm.)

g. (Cover the numerals after **4**, using the arrow card:)

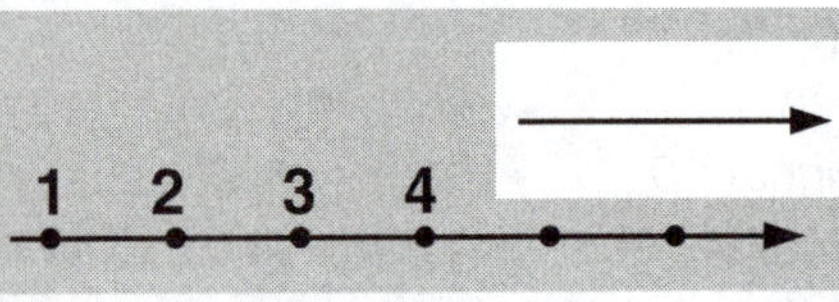

- Now we'll play the great cover-up game. I'll say the numbers that are in front of the arrow card: 1, 2, 3, 4. (Touch **4.**) Here's the last number that's showing. Listen: What's the **last** number showing? (Signal.) *4.*

- I know the next number. It's 5. Watch. (Uncover **5.**)
- I'm really good at the great cover-up game.
- Let's see if you can do it.

h. (Cover the numerals after **2**:)

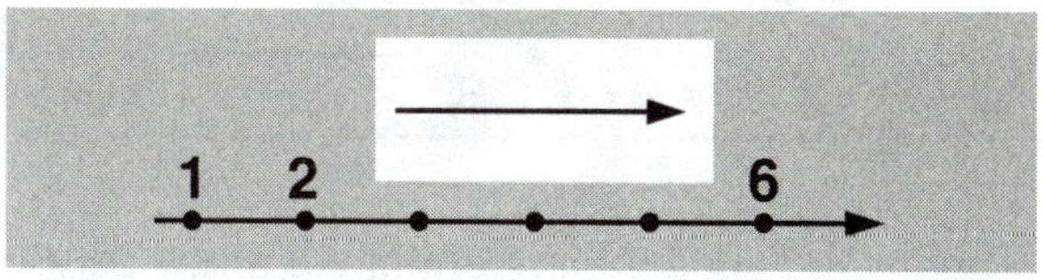

- New game. I'll say the numbers that are in front of the arrow card: 1, 2. (Touch **2.**) Here's the last number that's showing. Listen: What's the **last** number showing? (Signal.) *2.*
- So what's the next number? (Signal.) *3.*
- (Uncover **3.**) Were you right?

i. (Cover **6.**)

- New game. I'll say the numbers that are in front of the arrow card: 1, 2, 3, 4, 5. What's the **last** number showing? (Signal.) *5.*
- So what's the next number? (Signal.) *6.*
- (Uncover **6.**) Were you right?

j. (Cover the numerals after **3**.)

- New game. I'll say the numbers that are in front of the arrow card: 1, 2, 3. What's the last number showing? (Signal.) *3.*
- So what's the next number? (Signal.) *4.*
- (Uncover **4.**) Were you right?

k. You're pretty good at playing the great cover-up game.

The pacing for the activity should be fast. All games, starting at step G, are the same. You cover numbers after a specified number (making sure that the arrow points right). You say the numbers in front of the card. You touch the last number showing. Then you ask two questions:

"What's the last number showing?"
"So what's the next number?"

You uncover the next number and ask, "Were you right?"

Practice presenting this activity, because a lot of variations are presented in Level A. If you can present the activity in Lesson 3 with good timing, you won't have much trouble with subsequent variations.

The first variation occurs in Lesson 6. In this variation, children identify the numbers that are more. They identify all the numbers that are covered (as well as those that may be visible after the arrow card).

Here's the first part of the exercise from Lesson 6:

a. (Write on the board:)

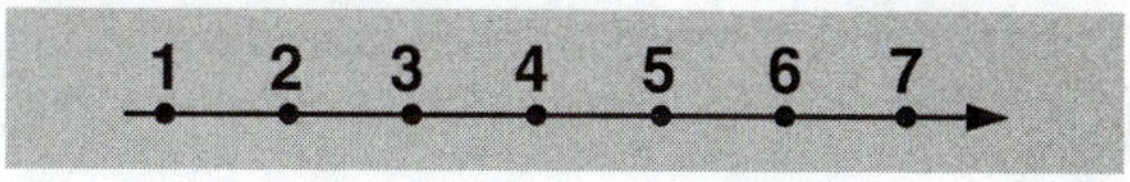

- I'll touch the numerals on this number line. You say them.
- (Point to **1.**) Get ready. (Touch the dot for each numeral as children say:) *1, 2, 3, 4, 5, 6, 7.*

b. We're going to play a new kind of cover-up game. This game is different, because you'll have to tell me the numbers that are **more.** I'll show you how it works.

- (Cover the numerals after **4,** using the arrow card:)

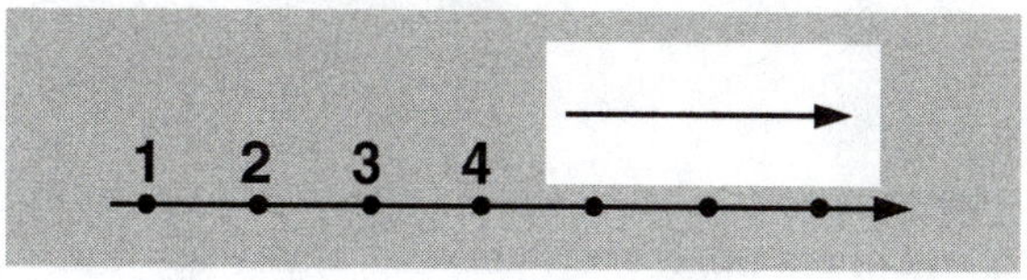

Look at the numbers in front of the arrow card. Everybody, what's the last number showing? (Signal.) 4.

- Listen: All the numbers that are covered up are more than 4. And I can say all the numbers on this number line that are more than 4. Here are the numbers that are more than 4: 5, 6, and 7. Let's see if I'm right.
- (Uncover the numerals and say:) 5, 6, 7. I was right. I'm really good at this game. But now it's your turn.

c. (Cover the numerals after **4.**) What's the last number showing? (Signal.) *4.*

- All the numbers that are covered up are more than 4. Say the numbers that are more than 4. Get ready. (Signal.) *5, 6, 7.*
- Let's see if you were right. Say the numbers that are more than 4 as I uncover them. Get ready. (Uncover each numeral as children say:) *5, 6, 7.*

d. (Cover the numerals after **3.**) New game. What's the last number showing? (Signal.) *3.*
Let's do a harder game. Say the numbers that are more than 3. Get ready. (Signal.) *4, 5, 6, 7.*

- Let's see if you were right. Say the numbers as I uncover them. Get ready.
(Uncover each numeral as children say:) *4, 5, 6, 7.*

e. (Cover the numerals after **6.**) New game. On this number line there's one number that's more than 6. But I'll bet you don't know what it is. What is it? (Signal.) *7.* Let's see if you were right.
(Uncover **7.**) Raise your hand if you were right.

f. (Erase the number line.)

- Now comes the hardest of all games. I'll tell you the last number showing, but you won't be able to see it. Then you'll tell me numbers that are more.

g. Listen: The last number showing is 5. Say the numbers that are more than 5. Get ready. (Signal.) *6, 7.*

- New problem: The last number showing is 3. Say the numbers that are more than 3. Get ready. (Signal.) *4, 5, 6, 7.*
- Last problem: The last number showing is 4. Say the numbers that are more than 4. Get ready. (Signal.) *5, 6, 7.*
(Repeat step g until firm.)

h. You're getting pretty smart.

The next variation, which occurs in Lesson 9, involves identifying the number that is 1 more. Here's the exercise from Lesson 9:

a. (Write on the board:)

5
3
2
7

- Here's a rule. Listen: When you say the number that comes next when you count, you say the number that is **1 more.**

b. (Point to **5.**) Here's 5. My turn to say the next number: 6. My turn to say the number that is **1 more than 5:** 6. The number that's 1 more is the number that comes next.

c. (Point to **3.**) Everybody, what is this? (Signal.) *3.*
- Say the number that is 1 more than 3. (Signal.) *4.*
- (Point to **2.**) What is this? (Signal.) *2.*
- Say the number that is 1 more than 2. (Signal.) *3*
- (Point to **7.**) What is this? (Signal.) *7.*
- Say the number that is 1 more than 7. (Signal.) *8.*

(Repeat step c until firm.)

d. Let's see if you can do it with some other numbers.

e. Listen: 9. Everybody, say the number that is 1 more than 9. (Signal.) *10.*
- Listen: 4. Say the number that is 1 more than 4. (Signal.) *5.*
- Listen: 6. Say the number that is 1 more than 6. (Signal.) *7.*

(Repeat step e until firm.)

f. Are you ever getting smart!

Note that you present numbers that are shown on the board and other numbers that are presented orally (step E). The activity is not difficult for children; however, it introduces the notion of 1 more. The next step is to introduce plus 1 (Lesson 11). Plus 1 on the number line is simply the number that is 1 more than the last number showing in front of the arrow card.

The next "more" activity occurs in Lesson 19. Children learn to identify the number that is 2 more than the last number showing. Children first identify the number that is 1 more, then the number that is 2 more.

Here's the introduction from Lesson 19:

a. (Write on the board:)

0 1 2 3 4 5 6 7 8 9 10

- We're going to play a new cover-up game. I'll show you how it works.

b. (Cover the numerals after **6,** using the arrow card:)

0 1 2 3 4 5 6 → 10

- Look at the numbers in front of the arrow card. Everybody, what's the last number showing? (Signal.) *6.*
- My turn: What's **1 more** than 6? 7. What's **2 more** than 6? 8. Listen again: What's 1 more than 6? 7. Your turn: What's **2 more** than 6? (Signal.) *8.*
- Let's see if you're right. (Uncover **7.**) Here's 1 more than 6.
- (Uncover **8.**) Here's **2** more than 6. Did we get them right?

c. (Cover the numerals after **4.**)
- New game. Let's see if you can do it.

d. Listen: What's the last number showing? (Signal.) *4.*
- What's 1 more than 4? (Signal.) *5.*
- What's 2 more than 4? (Signal.) *6.*

(Repeat step d until firm.)

e. Let's see if you're right. (Uncover **5.**) Here's 1 more than 4.

(Uncover **6.**)

Here's **2** more than 4. Who got it right?
- Wow!

f. (Cover the numerals after **8.**) New game.

g. What's the last number showing? (Signal.) *8.*
- What's 1 more than 8? (Signal.) *9.*
- What's 2 more than 8? (Signal.) *10.*

(Repeat step g until firm.)

h. Let's see if you're right. (Uncover **9.**) Here's 1 more than 8.
- (Uncover **10.**) Here's **2** more than 8. Who got it right?
- Yea.

i. (Cover the numerals after **3.**) Last game.

j. What's the last number showing? (Signal.) *3.*
- What's 1 more than 3? (Signal.) *4.*
- What's 2 more than 3? (Signal.) *5.*

(Repeat step j until firm.)

k. Let's see if you're right. (Uncover **4.**) Here's 1 more than 3.
- (Uncover **5.**) Here's **2** more than 3. Who got it right?

l. Raise your hand if you got all the cover-up problems right.

m. (Do **not** erase the number line.)

The steps involved in presenting the cover-up tasks are very similar to those presented for earlier exercises.

In subsequent lessons, children identify the number that is 2 more without first identifying the number that is 1 more. Children also write the number that is 2 more than the last number showing. Following this work, students are introduced to plus-2 problems.

The concept of less parallels that of more but it starts later, after children have had a lot of practice with more. The first activity is presented in Lesson 23 and is related to counting backward. Children play a variation of the cover-up game in which the arrow points toward the smaller numbers. They identify the number that is next to the card (the number to the right of the card) and then identify the number that comes just before that number. Here's the introduction:

a. My turn to count backward from **10.** Here I go: 10, 9, 8, 7, 6, 5, 4, 3, 2, 1, zero.
b. Your turn: Count backward from **10.** Get ready. (Signal.) *10, 9, 8, 7, 6, 5, 4, 3, 2, 1, zero.* (Repeat step b until firm.)
c. I can count backward from **7**. Here I go: 7, 6, 5, 4, 3, 2, 1, zero.
d. Your turn: Count backward from **7**. Get ready. (Signal.) *7, 6, 5, 4, 3, 2, 1, zero.* (Repeat step d until firm.)
e. We're going to play a new kind of cover-up game. For this game, you'll tell me the number that comes just **before** the number next to my paper.
f. (Cover the numerals before **8,** using the arrow card. Arrow must point left:)

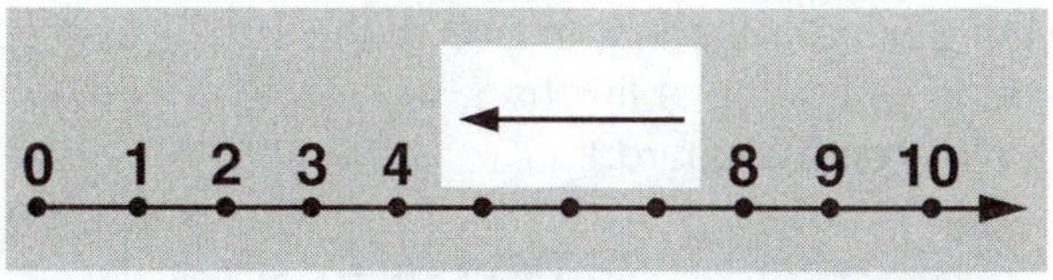

- Look at the arrow. It's pointing toward zero. That means we're counting backward. Here are the numbers you can see, starting with **10**: 10, 9, 8. My turn: What number comes just **before 8**? It's 7. Watch.
- (Uncover **7**.) I was right.

g. (Cover the numerals before **6**:)

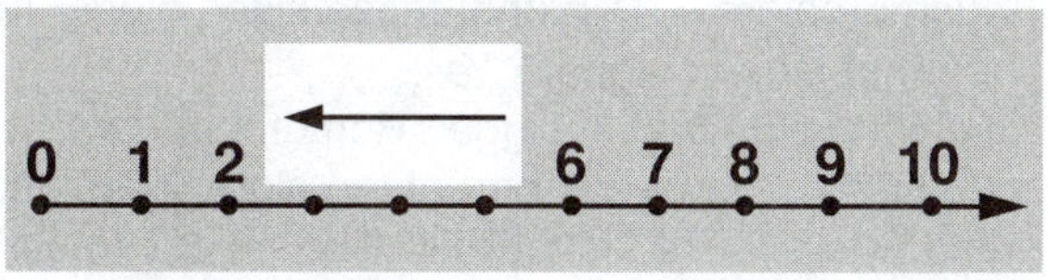

- Here are the numbers you can see: 10, 9, 8, 7, 6. Everybody, what number comes just **before 6**? (Signal.) *5.*
- (Uncover **5.**) Were you right?
- I'll make it tougher.

h. (Cover the numerals before **4**.) What's the number next to the card? (Signal.) *4.*
- Raise your hand when you know the number that comes just before 4.
- Everybody, what number comes just before **4**? (Signal.) *3.*
- (Uncover **3.**) Were you right?

i. (Cover the numerals before **8**.) What's the number next to the card? (Signal.) *8.*
- Raise your hand when you know the number that comes just before 8.
- Everybody, what number comes just before **8?** (Signal.) *7.*
- (Uncover **7.**) Were you right? I can't seem to fool you.

In step H, children may make the mistake of identifying the wrong number when you ask, "What's the number next to the card?" Children sometimes identify the number to the left of the card, not to the right. Correct by pointing to the number to the right of the card and saying, "Here's the number next to the card." You can also call attention to the arrow on the card. "Remember, the arrow shows that we're going toward zero."

In Lesson 32, children play a new cover-up game. They identify numbers that are 1 less.

a. (Write on the board:)

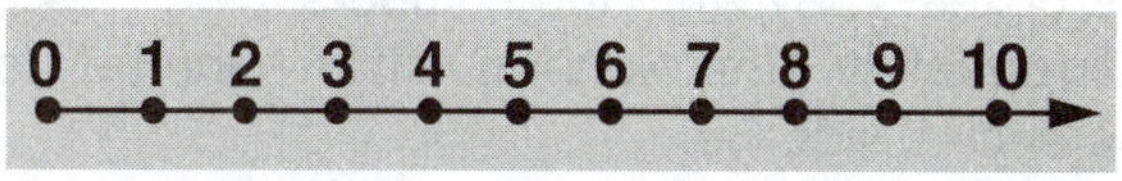

- You're going to tell me the number that is **1 less** than the number next to the card. That's the first number you say when you count backward.

b. (Cover the numerals before **7,** using the arrow card. Arrow must point left:)

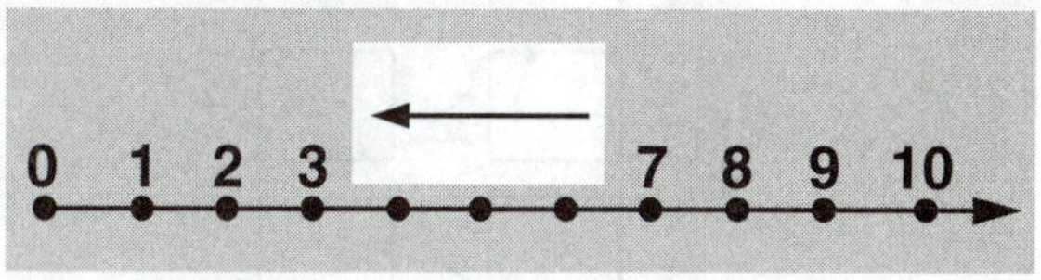

- Everybody, what's the number next to the card? (Signal.) *7.*
- What's the number that is **1 less** than 7? (Signal.) *6.*
- (Uncover **6.**) Were you right?

c. (Cover the numerals before **9.**) New game. What's the number next to the card? (Signal.) *9.*
- What's the number that is 1 less than **9**? (Signal.) *8.*
- (Uncover **8.**) Were you right?

Note that in this and other lessons, children count backward before working on the number line.

As with addition, subtraction problems are introduced for minus 1 after children have worked with values that are 1 less.

In Lesson 62, the cycle is repeated with 2 less. Children first identify values on the number line that are 2 less. In Lesson 65, they respond to questions involving minus 2: "What's 6 minus 2?"

The final activities involving more and less are associated with completing equality and inequality signs. These activities start in Lesson 91. By this time, children have identified values that are more and less. They've worked with groups of symbols and followed instructions such as: "Cross out all the values that are more than 5. Circle all the values that are less than 5." Children have also worked with the equal sign.

In Lesson 91, children learn about the greater-than sign. Children learn that the bigger end of the sign is close to the bigger number. If the numbers are the same, the equal sign connects them.

In Lesson 92, the teacher first reviews the rule about the sign. Then children work problems in which the sign is shown between two boxes. If the sign is not an equal sign, children circle the "side" (the box) that's bigger. That's the box close to the bigger end of the sign. After children have circled the side that's bigger for each inequality, they are told the numbers that go in the boxes. They write the numbers appropriately—the bigger number in the box for the circled side.

Here's the activity:

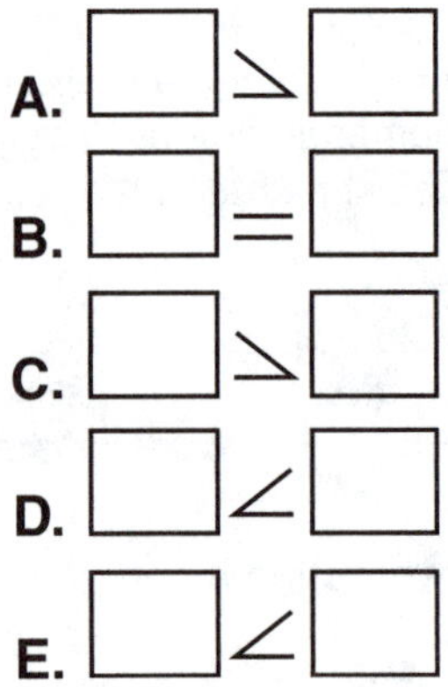

a. (Write on the board:)

6 – 5
5 – 5
4 – 5

- Remember how the signs work. The bigger end of the sign is close to the bigger number. If the numbers are the same on both sides, you write an equal sign.

b. (Point to **6 – 5.**) Everybody, which number is bigger in this problem, 6 or 5? (Signal.) *6.*

- So I make the sign bigger close to the 6.

(Complete the sign:)

>

c. (Point to **5 – 5.**) (Call on a child.) Which number is bigger in this problem, 5 or 5? (Idea: *They are equal.)*
The numbers are the same size, so I write an equal sign.
(Complete the sign:)

=

d. (Point to **4 – 5.**) Which number is bigger in this problem, 4 or 5? (Signal.) *5.*

- So I'll make the sign bigger next to one of the numbers. Which number is that? (Signal.) *5.*
(Complete the sign:)

<

Workbook Practice

a. Open your workbook to Lesson 92 and find part 1. √

- Each problem has two boxes with the sign between them. Some of those signs have a big end and a small end.

b. Touch problem A. Touch the end of the sign that is bigger. √

- Circle the side that's bigger. You do that by circling the box near the bigger end of the sign. Raise your hand when you're finished. √
- (Write on the board:)

A. 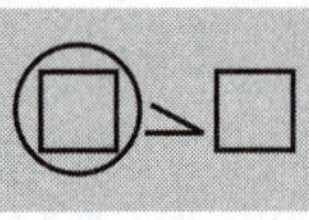

- Here's what you should have for problem A.

c. Touch problem B. Is one of those sides bigger than the other side? (Signal.) *No.*

- The equal sign shows that the number on each side is the same size.

d. Touch problem C. Is one of those sides bigger than the other side? (Signal.) *Yes.*

- Circle the side that is bigger. Remember, that's the side next to the bigger end of the sign. Raise your hand when you're finished. √
- (Write on the board:)

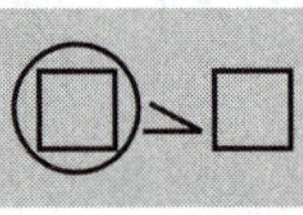

- Here's what you should have for problem C.

e. Touch problem D. Is one of those sides bigger than the other side? (Signal.) *Yes.*

- Circle the side that is bigger. Raise your hand when you're finished. √

- (Write on the board:)

□ < (□)

- Here's what you should have for problem D.

f. Touch problem E. Is one of those sides bigger than the other side? (Signal.) *Yes.*

- Circle the side that is bigger. Raise your hand when you're finished. √
- (Write on the board:)

E. □ < (□)

- Here's what you should have for problem E.

g. I'll tell you the numbers for each problem. You'll put them where they belong. You'll put the bigger number on the side that's bigger. That's the side you circled.

h. Problem A. The numbers are **3** and **5.** Which number is bigger? (Signal.) *5.*

- Put **5** on the side that's bigger. Put **3** on the side that's smaller. Raise your hand when you're finished. √
- (Write on the board:)

A. ([5]) > [3]

- Here's what you should have for problem A.

i. Problem B. The numbers are **3** and **3.** Put them in boxes. Raise your hand when you're finished. √

- (Write on the board:)

B. [3] = [3]

- Here's what you should have for problem B.

j. Problem C. The numbers are zero and **2.** Which is bigger? (Signal.) *2.*

- Put **2** on the side that's bigger. Put zero on the side that's smaller. Raise your hand when you're finished. √
- (Write on the board:)

C. ([2]) > [0]

- Here's what you should have for problem C.

k. Problem D. The numbers are **7** and **11**. Which is bigger? (Signal.) *11.*

- Put **7** and **11** where they belong. Remember, the bigger number goes on the side that's bigger. Raise your hand when you're finished. √
- (Write on the board:)

D. [7] < ([11])

- Here's what you should have for problem D.

l. Problem E. The numbers are 6 and 7. Which is bigger? (Signal.) *7.*

- Put **6** and **7** where they belong. Raise your hand when you're finished. √
- (Write on the board:)

E. [6] < ([7])

- Here's what you should have for problem E.

Addition

Level A teaches the foundation facts—plus-zero facts, plus-1 facts, plus-2 facts, plus-3 facts, and "doubles" through 6 + 6. The facts are:

	0+1	0+2	0+3	0+4	0+5	0+6	0+7	0+8	0+9
1+0	1+1	1+2	1+3	1+4	1+5	1+6	1+7	1+8	1+9
2+0	2+1	2+2	2+3	2+4	2+5	2+6	2+7	2+8	2+9
3+0	3+1	3+2	3+3	3+4	3+5	3+6	3+7	3+8	3+9
4+0	4+1	4+2	4+3	4+4					
5+0	5+1	5+2	5+3		5+5				
6+0	6+1	6+2	6+3			6+6			
7+0	7+1	7+2	7+3						
8+0	8+1	8+2	8+3						
9+0	9+1	9+2	9+3						

The addition activities are extensions of activities involving more, numbers that are more, and the next number on the number line. Instruction in plus 1 follows work with "1 more." Work with plus 2 follows "2 more." Then the plus-1 and plus-2 relationships are extended to 2-digit values: 45 plus 2. Children express these relationships in equations: 61 + 1 = 62.

Next, children are shown that the numbers in addition facts can be "turned around." They learn 1-plus and 2-plus facts and do turn-around problems with 2-digit numbers, such as: 2 + 45 = 47.

Plus-3 facts are derived from plus-2 facts: 5 + 2 = 7, so 5 + 3 = 8. Children also do turn-around problems with 3, such as 3 + 5 = 8.

The children learn several "doubles" facts: 1 + 1, 2 + 2, 3 + 3, 4 + 4, and 5 + 5.

Children learn that 3 numbers can be combined through addition.

Finally, they learn column addition and apply it to familiar facts, to 3 addends, and to 2-digit values.

The introduction addition statements occurs in Lesson 11. Structured work on the plus sign and expressing reading (5 + 2) is presented. The next activity is a cover-up game similar to those used for "next number" and "1 more." This exercise teaches that "plus 1" means "one more."

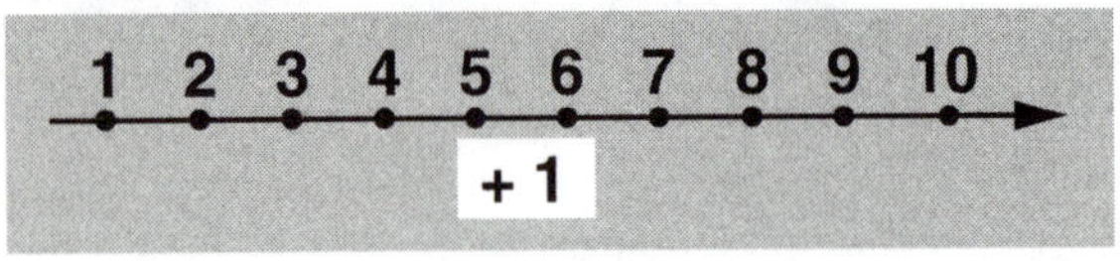

- Here's that new sign you learned—the plus sign. This says **plus 1.** What does it say? (Signal.) *Plus 1.*
- (Change + **1** to + **2**:)

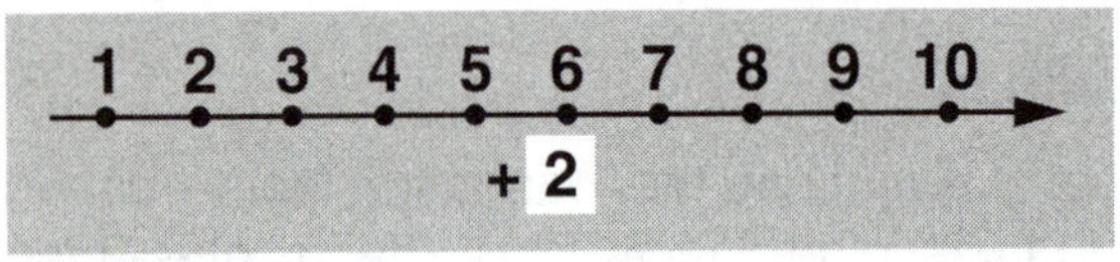

- What does it say now? (Signal.) *Plus 2.*
- (Change + 2 to + 1:)

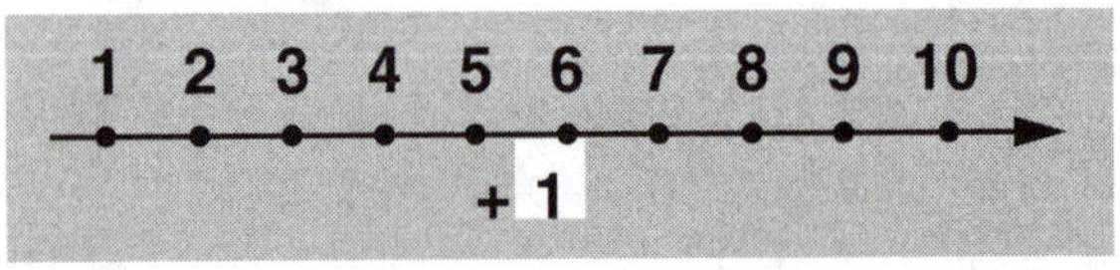

- What does it say now? (Signal.) *Plus 1.*

e. I'll show you how to plus 1. You just say the number that is 1 more.
- (Cover **10.**) My turn: The last number showing is 9. So 9 **plus 1** is the number that's 1 more than 9. What number is that? It's 10.
- (Uncover **10.**) There it is. 10.

f. (Cover the numerals after **4.**) New game. Look at the numbers in front of the arrow card. What's the last number showing? (Signal.) *4.*
- My turn: What's 4 **plus 1**? It's 5. Watch.
- (Uncover **5.**)

g. (Cover the numerals after **4.**) Your turn: Look at the numbers in front of the arrow card. What's the last number showing? (Signal.) *4.*
- Listen: What's 4 **plus 1**? (Signal.) *5.*
- (Uncover **5.**)
  Yes, 5.

h. (Cover the numerals after **6.**) New game. Look at the numbers in front of the arrow card. What's the last number showing? (Signal.) *6.*
- Listen: What's 6 **plus 1**? (Signal.) *7.*
- (Uncover **7.**) Yes, 7.

i. What's the last number showing now? (Signal.) *7.*
- Listen: What's 7 **plus 1**? (Signal.) *8.*
- (Uncover **8.**) Yes, 8.

j. What's the last number showing now? (Signal.) *8.*
- What's 8 **plus 1**? (Signal.) *9.*
- (Uncover **9.**) Yes, 9.

k. What's the last number showing now? (Signal.) *9.*
- What's 9 **plus 1**? (Signal.) *10.*
- (Uncover **10.**) Yes, 10.

l. (Cover the numerals after **3.**) New game. Look at the numbers in front of the arrow card. What's the last number showing? (Signal.) *3.*
- What's 3 plus 1? (Signal.) *4.*
  (Uncover **4.**) It's 4, all right.

m. Raise your hand if you think you know how to plus 1.
- Remember, when you plus 1, you just tell the number that is 1 more.

Note: For some children, Lesson 11 is a starting point, the first lesson in the program. These children have the counting skills and knowledge that permit them to skip the first ten lessons of the program.

Beginning in Lesson 15, children write answers to plus-1 problems the teacher shows on the number line. Starting in Lesson 17, children write answers to plus-1 problems when no number line is present. In this lesson, they are taught to translate a box in a problem as "What number?" (Later in the program, they will learn that the box can also be interpreted as "How many?")

a. (Write on the board:)

4 + 1 = □

- Here's a plus-1 question written with an equal sign.

b. (Touch □.) When you read the question, you say **what number** for the box. What do you say for the box? (Signal.) *What number.*
- My turn to read the whole question. (Touch the symbols as you say:) 4 plus 1 equals what number?

c. Your turn to read the question. (Touch the symbols as children say:) *4 plus 1 equals what number?* (Repeat step c until firm.)

d. That question is just another way of saying: What number is 4 plus 1? Everybody, what's the answer? (Signal.) *5.*
- That's what I write in the box.
  (Write **5**:)

4 + 1 = [5]

- Now we've answered the plus-1 question: 4 plus 1 equals 5.

e. (Write on the board:)

$4 + 1 = \boxed{5}$

$6 + 1 = \boxed{}$

- Here's a new plus-1 question. (Point to **6.**)

f. Everybody, read the plus-1 question. (Touch the symbols as children say:) *6 plus 1 equals what number?*
(Repeat step f until firm.)

g. Remember, that's just like the question: What number is 6 plus 1? Everybody, what's the answer? (Signal.) *7.*

- So I write **7** in the box. (Write **7**:)

$4 + 1 = \boxed{5}$

$6 + 1 = \boxed{7}$

- Now we've answered the question: 6 plus 1 equals **7.**

h. (Write on the board:)

$4 + 1 = \boxed{5}$

$6 + 1 = \boxed{7}$

$8 + 1 = \boxed{}$

- Here's a new plus-1 question. (Point to **8.**)

i. Everybody, read the plus-1 question. (Touch the symbols as children say:) *8 plus 1 equals what number?*
(Repeat step i until firm.)

j. Remember, that's just like the question: What number is 8 plus 1? Everybody, what's the answer? (Signal.) *9.*

- So I write **9** in the box.
(Write **9**:)

$4 + 1 = \boxed{5}$

$6 + 1 = \boxed{7}$

$8 + 1 = \boxed{9}$

- Now we've answered the question.

k. (Erase the problems.)

In step C, make sure that the children are saying the statement one part at a time and are responding when you point to the symbols.

Following the board demonstration, children write answers to problems presented in their workbook.

A similar set of practice exercises is presented for plus 2. Beginning in Lesson 24, children work plus-2 problems on a number line. Beginning in Lesson 26, they work problems without the number line. The sequence is designed to give the children lots of practice with individual facts so they develop facility to answer plus-1 and plus-2 questions without counting on their fingers. If you observe children counting when trying to work plus-2 problems, tell them, "Don't do it that way. Get a picture of that number line in your mind. Go to 5 and then plus 2." If you use that reminder and praise children who are performing quickly and accurately, children will learn the basic plus-1 and plus-2 facts. With this foundation, they are in a good position to learn other facts without incredible amounts of practice.

Children are introduced to the notion of zero plus in Lesson 37. The demonstration shows that zero plus a number equals the number you plus. Here's the initial board demonstration:

a. (Write on the board:)

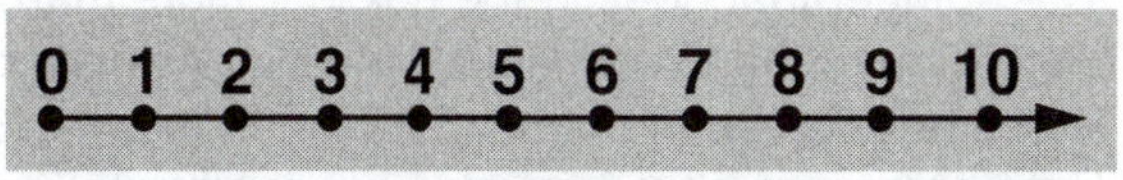

- I'll show you how to figure out numbers that are **more than** zero. It's easy.

b. (Cover the numerals after **0**:)

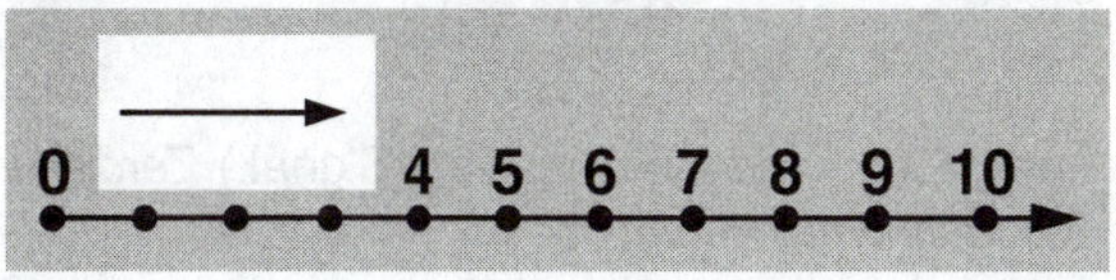

- What's the last number showing? (Signal.) *Zero.*
- My turn: What's 1 more than zero? It's 1. Watch. (Uncover **1.**)

c. (Cover the numerals after **0.**)

- New problem. What's the last number showing? (Signal.) *Zero.*
- My turn: What's 2 more than zero? It's 2. Watch.
- (Uncover **1** and **2** as you say:) 1 more, 2 more.

d. (Cover the numerals after **0.**)

- New problem. What's the last number showing? (Signal.) *Zero.*
- My turn: What's 3 more than zero? It's 3. Watch. (Uncover **1, 2,** and **3** as you say:) 1 more, 2 more, 3 more.
- Do you think you can do that?

e. (Cover the numerals after **0.**)

- What's the last number showing? (Signal.) *Zero.*

- What's 3 more than zero? (Signal.) *3.*
- (Uncover the numerals as you say:) 1 more, 2 more, 3 more.
- It's **3.**

f. (Cover the numerals after **0.**)
- New problem. What's the last number showing? (Signal.) *Zero.*
- Listen: What's 5 more than zero? (Signal.) *5.*
- (Uncover the numerals as you say:) 1 more, 2 more, 3 more, 4 more, 5 more.
- It's **5.**

g. (Cover the numerals after **0.**)
- Last problem. What's the last number showing? (Signal.) *Zero.*
- Listen: What's 6 more than zero? (Signal.) *6.*
- (Uncover the numerals as you say:) 1 more, 2 more, 3 more, 4 more, 5 more, 6 more.
- It's **6.** Raise your hand if you got all the problems right.

h. (Write below the number line:)

0 1 2 3 4 5 6 7 8 9 10

0 + 4 = □

- Here's a question that starts with zero. (Point to each symbol as you say:) Zero **plus 4** equals what number?
- The number that goes in the box is 4 more than zero. 4 more than zero. Raise your hand when you know the answer.
- Everybody, zero plus 4 equals what number? (Signal.) *4.*

i. (Change the problem to show:)

0 + 2 = □

- Everybody, read the question. (Signal.) *Zero plus 2 equals what number?*
- Remember, the number that goes in the box is 2 more than zero. Everybody, what number? (Signal.) *2.*
- Yes, zero plus 2 equals 2.

j. (Change the problem to show:)

0 + 6 = □

- Everybody, read the question. (Signal.) *Zero plus 6 equals what number?*
- The number that goes in the box is 6 more than zero. Everybody, what number? (Signal.) *6.*
- Yes, zero plus 6 equals 6.

k. (Change the problem to show:)

0 + 9 = □

- Everybody, read the question. (Signal.) *Zero plus 9 equals what number?*
- The number that goes in the box is 9 more than zero. Everybody, what number? (Signal.) *9.*
- Yes, zero plus 9 equals 9.

Following the demonstration, children work problems in the workbook. During this work, they are able to view the number line left from the board demonstration. In later lessons the number line is removed and children work problems with fewer prompts. They also learn that zero plus a number and a number plus zero describe the same value. Plus zero is treated as a joke. The problem tells you to plus, but it tells you to plus zero. That's none at all.

Although zero may have been a difficult concept in the development of modern arithmetic, it is not a difficult concept for children to learn.

Beginning in Lesson 27, children write problems from dictation. The first problem they work is prompted with dotted symbols on their worksheet. Here's the exercise from Lesson 27:

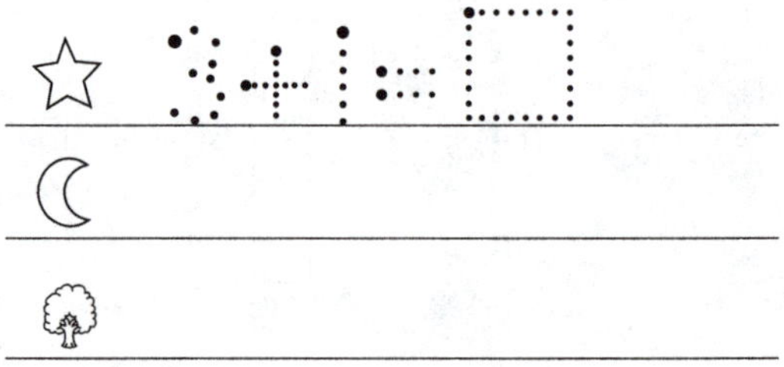

a. Find part 2. You're going to write plus-1 questions. First you'll say the question. Then you'll write it.

b. Touch the star. Here's the question for the star: 3 plus 1 equals what number?

c. Your turn: Say the question. Get ready. (Signal.) *3 plus 1 equals what number?*
(Repeat step c until firm.)

d. That question is already written with dotted symbols. Trace all the symbols. Remember, the box is what you write for **what number.** Raise your hand when you've traced the question for the star.
(Observe children and give feedback.)

e. Touch the moon. Here's the question for the moon. Listen: 7 plus 1 equals what number?

f. Everybody, say the question. Get ready. (Signal.) *7 plus 1 equals what number?*
(Repeat step f until firm.)

g. Your turn: Write the whole question. Remember to write a box for **what number.** Listen to the whole question again: 7 plus 1 equals what number? Raise your hand when you're finished.
(Observe children and give feedback.)

- (Write on the board:)

7 + 1 = □

- Here's what you should have for the moon question: 7 plus 1 equals what number? Raise your hand if you got it right.

h. Touch the tree. Here's the question for the tree. Listen: 6 plus 1 equals what number?

i. Everybody, say the question. Get ready. (Signal.) *6 plus 1 equals what number?*
(Repeat step i until firm.)

j. Your turn: Write the whole question. Raise your hand when you're finished.
(Observe children and give feedback.)

- (Write on the board:)

7 + 1 = □
6 + 1 = □

- (Point to 6 + 1 = □.) Here's what you should have for the tree question: 6 plus 1 equals what number? Raise your hand if you got it right.

k. Your turn again: Start with the star question. Read each question to yourself and write the answer. Raise your hand when you're finished.
(Observe children and give feedback.)

l. (Write to show:)

3 + 1 = [4]
7 + 1 = [8]
6 + 1 = [7]

- (Point to **3** + 1 = 4.) Check your work. Here's what you should have for the star: 3 plus 1 equals 4. Raise your hand if you got it right.
- (Point to **7** + 1 = 8.) Here's what you should have for the moon: 7 plus 1 equals 8. Raise your hand if you got it right.
- (Point to **6** + 1 = 7.) Here's what you should have for the tree: 6 plus 1 equals 7.

m. Raise your hand if you got all the answers right.

Note that children first write the questions, then answer them. If children write the problem and the answer, tell them to erase the answer and wait for you to tell them to write the answer.

Praise children who write the symbols in the problems for the moon and the tree directly under the prompted symbols:

"Good writing. That's a nice, big box and all those numerals go down to the line. Nice job."

Children learn to apply plus 1 and plus 2 to 2-digit numbers. They work two types of problems—written problems and orally presented problems. Starting in Lesson 29, children write answers to orally presented questions involving teen numbers:

"13 plus 1 equals what number?"

Starting in Lesson 40, children write answers to questions that have 20s numbers. Here's the exercise from Lesson 40:

A. 24+1= □　　**C.** 26+1= □

B. 28+1= □

a. (Write on the board:)

27 + 1 = □
23 + 1 = □
25 + 1 = □

- Here are plus-1 questions that start with twenties numbers.

b. (Point to **27** + 1 = □.)

- Everybody, read the question. (Signal.) *27 plus 1 equals what number?*
- What's the answer? (Signal.) *28.*
- (Write **28**:)

27 + 1 = [28]
23 + 1 = □
25 + 1 = □

- Yes, 27 plus 1 equals 28.

c. (Point to **23** + 1 = □.)

- Everybody, read the question. (Signal.) *23 plus 1 equals what number?*
- What's the answer? (Signal.) *24.*
- (Write **24**:)

27 + 1 = [28]
23 + 1 = [24]
25 + 1 = □

- Yes, 23 plus 1 equals 24.

d. (Point to **25** + 1 = □.)

- Everybody, read the question. (Signal.) *25 plus 1 equals what number?*
- What's the answer? (Signal.) *26.*

- (Write **26**:)

27 + 1 = [28]
23 + 1 = [24]
25 + 1 = [26]

- Yes, 25 plus 1 equals 26.

Workbook Practice

a. Open your workbook to Lesson 40 and find part 1. √
- These are different plus-1 questions.

b. Touch question A. I'll read the question: 24 plus 1 equals what number? Your turn: Write the answer. Raise your hand when you're finished.
(Observe children and give feedback.)
- Everybody, 24 plus 1 equals what number? (Signal.) *25.*
- (Write on the board:)

25

- Here's what you should have. Raise your hand if you got it right.

c. Touch question B. I'll read the question: 28 plus 1 equals what number? Your turn: Write the answer. Raise your hand when you're finished. √
- Everybody, 28 plus 1 equals what number? (Signal.) *29.*
- (Write 29:)

29

- Here's what you should have. Raise your hand if you got it right.

d. Touch question C. I'll read the question: 26 plus 1 equals what number? Your turn: Write the answer. Raise your hand when you're finished. √
- Everybody, 26 plus 1 equals what number? (Signal.) *27.*
- (Write **27**:)

27

- Here's what you should have.

e. Let's see who did a super job. Raise your hand if you got all of them right.

Later in the program, children do a lot of work with orally-presented problems:

"60 plus 3. Everybody, what's the answer?"
"62 plus 2. Everybody, what's the answer?"

Children also learn to apply basic plus-1 and plus-2 fact knowledge to adding pairs of 10s values. The introduction shows children that these facts are generated simply by converting the numbers in a simple fact to 2-digit numbers that end in zero.

Here's the first part of the introduction, which appears in Lesson 57:

A. 4+2= [ ]   **C.** 2+5= [ ]

B. 7+1= [ ]   **B.** 8+1= [ ]

a. (Write on the board:)

40 41 42 43 44 45 46 47 48 49 50

4 + 1 = [ ]

- I'll show you something that's very tricky.

b. Everybody, read this problem. Get ready. (Signal.) *4 plus 1 equals what number?*
- Everybody, what's the answer? (Signal.) *5.*
- (Write **5** in the box:)

4 + 1 = [5]

c. (Write below:)

4 + 1 = [5]
4 + 1 = 5

- Here's the same fact, but I'm going to change it to show you a new fact. I'll just write a zero after every numeral. Watch.
- (Write a zero after each numeral:)

4 + 1 = [5]
40 + 10 = 50

d. Everybody, say the new fact. Get ready. (Signal.) *40 plus 10 equals 50.*
(Repeat step d until firm.)

e. That's true. 40 plus 10 equals 50. I'll show you on the number line. What number do I start with? (Signal.) *40.*
- (Touch **40** on the number line.) And how many do I plus? (Signal.) *10.*
- I'll plus 10. Watch. (Say **plus 1, 2, 3, 4, 5, 6, 7, 8, 9, 10** as you touch the dot for each numeral.)
- Everybody, what number did I end up with? (Signal.) *50.*
- So it's true. 40 plus 10 equals 50. Let's do one more.

f. (Write on the board:)

$$7 + 1 = \boxed{}$$

- Here's 7 plus 1. Everybody, what does 7 plus 1 equal? (Signal.) *8.*
- (Write **8** in the box:)

$$7 + 1 = \boxed{8}$$

- (Write below:)

$$7 + 1 = \boxed{8}$$
$$7 + 1 = 8$$

- Here's the same fact, but I'm going to change it to show you a new fact. I'll just write a zero after every numeral. Watch.
- (Write a zero after each numeral:)

$$4 + 1 = \boxed{8}$$
$$70 + 10 = 80$$

g. Everybody, say the new fact. Get ready. (Signal.) *70 plus 10 equals 80.*
(Repeat step g until firm.)

h. That fact is true. 70 plus 10 equals 80.

Workbook Practice

a. Find part 3.

b. Problem A is: 4 plus 2. Listen: Write the answer in the answer box. Raise your hand when you're finished.
(Observe children and give feedback.)

- Everybody, what does 4 plus 2 equal? (Signal.) *6.*
- Listen: Below that fact, you're going to write a fact that has 2-digit numerals that end in zero. The first number in the fact is **4.** Below **4,** you're going to write **4** with a zero. That's **40.** What are you going to write below the 4? (Signal.) *40.*
- The next number in the fact is **2**. Below **2,** you're going to write **2** with a zero. What number is that? (Signal.) *20.*
- The last number in the fact is **6.** Below **6,** you're going to write **6** with a zero. What number is that? (Signal.) *60.*
- Write the new fact below. 40 plus 20 equals 60. Raise your hand when you're finished.
(Observe children and give feedback.)
- (Write on the board:)

A. $4 + 2 = \boxed{6}$
$40 + 20 = 60$

- Here's what you should have for problem A: 40 plus 20 equals 60.

c. Everybody, say that fact. (Signal.) *40 plus 20 equals 60.*
(Repeat step c until firm.)

Relationships are difficult for children to learn. Part of the problem with their learning stems from lack of familiarity with benchmarks of knowledge. Level A attempts to provide children with enough practice in each type of "extension" of basic knowledge to provide bench marks. Children work a lot of problems that are based on this extension:

$6 + 2 = \square$
$56 + 2 = \square$

They also work many of these extensions:

$6 + 2 = \square$
$60 + 20 = \square$

Even though much of the work may seem easy, don't skip exercises or present in a greatly abbreviated manner. Children will learn the relationships only through a lot of exposure and work in which they do not make mistakes. Provide the practice and you will observe fewer "silly" errors, such as:

$60 + 20 = 62$
or
$56 + 2 = 80$

A relationship that is particularly important and often difficult for children is "turn around," the idea that 4 plus 1 equals 1 plus 4.

Turn arounds are introduced in Lesson 42. A board demonstration shows that you get the same answer to problems that are turned around. Following the board work, children write turned-around problems and answers. Here's the board demonstration and the first part of the workbook activity:

A. $5+2= \boxed{}$

____

a. Listen: 5 plus 2 and 2 plus 5 equal the same number. My turn: 5 plus 2. Say it the other way: 2 plus 5.

- Your turn: 5 plus 2. Say it the other way. (Signal.) *2 plus 5.*
(Repeat step a until firm.)

b. Listen: What does 5 plus 2 equal? (Signal.) *7.*

- 2 plus 5 equals the same number. So what does 2 plus 5 equal? (Signal.) *7.*
- Say the whole fact for 2 plus 5. (Signal.) *2 plus 5 equals 7.*
(Repeat step b until firm.)

c. New problem: 7 plus 1. Say it the other way. (Signal.) *1 plus 7.*
(Repeat step c until firm.)

d. Listen: What does 7 plus 1 equal? (Signal.) *8.*
- So what does 1 plus 7 equal? (Signal.) *8.*
- Say the fact for 1 plus 7. (Signal.) *1 plus 7 equals 8.*

(Repeat step d until firm.)

e. New problem: 8 plus 2. Say it the other way. (Signal.). *2 plus 8*
(Repeat step e until firm.)

f. Listen: What does 8 plus 2 equal? (Signal.) *10.*
- So what does 2 plus 8 equal? (Signal.) *10.*
- Say the fact. (Signal.) *2 plus 8 equals 10.*

(Repeat step f until firm.)

g. Last problem: 4 plus 1. Say it the other way. (Signal.) *1 plus 4.*
(Repeat step g until firm.)

h. Listen: What does 4 plus 1 equal? (Signal.) *5.*
- So what does 1 plus 4 equal? (Signal.) *5.*
- Say the fact. (Signal.) *1 plus 4 equals 5.*

(Repeat step h until firm.)

i. (Write on the board:)

4 + 1 = □

- I'll show you that 4 plus 1 and 1 plus 4 equal the same number.
- (Point to **4** + 1 = □.) Read this problem. Get ready. (Signal.) *4 plus 1 equals what number?*
- What's the answer? (Signal.) *5.*
- (Write **5**:)

4 + 1 = [5]

- This problem starts with 4 plus 1. Say that part the other way. (Signal.) *1 plus 4.*
- (Write on the board:)

4 + 1 = [5]
1 + 4 = □

- Now we'll see if we end up with the same number when we start with 1 and plus 4. What number are we going to start at on the number line? (Signal.) *1.*
- And how many are we going to plus? (Signal.) *4.*
- We start at **1.** So I'll touch that number on the number line.
- (Touch 1 on the number line.) Now we plus. How many do we plus? (Signal.) *4.*
- I'll make a hump for each place I plus. Here I go. (Draw humps as you say:) Plus 1, plus 2, plus 3, plus 4.

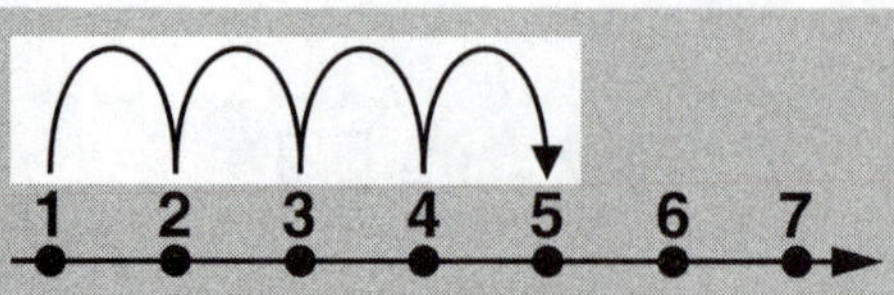

4 + 1 = [5]
1 + 4 = □

- I started with 1 and plussed 4. You can see what number on the number line I ended up at. What number? (Signal.) *5.*
- I ended up at **5.** That's the answer.
(Write **5**:)

1 + 4 = [5]

- Look: 4 plus 1 equals 5. And 1 plus 4 equals 5.

Workbook Practice

a. Open your workbook to Lesson 42 and find part 1. √
- You're going to rewrite the first part of each problem. Then you'll write the answers to the problems.

b. Touch problem A. The first part of the problem is: 5 plus 2. Say that part the other way. (Signal.) *2 plus 5.*
- On the line below, write: 2 plus 5 equals what number? Once more: Write 2 plus 5 equals what number? Raise your hand when you're finished.
(Observe children and give feedback.)
- (Write on the board:)

A. 5 + 2 = □
2 + 5 = □

- Here's what you should have for problem A.

c. Now write the answer to both problems. Remember, if you know the answer to 5 plus 2, you know the answer to 2 plus 5. It's the same answer. Write your answers. Raise your hand when you're finished.
(Observe children and give feedback.)
- (Write to show:)

A. 5 + 2 = [7]
2 + 5 = [7]

- Here's what you should have: 5 plus 2 equals 7; 2 plus 5 equals 7.

Notice that children are required to write the turned-around problems and answers. By writing the entire fact, children more quickly learn the relationship of the component symbols.

Following the introduction to turned-around facts, children are provided with a great deal of practice with turned-around problems. The practice involves all the basic facts and problems with 2-digit numbers:

"2 + 34. Everybody, what's the answer?"
"2 + 36. Everybody, what's the answer?"
"2 + 76. Everybody, what's the answer?"

The procedure for plus-3 facts parallels that of plus 1 and plus 2. Three-more is demonstrated on the number line (starting at Lesson 70). Plus-3 facts are presented in which children count 3 places (starting at Lesson 77).

Beginning in Lesson 81, children learn a relationship that is unique to plus-3 facts. They learn how to relate plus-3 problems to familiar plus-2 facts. By Lesson 81, children have worked with plus-2 facts for nearly 60 lessons, so these facts are familiar. The fact-derivation exercises for plus 3 are particularly important. While children should understand that plus 3 is 3 more, and that it is possible to count to figure out the answer to a plus-3 problem, the fact-derivation exercises provide an alternative and faster method of handling plus-3 problems. Here's the introduction from Lesson 81:

A. 5 + 2 = ☐	**B.** 7 + 2 = ☐
5 + 3 = ☐	7 + 3 = ☐
C. 4 + 2 = ☐	**D.** 6 + 2 = ☐
4 + 3 = ☐	6 + 3 = ☐

a. Open your workbook to Lesson 81 and find part 1. √

b. Touch pair A. The problems are: 5 plus 2 and 5 plus 3. Listen: 5 plus **2** equals what number? (Signal.) *7.*
- So 5 plus **3** equals what number? (Signal.) *8.*
- Right. The answer is 1 more than 5 plus 2. 5 plus 2 equals 7. So 5 plus 3 equals 8.

c. Touch pair B. The problems are: 7 plus 2 and 7 plus 3. Listen: 7 plus 2 equals what number? (Signal.) *9.*
- So 7 plus **3** equals what number? (Signal.) *10.*
- Yes, 7 plus 2 equals 9. So 7 plus 3 equals 10.

d. Touch pair C. The problems are: 4 plus 2 and 4 plus 3. Listen: 4 plus **2** equals what number? (Signal.) *6.*
- So 4 plus **3** equals what number? (Signal.) *7.*
- Yes, 4 plus 2 equals 6. So 4 plus 3 equals 7.

e. Touch pair D. Listen: 6 plus **2** equals what number? (Signal.) *8.*
- So 6 plus **3** equals what number? (Signal.) *9.*
- Yes, 6 plus 2 equals 8. So 6 plus 3 equals 9.

f. Your turn: Write answers to all the problems in part 1. Raise your hand when you're finished. (Observe children and give feedback.)

g. Check your work. You're going to read the problems and the answers.
- Touch pair A. Read the top fact. (Signal.) *5 plus 2 equals 7*
- Read the bottom fact. (Signal.) *5 plus 3 equals 8.*
- Touch pair B. Read the top fact. (Signal.) *7 plus 2 equals 9.*
- Read the bottom fact. (Signal.) *7 plus 3 equals 10.*
- Touch pair C. Read the top fact. (Signal.) *4 plus 2 equals 6.*
- Read the bottom fact. (Signal.) *4 plus 3 equals 7.*
- Touch pair D. Read the top fact. (Signal.) *6 plus 2 equals 8.*
- Read the bottom fact. (Signal.) *6 plus 3 equals 9.*

h. Remember how plus-3 problems work. If you know what a number plus 2 equals, you can figure out what number plus 3 equals.

The workcheck for fact derivation, starting with step G, is particularly important. The more children say the pairs of facts, the easier it becomes for them to clarify the relationship. Make sure that children are firm in their reading.

Following the initial work with plus 3, children do a lot of fact work and fact review involving plus-1, plus-2, and plus-3 problems. An objective of the program is for children to be pretty automatic with these facts (possibly not completely automatic with plus-3 facts). The last group of facts introduced in Level A are "doubles." These are facts that have the same number twice: 4 + 4, 2 + 2, etc. Doubles are introduced as "double jumps" a bug makes on the number line. Here's the introduction from Lesson 89. Following the board work, children complete double-jump problems in their workbook and write the facts for the double jumps. The new double facts (4 + 4 and 5 + 5) are then integrated with other facts (+1, +2, +3).

a. (Write on the board:)

- This is a new kind of bug problem. There was a bug who was called the "double jumper" because the bug always made 2 jumps that were the same number of places. If that bug jumped 2 places, it would jump 2 places again. If that bug jumped 5 places, it would jump 5 places again. Here's a jump that bug made.

b. (Draw arrow to show:)

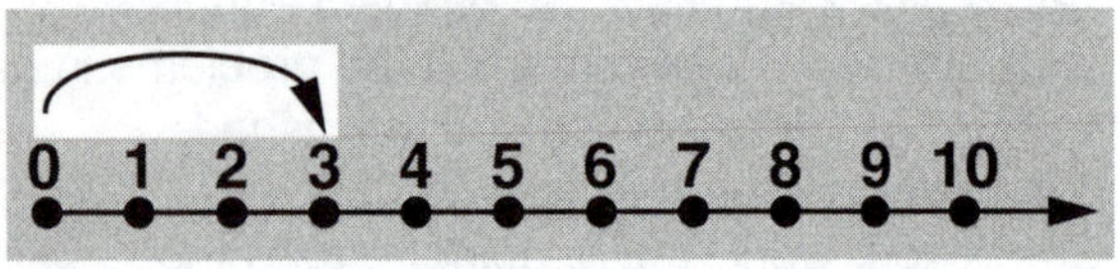

- Raise your hand when you know how many places the bug jumped.
- Everybody, how many places? (Signal.) *3.*
- So how many places will the bug jump next? (Signal.) *3.*
- Raise your hand when you know what number the bug will end up at.
- Everybody, what number? (Signal.) *6.*
- (Draw arrow to show:)

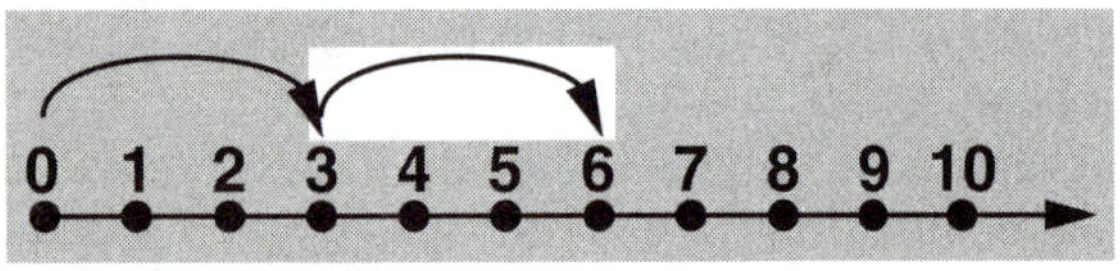

- Were you right? The bug jumped 3 plus 3. So here's the fact: 3 plus 3 equals 6. Everybody, say it. (Signal.) *3 plus 3 equals 6.*

c. (Change to show:)

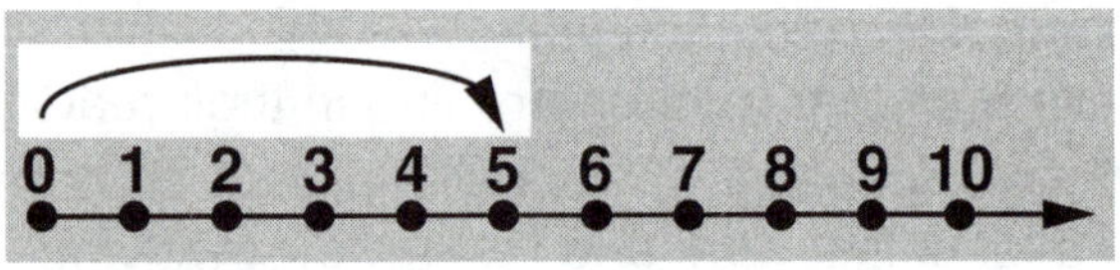

- New problem. Here's the bug's first jump. How many places did it jump? (Signal.) *5.*
- So how many places will the bug jump next? (Signal.) *5.*
- Raise your hand when you know what number the bug will end up at.
- Everybody, what number? (Signal.) *10.*
- (Draw arrow to show:)

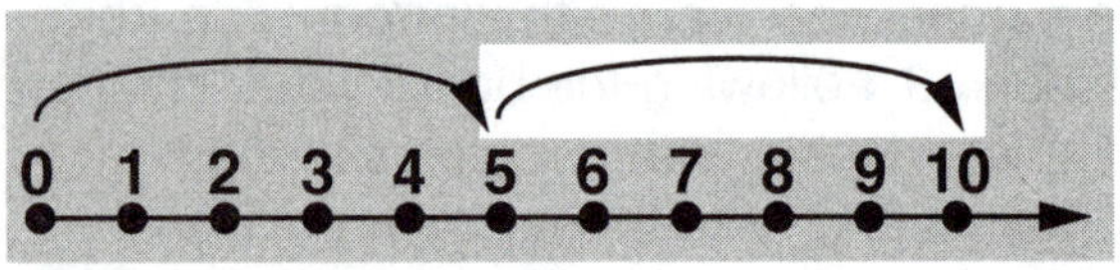

- Were you right? The bug jumped 5 plus 5.

d. Say the fact for the double jump. Get ready. (Signal.) *5 plus 5 equals 10.*
(Repeat step d until firm.)

e. (Change to show:)

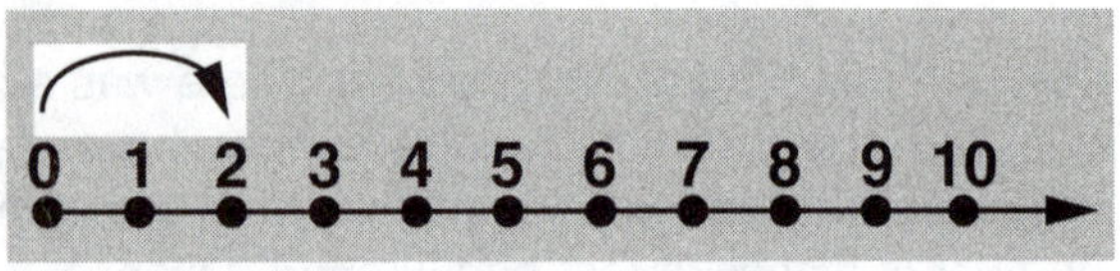

- New problem. Here's the bug's first jump. How many places did it jump? (Signal.) *2.*
- So how many places will the bug jump next? (Signal.) *2.*
- Raise your hand when you know what number the bug will end up at.
- Everybody, what number? (Signal.) *4.*
- (Draw arrow to show:)

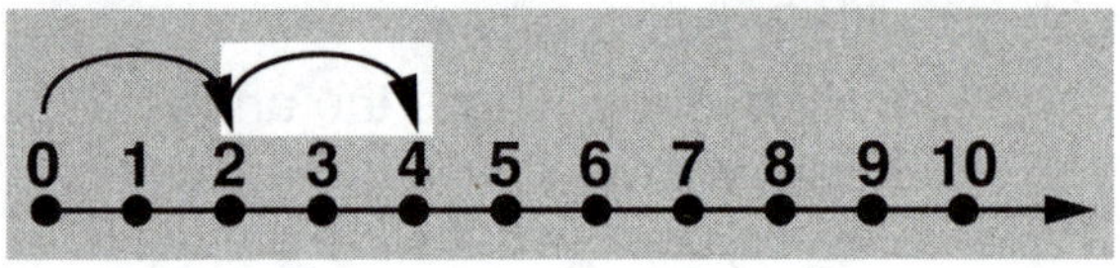

- Were you right?

f. Say the addition fact for the double jump. Get ready. (Signal.) *2 plus 2 equals 4.*
(Repeat step f until firm.)

Children learn two other important skills involving addition in Level A. They are:

a) working problems with three addends, and
b) working column-addition problems.

The work with three addends begins in Lesson 85 in which the children are shown how to keep a running total. The most difficult part for the children to learn is that after two numbers are added (4 + 1), you're no longer at either 4 or 1. You're at 5. Here's the board demonstration that appears in Lesson 85:

a. (Write on the board:)

A.		B.		C.	
	4		3		7
	+1		+2		+1
	+1		+1		+2

- These are problems that plus two numbers. I'll show you how to work them.

b. Problem A is: 4 plus 1 plus 1. I start by working the first part: 4 plus 1. How many is that? (Signal.) *5.*

- I'm at **5.** The problem tells me to plus 1 more. So I start at **5** and plus 1 more. What's the answer? (Signal.) *6.*
- (Write 6:)

A.	
	4
	+1
	+1
	6

- 4 plus 1 plus 1 more equals 6.

c. Problem B is: 3 plus 2 plus 1. Here's the first part of the problem: 3 plus 2. Everybody, say the first part. (Signal.) *3 plus 2.*

- What's the answer? (Signal.) *5.*
- You're at **5.** How many more are you going to plus? (Signal.) *1.*
- You're at **5** and you plus 1 more. What's the answer? (Signal.) *6.*

- (Write 6:)

```
B.   3
   + 2
   + 1
   ---
     6
```

- 3 plus 2 plus 1 more equals 6.

d. Problem C is: 7 plus 1 plus 2.
Everybody, say the first part of the problem. Get ready. (Signal.) *7 plus 1.*

- What's the answer? (Signal.) *8.*
- You're at **8.** How many more are you going to plus? (Signal.) *2.*
- What's the answer? (Signal.) *10.*
- (Write 10:)

```
C.    7
    + 1
    + 2
    ---
     10
```

- Yes, 7 plus 1 plus 2 more equals 10.

Following the board demonstration, children work problems of the type just demonstrated. One problem involves 2-digit numbers.

The work on column addition begins in Lesson 77 and parallels the work done on facts. Different types of problems are presented—familiar facts, problems with 2-digit numbers, problems with three addends, and problems involving tens values (30 + 10).

Initially, children are taught how to transform equations into column problems. The first number goes on top. The plus sign goes in front of the second number. The equal sign becomes a line.

```
6 + 2 = 6
       +2
```

In lessons 79 through 110, children rewrite fact problems as column problems.

Beginning in Lesson 101, children work with column addition involving two 2-digit addends. These problems are different from others the children have worked because they include two separate problems, one for the ones column and another for the tens column. Since none of these problems involve carrying, the great danger is that children may develop the habit of working the problem in the tens column first, then the problem for the ones. The children will get the right answer working these problems in that manner; however, they will have trouble when problems that require carrying are introduced.

To guard against possible mislearning, columns are marked, and the routine that you follow to present these problems very strongly stipulate that you start with the ones column. The children have learned that the ones column shows the "leftovers" and that the tens column shows tens. Note that children are familiar with the concept of "tens" and "leftovers" from their work from T's and lines. Here's the introduction from Lesson 101:

```
A.   41     B.   82     C.   21     D.   32
   + 27        + 16        + 75        + 34
```

a. (Write on the board:)

```
  3|8
+ 2|1
```

- Here's a new kind of problem: 38 plus 21. That's a hard problem. But there's a trick for working it. You add the leftovers first. Then you add the tens. Remember; add in the leftovers column first.

b. The top number is 38. How many tens in 38? (Signal.) *3.*

- How many leftovers in 38? (Signal.) *8.*
- The other number is 21. How many tens in 21? (Signal.) *2.*
- How many leftovers in 21? (Signal.) *1.*
(Repeat step b until firm.)

c. When you add the leftovers, you add the **8** leftovers for the top number and the **1** leftover for the bottom number. My turn to say the addition problem for the leftovers: 8 plus 1.

- Everybody, what's 8 plus 1? (Signal.) *9.*
- I write **9** in the leftovers column.
- (Write **9**:)

```
  3|8
+ 2|1
   |9
```

- Now I add the tens. 3 tens plus 2 tens. How many tens is that? (Signal.) *5.*
- So I write **5** for the tens.
- (Write **5**:)

```
  3|8
+ 2|1
  5|9
```

- All done. We figured out what 38 plus 21 equals. Everybody, what does it equal? (Signal.) *59.*

d. (Write on the board:)

$$\begin{array}{r} 5|4 \\ +2|4 \\ \hline \end{array}$$

- New problem: 54 plus 24. We add the leftovers first.

e. Everybody, say the problem for the leftovers. (Signal.) *4 plus 4.*

- What's the answer? (Signal.) *8.*
- (Write **8**:)

$$\begin{array}{r} 5|4 \\ +2|4 \\ \hline |8 \end{array}$$

- The problem for the tens is 5 tens plus 2 tens. How many tens is that? (Signal.) *7.* (Write **7**:)

$$\begin{array}{r} 5|4 \\ +2|4 \\ \hline 7|8 \end{array}$$

- We figured out what 54 plus 24 equals. Everybody, what does it equal? (Signal.) *78.*

Workbook Practice

a. Open your workbook to Lesson 101 and find part 1. √

b. Touch problem a. Everybody, read the problem. (Signal.) *41 plus 27.*

- Remember, you add the leftovers first. Listen: How many **leftovers** does 41 have? (Signal.) *1.*
- How many **leftovers** does 27 have? (Signal.) *7.*
- Say the problem for the leftovers. Get ready. (Signal.) *1 plus 7.*

c. Your turn: Write the answer in the leftovers column. Don't do anything to the tens. Just work the leftovers. Raise your hand when you're finished. (Observe children and give feedback.)

- Everybody, read the problem and the answer for the leftovers. (Signal.) *1 plus 7 equals 8.*
- (Write on the board:)

A.
$$\begin{array}{r} 4|1 \\ +2|7 \\ \hline |8 \end{array}$$

- Here's what you should have for problem A. The **8** should be right under the other leftovers. Raise your hand if you got it right.
- Now add the tens. Add **4** and **2.** Write the answer in the tens column. Raise your hand when you're finished. √
- (Write **6**:)

A.
$$\begin{array}{r} 4|1 \\ +2|7 \\ \hline 6|8 \end{array}$$

- Here's what you should have. Raise your hand if you got it right.
- You figured out what 41 plus 27 equals. Everybody, what's the answer? (Signal.) *68.*

First you demonstrate how to work the problems. Then you direct workbook practice. The exercise above takes you through the presentation of the first workbook problems. Note that in the workbook, the ones columns are shaded. Note also that in step C of the workbook practice, you direct the children to work the "leftovers" first. Observe them carefully. Praise those who do it the right way.

In later lessons, the structure is dropped and children work problems with less guidance. It's a good idea, however, to check them from time to time and make sure that they are following the convention of starting with the leftovers column.

Subtraction

The work on subtraction largely parallels that on addition. Children extend knowledge of 1 less to problems that minus 1 (starting in Lesson 36). The term used is "minusing," not "subtracting," which is not introduced until Lesson 103. To minus 1 is to go one place in the minus direction.

Minus zero is presented next (Lesson 52). It is explained as being like plus zero. "You've learned that when you plus zero, you don't plus anything at all. It works the same way when you minus zero. Zero is nothing. So when you minus zero, you don't minus anything at all."

Minus 2 begins in Lesson 64, first with the number line, then with various fact problems. Work with 2-digit numbers that minus 1 or 2 begins in Lesson 72. Work with tens numbers (50–10 begins in Lesson 73. Column subtraction with 2-digit numbers begins in Lesson 106.

The "double jump" in addition has something of a parallel in subtraction. If you minus the number you begin with, you'll end up at zero.

$7 - 7 = 0$

This concept is very important because it sets the stage for borrowing and rewriting. Borrowing is needed because the problem in a column may start with the smaller number.

$$\begin{array}{r} 27 \\ -18 \\ \hline \end{array}$$

The rule is that you have to rewrite to correct this situation, making the top of the 1s column a 2-digit number. Children frequently have trouble with borrowing because they don't understand that they can't go "past zero" on the number line (subtract more than they start out with).

Another concept is that of ending up with 1 or 2:

$7 - 5 = 2$

This relationship is difficult for many children. Level A prompts it in this manner. If you start at 7 and minus all 7, you end up at zero. If you minus 1 less than 7, you end up at 1. If you minus 2 less than 7, you end up with 2.

The notion of minusing to end up at zero is introduced in Lesson 100. The context is the bug on the number line. This bug wants to go to zero.

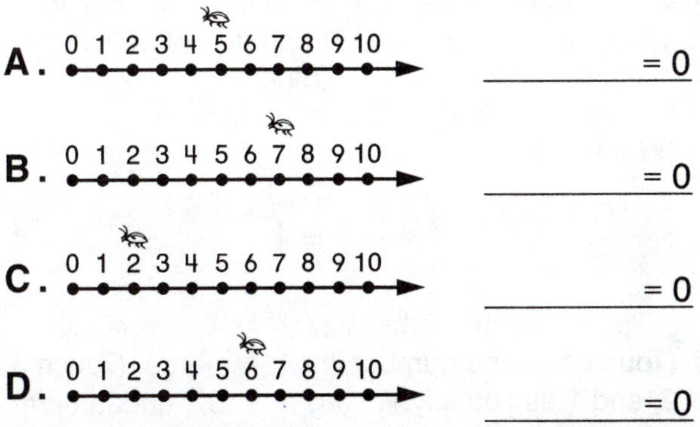

a. (Write on the board:)

0 1 2 3 4 5 6 7 8 9 10

- You're going to learn how many you minus to end up at zero.

b. (Touch **3.**) What number am I starting at? (Signal.) *3.*

- If I start at **3**, I have to minus 3 places to get to zero. Watch.
- (Touch **2, 1, 0** as you say:) Minus 1, minus 2, minus 3. I'm at zero and I minused 3 places. 3 minus 3 equals zero. Everybody, say it. (Signal.) *3 minus 3 equals zero.*

c. (Touch **5** on the number line.) What number am I starting at? (Signal.) *5.*

- I want to end up at zero. If I start at **5**, I have to minus 5 places to get to zero. Watch.
- (Touch **4, 3, 2, 1, 0** as you say:) 1, 2, 3, 4, 5. I'm at zero and I minused 5 places. 5 minus 5 equals zero. Everybody, say it. (Signal.) *5 minus 5 equals zero.*

d. (Touch **8** on the number line.) What number am I starting at? (Signal.) *8.*

- I want to end up at zero. How many places do I have to minus? (Signal.) *8.*
- If I start at **8,** I have to minus 8 places to get to zero. 8 minus 8 equals zero. Everybody, say it. (Signal.) *8 minus 8 equals zero.*
- (Make an **X** at **7** on the number line:)

0 1 2 3 4 5 6 7 8 9 10 (X at 7)

- The X shows where you start on the number line. You're going to tell me how to write the fact for ending up at zero. What number am I starting at? (Signal.) *7.*
- So I write **7.**
- (Write **7**:)

7

- Everybody, how many places do I minus to end up at zero? (Signal.) *7.*
- (Write to show:)

7 – 7 = 0

- Everybody, say the fact. Get ready. (Signal.) *7 minus 7 equals zero.*

Workbook Practice

- Find part 2. Each problem shows a number line with a bug on it. That bug wants to go to zero. You're going to complete the fact to show where the bug starts out and what the bug does to get to zero.

b. Touch number line A. What number is the bug starting at? (Signal.) *5.*

- So the first number in the fact is **5.** What does the bug have to do to get to zero? (Signal.) *Minus 5.*
- So the fact should say: 5 minus 5 equals zero. Complete the fact so it says: 5 minus 5 equals zero. Raise your hand when you're finished. (Observe children and give feedback.)

c. Touch number line B. What number is the bug starting at? (Signal.) *7.*

- So what's the first number of the fact? (Signal.) *7.*
- What does the bug have to do to get to zero? (Signal.) *Minus 7.*
- Complete the fact so it says: 7 minus 7 equals zero. Raise your hand when you're finished. (Observe children and give feedback.)

d. Your turn: Complete the rest of the facts in part 2. Remember, this bug always wants to end up at zero. You have to tell where the bug starts out and what the bug does to get to zero. Raise your hand when you're finished. (Observe children and give feedback.)

e. Check your work.

- Problem C. Where does the bug start out? (Signal.) *2.*
- Read the fact for problem C. (Signal.) *2 minus 2 equals zero.*
- Problem D. Where does the bug start out? (Signal.) *6.*
- Read the fact for problem D. (Signal.) *6 minus 6 equals zero.*

f. Raise your hand if you got everything right.

Three lessons later, in 103, children learn the relationship for ending up at 1. The context again is the bug on the number line. The board demonstration begins with a review of how many to minus if you want to end up at zero. Next, the procedure for ending up at 1 is presented.

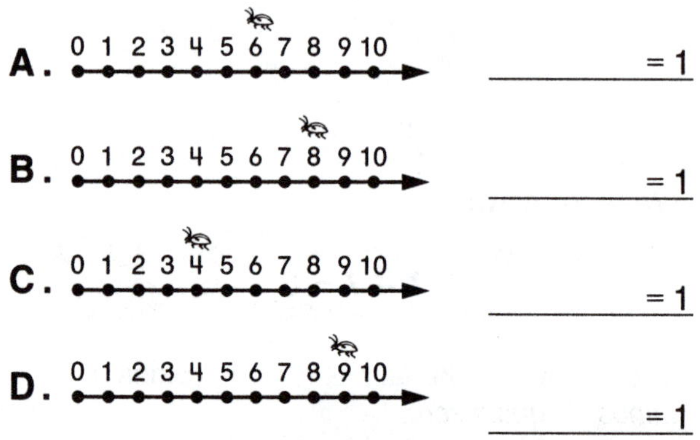

0 1 2 3 4 5 6 7 8 9 10

c. (Underline **1** on the number line.) Now we're going to play a much harder game. I don't want to go all the way to zero. I want to go to **1** on the number line. Here's the rule: To end up at 1, you don't minus the same number you start with. You minus **1 less** than that number.

d. (Put an **X** above **5** on the number line.) The **X** shows where I'm starting. Everybody, what number? (Signal.) *5.*
- So I write **5.** (Write **5**:)

5

- I know that I want to end up at **1**. So I write **equals 1** at the end of the problem. (Write = **1**:)

5 = 1

- Listen: If I start at **5** and minus **5,** I end up at zero. If I minus 1 less than **5,** I'll end up at **1.** What number is 1 less than 5? (Signal.) *4.*
- So I write **minus 4.** (Write − **4**:)

5 − 4 = 1

- Let's see if that's right. I'll start at **5** and minus 4.
- (Touch **5** on the number line.) Here I go. (Touch **4, 3, 2,** and **1** as you say:) Minus 1, 2, 3, 4. I ended up at **1**. How many did I minus? (Signal.) *4.*

e. (Change number line to show **X** over the 4.) New problem. Where am I starting? (Signal.) *4.*
- (Write on the board:)

4

- What number do I want to end up at? (Signal.) *1.*
- (Write = **1**:)

4 = 1

- Listen: If I start at **4** and minus 4, I end up at zero. If I minus 1 less than 4, I'll end up at **1.** What number is 1 less than 4? (Signal.) *3.*
- So I write **minus 3**. 4 minus 3 equals 1. (Write − **3**:)

4 − 3 = 1

- Let's see if that's right. I'll start at **4** and minus 3.
- (Touch **4** on the number line.) Here I go. (Touch **3, 2,** and **1** as you say:) Minus 1, 2, 3. I ended up at **1.** How many did I minus? (Signal.) *3.*

Workbook Practice

a. Open your workbook to Lesson 103 and find part 1. √
- The **1** is very dark on these number lines because the bug will always end up at **1.** You're going to complete the facts to show where the bug starts and what the bug does.

b. Problem A. What number is the bug starting at? (Signal.) *6.*
- So what's the first number of the fact? (Signal.) *6.*
- The bug starts at **6** If you minus 6, you end up at zero. So you want to minus 1 less than 6.
- Everybody, what number is that? (Signal.) *5.*
- So you write **6 minus 5** for problem A. Do it. Raise your hand when you're finished. √
- Everybody, read the fact for problem A. (Signal.) *6 minus 5 equals 1.*

c. Problem B: What number is the bug starting at? (Signal.) *8.*
- What number is 1 less than 8? (Signal.) *7.*
- Complete the fact for problem B. Raise your hand when you're finished. (Observe children and give feedback.)

- (Write on the board:)

B. 8 – 7 = 1

- Here's what you should have for problem B. Everybody, read the fact. (Signal.) *8 minus 7 equals 1.*

d. Your turn: Complete the rest of the facts in part 1. Write where the bug starts out and what the bug has to do to end up at **1.** Remember, minus 1 less than you start out with and you'll always end up at **1.** Raise your hand when you're finished.
(Observe children and give feedback.)

e. Check your work.

- Problem C. What number is the bug starting at? (Signal.) *4.*
- Read the fact. (Signal.) *4 minus 3 equals 1.*
- Problem D. What number is the bug starting at? (Signal.) *9.*
- Read the fact. (Signal.) *9 minus 8 equals 1.*

For children to become facile with these "turn-around" facts, they must have a great deal of practice. Do not expect children to be perfectly facile by the end of Level A. Children who complete the program, however, should be accurate on minus-1 problems and those that end up at 1.

In Level A, children do not merely learn the concepts and relationships described above. Exercises are presented to assure that children learn to discriminate between concepts that are easily confused.

Each of the discrimination exercises involves a mix of addition and subtraction problems. For some, children work with a number line and either plus or minus a number (starting at Lesson 45). Some discrimination sets involve tens (Lesson 85):

50 + 10   50 – 10

Mental arithmetic problems involving addition and subtraction are introduced in Lesson 93. Column addition and subtraction problems first appear together in Lesson 109. Independent practice exercises also review the operations, facts, and relationships that are taught in the program.

Children create problems that show the relationship between addition and subtraction. The vehicle is once more the ubiquitous bug on the number line. This bug changes its mind, first plussing so many places, then deciding to return to the starting point. Children write the problems for both parts of the bug's journey.

Here's the first part of the introductory exercise from Lesson 64:

A. ______________ B. ______________

______________ ______________

a. (Draw to show:)

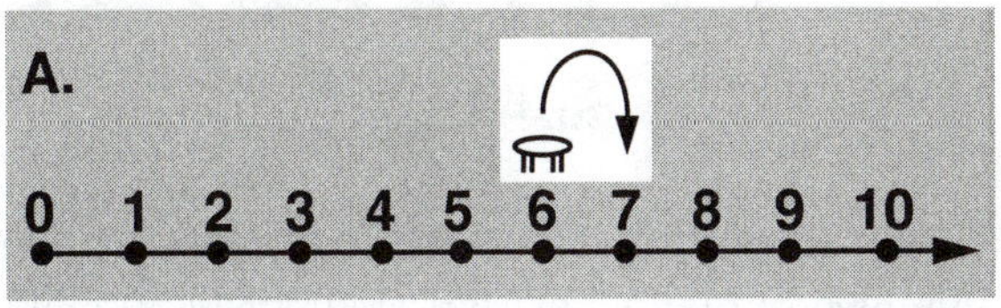

- The arrow shows a bug problem. Where does the bug start out? (Signal.) *6.*
- Does the bug plus or minus? (Signal.) *Plus.*
- How many places does the bug plus? (Signal.) *1.*
- What number does the bug end up at? (Signal.) *7.*

Workbook Practice

a. Find part 3. Your turn: Write the fact for this problem on the top line for problem A. Raise your hand when you're finished.
(Observe children and give feedback.)

- (Write **6 + 1 = 7**:)

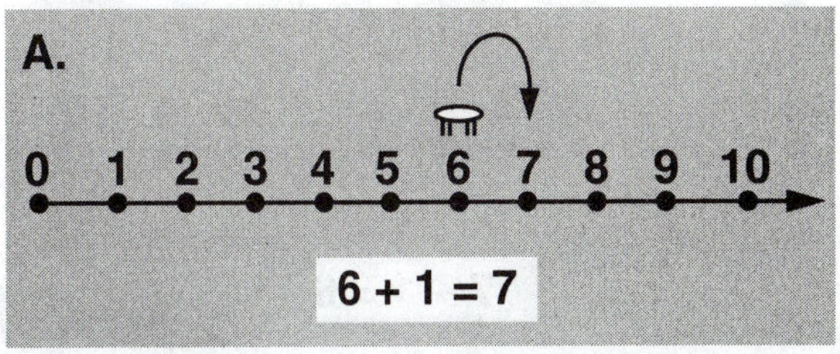

- Check your work. Here's the first fact for problem A. Raise your hand if you got it right.

b. Listen: Where was the bug at the end of this problem? (Signal.) *7.*

- I'll draw the bug there.
(Change bug to show:)

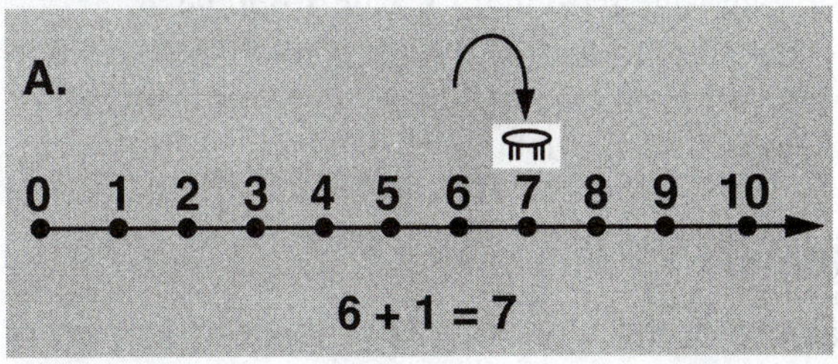

c. Listen: The bug decided that it didn't want to stay at **7** on the number line. It wanted to go back to where it started. Where did it start? (Signal.) *6.*

- So I just turn the arrow around. Watch.

(Change arrow:)

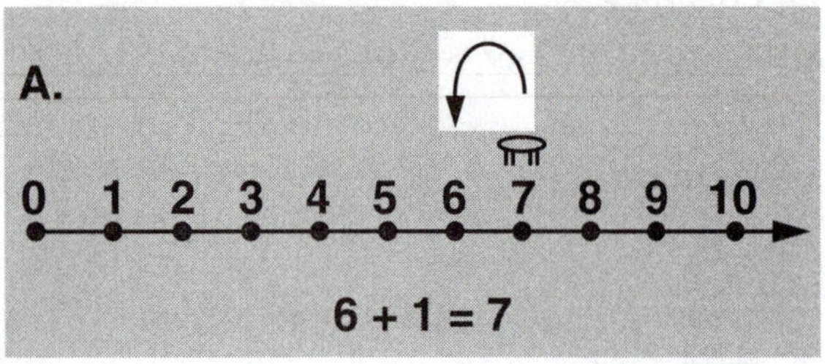

- Now you can write a new fact to tell how the bug got back to where it started. Remember, the bug is now at **7.** Does the bug plus or minus to get back to 6? (Signal.) *Minus.*

d. How many places does the bug minus? (Signal.) *1.*
- What number will the bug end up at? (Signal.) *6.* (Repeat step d until firm.)

e. Write the fact on the second line for problem A. Write it just under the other fact you wrote. Raise your hand when you're finished.
(Observe children and give feedback.)

(Write **7 – 1 = 6**:)

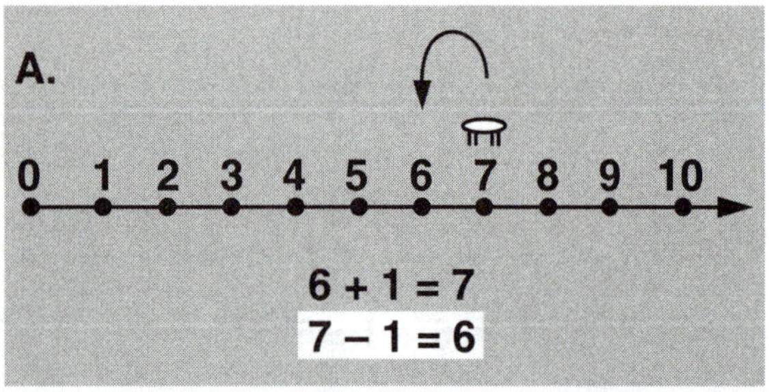

- Check your work. Here's the second fact for problem A. Raise your hand if you got everything right.
- For problem A, the bug started at **6** and went to **7.** Then the bug started at **7** and went back to **6.**

f. Everybody, say the fact for the bug going from **6** to **7.** Get ready. (Signal.) *6 plus 1 equals 7.*
- Now say the fact for the bug going back to where it started. Get ready. (Signal.) *7 minus 1 equals 6.* (Repeat step f until firm.)

Problem Solving

Some of the work that is presented as part of introducing addition and subtraction could be labeled problem solving (such as the bug on the number line). The primary purpose of these exercises in the program, however, is more to teach specific relationships than to apply knowledge to problem-solving situations. Level A does present problem-solving activities of two types: those that require children to apply their knowledge of an operation and those that require a reduction or translation from word problems.

Problem solving related to operations begins in Lesson 45. The first operational activities require children to use their operational knowledge about plussing to work problems such as 4 + □ = 6. Children know that when they plus, they go to the right on the number line. They also know that the first number in the problem is the starting number. The number after the equal sign is the number they end up with. With this information, they can operate on the number line and figure out the number of places to plus. Here's the introduction from Lesson 45.

a. (Write on the board:)

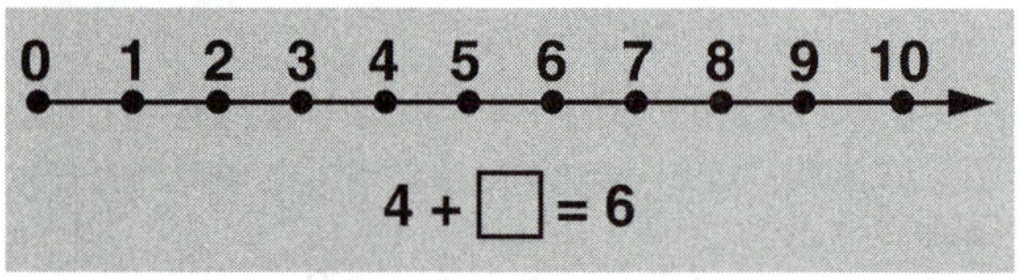

- Here's a brand new kind of problem. The middle number is missing. I'll point to each part of the problem and tell you what it says.
- (Point to each symbol as you say:) 4 plus **what number** equals 6?

b. Your turn: I'll touch. You tell me what the problem says. Remember, say **what number** for the box.

c. (Touch each symbol as children say:) *4 plus what number equals 6?*
(Repeat step c until firm.)

d. I'll show you how this problem works. The first number tells where to start out on the number line. What's the first number of the problem? (Signal.) *4.*
- So I start at **4.** And I'm plussing. So I'll draw a **plus** arrow over 4.
(Draw to show:)

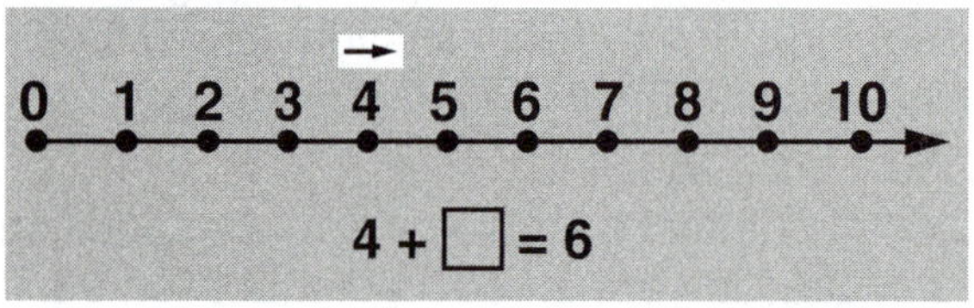

- The **last** number in the problem tells where I end up. What number do I end up at? (Signal.) *6.*
- So I'll circle 6.
(Circle **6**:)

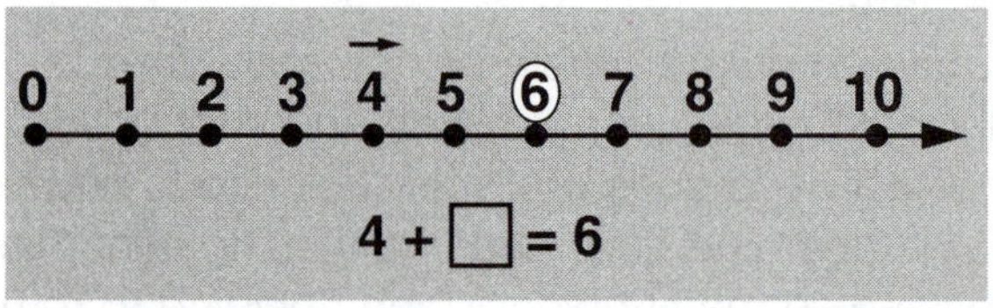

- Now all I have to do is figure out the number of places I plus to get from **4** to **6.** That's easy. I'll just make humps. (Make humps as you say:) Plus one, plus two.

- I plussed 2. That's the answer to the question. So I write **2** in the box.
  (Write **2**:)

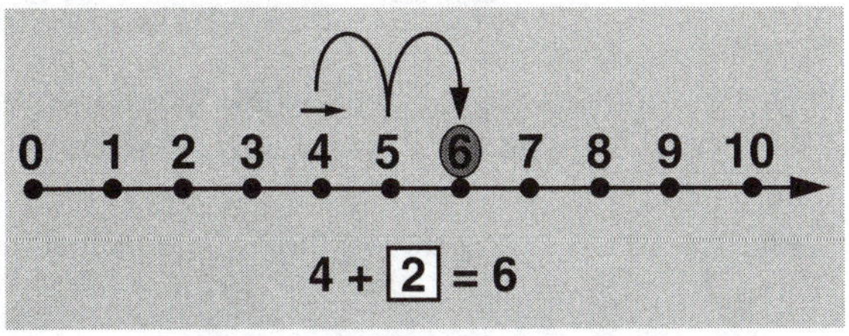

- I answered the question. Listen: 4 plus what number equals 6? The answer is 2. We plussed 2.

e. Your turn: 4 plus what number equals 6? (Signal.) *2.*
(Repeat step e until firm.)

f. (Change to show:)

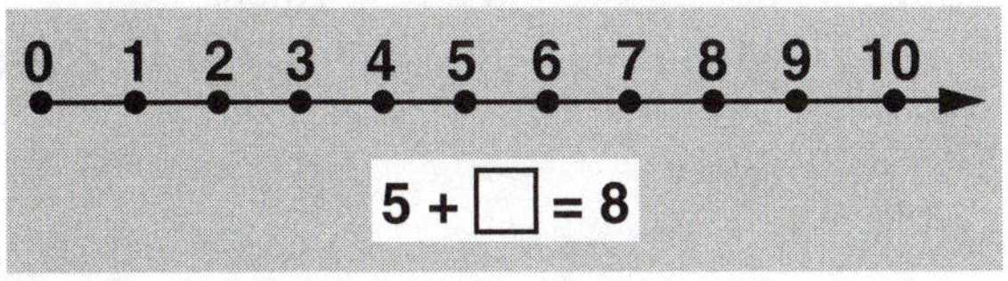

- Here's a new problem. I'll touch. You tell me what the problem says.

h. (Touch each symbol as children say:) *5 plus what number equals 8?*
(Repeat step h until firm.)

i. The problem tells the number we start at and the number we end up at. What number do we start at? (Signal.) *5.*

- What number do we end up at? (Signal.) *8.*
- I'll make an arrow to show the number we **start** at. What number? (Signal.) *5.*
  (Draw to show:)

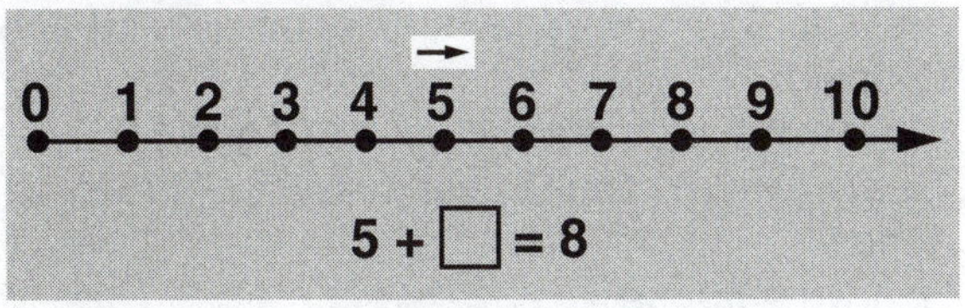

j. I'll circle the number we end up at. What number? (Signal.) *8.*
(Repeat step j until firm.)

k. (Circle **8**:)

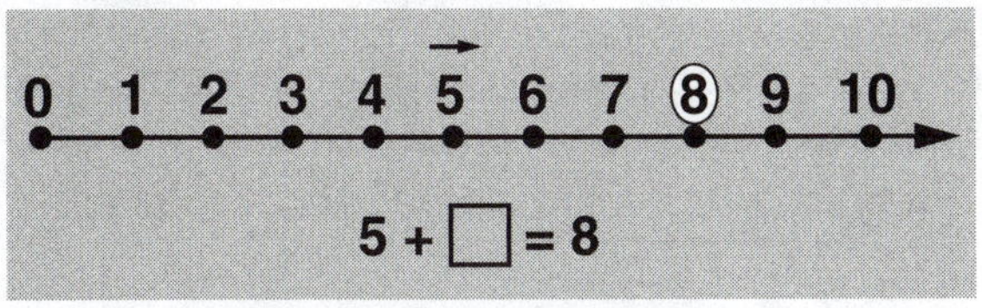

- Now all we have to do is figure out the number of places we plus to get from **5** to **8.** Count the places we plus. Raise your hand when you know how many places we plus.
- Everybody, how many places? (Signal.) *3.*
- Let's see if you're right. (Draw the humps as you say:) Plus one, plus two, plus three.

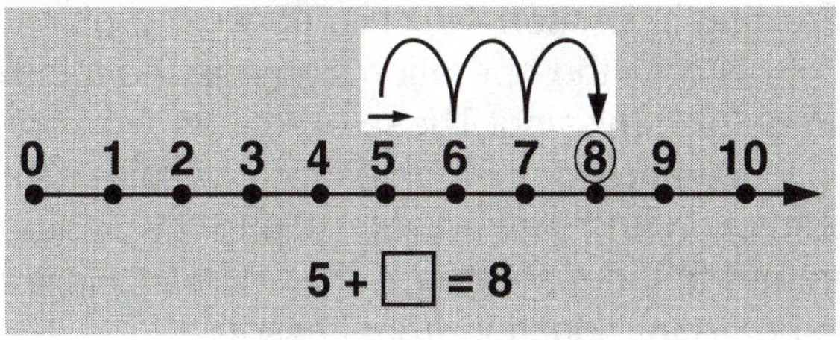

- How many places did we plus? (Signal.) *3.*
- That's the answer. We plussed 3. So I write **3** in the box.
  (Write **3**:)

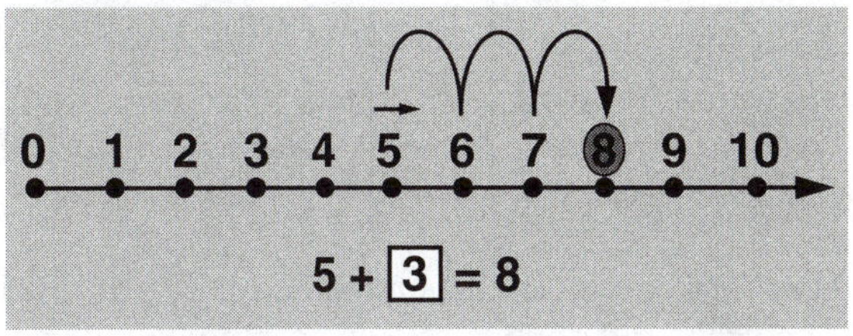

- Here was the question: 5 plus **what number** equals 8? Everybody, what's the answer? (Signal.) *3.*
- Yes, we plussed 3.

l. (Do **not** erase the board.)

Note the steps: After you read the problem, the children identify the starting number and identify the operation as plussing. You make an arrow over the starting number. Then you circle the ending number and make humps to determine the number of places plussed (one hump for each place).

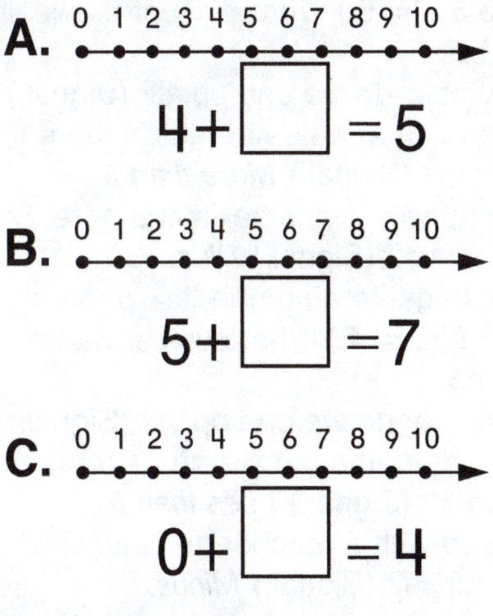

Sometimes when children work these problems, they have trouble making the humps. Some children try to make a single hump from the starting number to the ending number. If children make this kind of mistake, remind them to make a hump for each place they plus.

In Lesson 47, children work minus problems with the middle number missing.

Starting in Lesson 48, children work problems in which both the operation sign and the middle number are missing. These exercises are very important in reinforcing the logic of addition and subtraction and their relationship to the number line and to the statements of arithmetic. Here's the board introduction from Lesson 48.

a. (Write on the board:)

0 1 2 3 4 5 6 7 8 9 10 →

5 ☐ = 7

5 ☐ = 6

5 ☐ = 4

- Here are some new problems and they are tough. The problems don't tell you whether you plus or minus. And they don't have a number in the middle. But they tell you the number you start at and the number you end up at. So you can figure out the middle part.

b. (Point to **5** ☐= 7.) Look at this problem. What number do we start at? (Signal.) *5.*
- What number do we end up at? (Signal.) *7.*
- Do we end up at a number that's more than 5 or less than 5? (Signal.) *More than 5.*
- We end up with a number that's more. So do we plus or minus? (Signal.) *Plus.* We **plus** to get to a number that's more.
  (Repeat step b until firm.)

c. (Point to **5** ☐= 6.) What number do we start at? (Signal.) *5.*
- What number do we end up at? (Signal.) *6.*
- Do we end up at a number that's more than 5 or less than 5? (Signal.) *More than 5.*
- We end up with a number that's more. So do we plus or minus? (Signal.) *Plus.*
- We plus to get to a number that's more.

d. (Point to **5** ☐ = 4.) What number do we start at? (Signal.) *5.*
- What number do we end up at? (Signal.) *4.*
- Do we end up at a number that's more than 5 or less than 5? (Signal.) *Less than 5.*
- We end up with a number that's less. So do we plus or minus? (Signal.) *Minus.*
- We minus to get to a number that's less.

e. Let's figure out the answer to these problems. First, you'll tell me whether to write a plus sign or a minus sign. Then you'll tell me the missing number.

f. (Point to **5** ☐= 7.) What number do we start at? (Signal.) *5.*
- What number do we end up at? (Signal.) *7.*
- Do we plus or minus to get from 5 to 7? (Signal.) *Plus.*
- So I write **plus.**
  (Write +:)

5 [+] = 7

- Now the problem says: 5 plus what number equals 7? Raise your hand when you know how many we plus.
- Everybody, how many do we plus? (Signal.) *2.*
  (Write **2**:)

5 [+ 2] = 7

Now we have a fact you know: 5 **plus 2** equals 7.

g. (Point to 5 ☐= 6.) What number do we start at? (Signal.) *5.*
- What number do we end up at? (Signal.) *6.*
- Do we plus or minus to get from 5 to 6? (Signal.) *Plus.*
- So I write **plus.**
  (Write +:)

5 [+] = 6

- Now the problem says: 5 plus what number equals 6? Raise your hand when you know how many we plus.
- Everybody, how many do we plus? (Signal.) *1.*
  (Write **1**:)

5 [+ 1] = 6

- Now we have a fact you know: 5 **plus 1** equals 6.

h. (Point to **5** ☐= 4.) What number do we start at? (Signal.) *5.*
- What number do we end up at? (Signal.) *4.*
- Do we plus or minus to get from 5 to 4? (Signal.) *Minus.*
- So I write **minus.**
  (Write −:)

5 [−] = 4

- Now the problem says: 5 minus what number equals 4? Raise your hand when you know how many we minus.
- Everybody, how many do we minus? (Signal.) *1.*
  (Write **1**:)

5 [− 1] = 4

- Now we have a fact you know: 5 **minus 1** equals 4.

i. I'll show you that problem on the number line. What number do we start at? (Signal.) *5.*

- I'll make a minus arrow over the **5.**
  (Draw to show:)

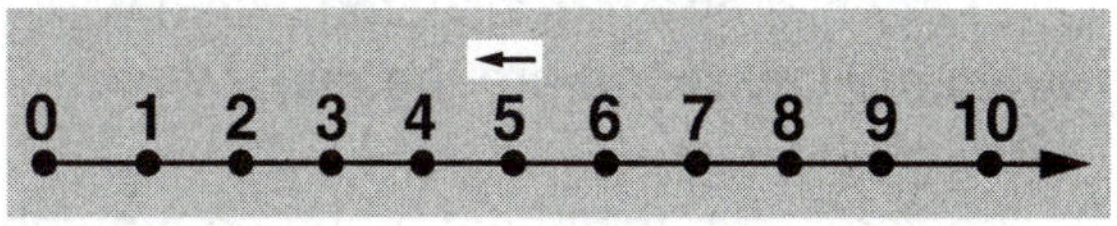

-
What number are we ending up at? (Signal.) *4.*
- I'll circle **4.**
  (Circle **4**:)

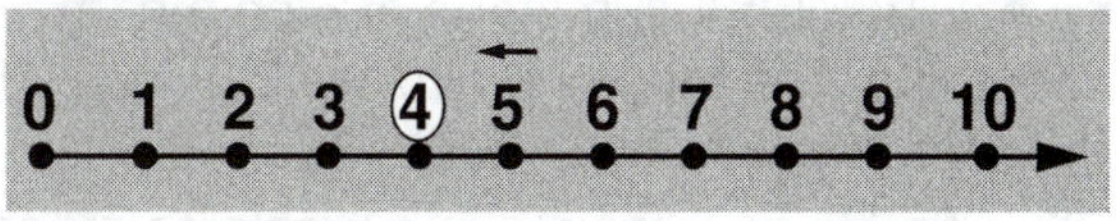

- You can see that you have to minus 1 to get from 5 to 4.

j. (Do **not** erase the number line.)

Following the board demonstration, children do workbook exercises. For the initial exercises, the number line is on the board so children can refer to it and confirm whether they are going to a smaller number or a bigger one and whether the arrow should point left or right.

A simpler variation is introduced later (starting in Lesson 104). For this variation, only the sign (+ or -) is missing.

The work with missing details in the middle of statements shows the children what kind of information is provided by the sign, the middle number, and the starting and ending numbers.

A final series of operational problems is associated with more and less. Starting in Lesson 109, children are introduced to the idea that statements may have a or sign instead of the equal sign. (When these activities are introduced, children have already received a lot of practice in working with the signs.) In Lesson 109, children are introduced to problem pairs:

A. 6+1 = □ **B.** 7+1 = □ **C.** 8−1 = □

6+1 ■ 8 7+1 ■ 10 8−1 ■ 6

Children complete the first problem in each pair. They then complete the sign for the second problem. Children must combine information in the problem with fact knowledge. To work pair A, for instance, children first indicate that 6 plus 1 equals 7. They then indicate that 6 plus 1 is less than 8.

A. 6 + 1 = 7

6 + 1 < 8

A variation is introduced in Lesson 112. Children solve a pair of column problems, then complete the sign between the answers.

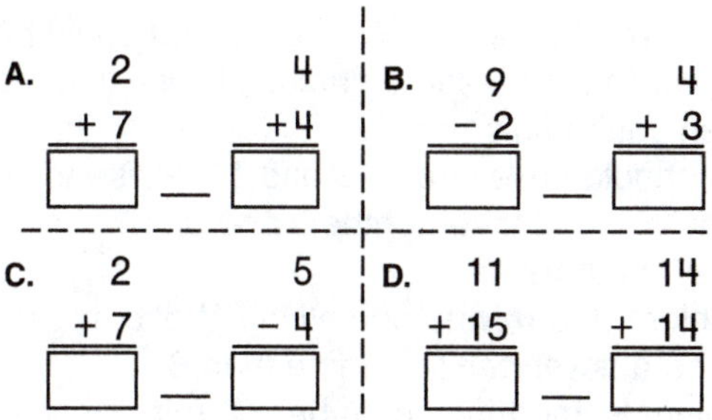

To work problems, children write answers to 2 plus 7 and 4 plus 4. They then compare the answers and complete the sign. 9 is more than 8.

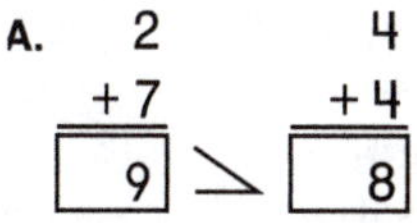

A final variation appears in Lesson 116. A problem with two unknowns appears above a group of numbers.

A. 8 + ■ = □

9	7	4	11

The first number is 8. The sign is a plus, indicating that the answer must be at least as big as 8. Children identify the numbers that could be answers to the problem. For this problem, 9 and 11 could be answers because they are more than 8. 7 and 4 could not be answers. Here's the introduction from Lesson 116:

a. In each problem, you can't see the number you're adding or subtracting.

b. Problem A: 8 plus some number equals some other number. We're adding and we're starting with 8. So we know that the answer can't be less than 8.

- Some of the numbers written under the answer box could be the answer because they are more than 8. Some of the numbers couldn't be the answer because they are less than 8.
- The first number is **9.** Could that be an answer if you were adding 8 and something else? (Signal.) *Yes.*

- The next number is **7.** Could that be an answer if you were adding 8 and something else? (Signal.) *No.*
- The next number is **4.** Could that be an answer if you were adding 8 and something else? (Signal.) *No.*
- The last number is **11**. Could that be an answer if you were adding 8 and something else? (Signal.) *Yes.*
- Your turn: Circle all the numbers that could be the answer to 8 plus some number. Raise your hand when you're finished. √
- You should have circled **9** and **11.** Raise your hand if you circled those numbers and didn't circle any other numbers.

c. Problem B: 8 **minus** something. We're minusing, so the answer can't be more than 8.
- 8 minus something could be 7. 8 minus something could **not** be 10. That's silly.
- Your turn: Circle all the numbers that could be the answer to the problem, 8 minus something. Raise your hand when you're finished. √
- You should have circled **7, 6,** and **2.** Raise your hand if you circled those numbers and didn't circle any other number.

d. Problem C: 14 **minus** something. Would the answer be more than 14 or less than 14? (Signal.) *Less than 14.*
- Circle all the numbers that could be the answer to 14 minus something. Raise your hand when you're finished. √
- You should have circled **6, 13, 7,** and **1.** Raise your hand if you circled all those numbers.

e. Problem D: 15 **plus** something. Would the answer be more than 15 or less than 15? (Signal.) *More than 15.*
- Circle all the numbers that could be the answer to 15 plus something. Raise your hand when you're finished. √
- You should have circled **16** and **34.** Raise your hand if you circled those numbers and didn't circle any other numbers.

f. Problem E: 23 minus something. Would the answer be more than 23 or less than 23? (Signal.) *Less than 23.*
- Circle all the numbers that could be the answer to 23 minus something. Raise your hand when you're finished. √
- You should have circled **22** and **19.** Raise your hand if you circled those numbers and didn't circle any other numbers.

g. Problem F: 23 plus something. Would the answer be more than 23 or less than 23? (Signal.) *More than 23.*
- Circle all the numbers that could be the answer to 23 plus something. Raise your hand when you're finished. √
- You should have circled **24** and **28.** Raise your hand if you circled those numbers and didn't circle any other numbers.

In addition to the operational problem solving in Level A, children are presented with a variety of word problems. Here are the major word-problem types:

a) Problems that tell about a bug on a number line or about movement along a number line (Lesson 47).

Some problems translate into problems of the form $5 + 2 = \square$: A bug starts at 5 on the number line. Then the bug plusses 2 places. The bug ends up at what number?

Other problems translate into problems of the form $5 + \square = 7$: A bug starts at 5 on the number line. Then the bug plusses some. The bug ends up at 7. How many places did the bug plus?

b) Problems that tell about a series of events in time (Lesson 78): Jan has 7 hats. Then she buys 2 more hats. How many hats does she end up with?

c) Problems that compare two values (Lesson 85): Bob has 12. Juanita has 1 less than Bob. How many does Juanita have? Or, Bob has 2. Juanita has 9 more than Bob. How many does Juanita have?

d) Problems that have an implied number 1 (Lesson 91): Mary walked to school with 8 other girls. How many girls walked to school?

e) Problems that involve all but 1 or all but 2 (Lesson 94): 5 bugs were on a leaf. All but 1 of the bugs flew home. How many bugs flew home?

f) Problems involving three numbers (Lesson 105). A man worked with 5 other men. Then another man joined them. How many men were working? Or: There were 8 bugs on a branch. Then 2 bugs flew away. Then 1 more flew away. How many bugs were still on the branch?

Before each problem is introduced, children are provided with a demonstration that shows the conceptual basis for the problem. These bases are particularly important for the children's understanding of comparisons and for problems involving all but 1 or all but 2.

Problems that compare two numbers are introduced in Lesson 84 with the number line. The teacher gives information about the teacher's number ("I have 8") and the relationship ("You have 2 fewer than I have"). The operation implied is explained this way: "You have 2 fewer than I have. If I go to your number, do I plus or do I minus?" Here's the introduction:

A. ____________________
B. ____________________
C. ____________________
D. ____________________
E. ____________________

a. (Write on the board:)

6 7 8 9 10 11 (number line)

- (Circle **8**.) I'm going to tell you problems about how many I have and how many you have. You'll tell me how to go from my number to your number. The circled number shows my number. What number? (Signal.) *8.*

b. (Touch **8** on the number line.) Here's how many I have. Listen: You have 2 fewer than I have. If I go to your number, do I plus or do I minus? (Signal.) *Minus.*
- You have 2 fewer than I have. So how many do I minus to get to your number? (Signal.) *2.*
- Your number is 2 fewer than **8.** Raise your hand when you know what your number is.
- Everybody, what's your number? (Signal.) *6.*
- Yes, your number is **6,** and I have to **minus 2** to go from my number to your number.

c. (Touch **8** again.) New problem. Here's how many I have. Listen: You have 3 more than I have. If I go to your number, do I plus or do I minus? (Signal.) *Plus.*
- You have 3 more than I have. So how many do I plus to get to your number? (Signal.) *3.*
- Your number is 3 more than **8.** Raise your hand when you know what your number is.
- Everybody, what's your number? (Signal.) *11.*
- Yes, your number is **11,** and I have to **plus 3** to go from my number to your number.

Workbook Practice

a. Find part 2. I'm going to tell you some super hard word problems. All the problems tell about my number and your number. You're going to write the problems and the answers.

b. Touch the line for problem A. Listen to the whole problem: I have 6. You have **2 more** than I have. How many do you have?
- The first part says that I have 6. So I start at **6.** You have **2 more.** So do I plus or minus to get to your number? (Signal.) *Plus.*
- How many do I plus? (Signal.) *2.*
- Tell me what to write. Listen: I have 6. What do I write? (Signal.) *6.*
- (Write **6**:)

6

- Next part: You have 2 more than I have. What do I write for that part? (Signal.) *Plus 2.* (Write + **2**:)

6 + 2

- Last part: How many do you have? That's like: What number do I end up at? I write **equals box.** (Write = □:)

6 + 2 = □

- Here's the whole problem. Your turn: Write problem A. Then write the answer. Raise your hand when you're finished. (Observe children and give feedback.)
- Everybody, if you have 2 more than I have, how many do you have? (Signal.) *8.*

c. Problem B: I have 9. You have **2 less** than I have. How many do you have?
- Listen again and write the whole problem: I have 9. Write that part. Raise your hand when you're finished. √
- Listen to the next part: You have 2 less than I have. Write that part. Raise your hand when you're finished. √
- Listen to the last part: How many do you have? Remember, that's **equals box.** Write it. Then write the answer. Raise your hand when you're finished. (Observe children and give feedback.)
- (Write on the board:)

B. 9 – 2 = [7]

Check your work. Here's what you should have: 9 minus 2 equals 7. I have 9 and you have 2 less than I have. So how many do you have? (Signal.) *7.*

The demonstration for problems about all but 1 or all but 2 appears in Lesson 94. Again, the number line is the basis for the demonstration, which shows that all but 1 is just 1 less than all. If the number line shows all, and all the numbers but one are circled, the number of circled numbers is 1 less than the number given. This relationship sounds complicated, but it can be shown as simple. Here's the introduction from Lesson 94:

A. ____ B. ____ C. ____ D. ____ E. ____

a. (Write on the board:)

1 2 3 4 5 (number line)

- Here's a number line that goes to **5.** I'll tell you a rule about the numbers. All the numbers are supposed to be circled. Raise your hand when you know how many numbers should be circled.
- Everybody, if all the numbers should be circled, how many should be circled? (Signal.) *5.*
- Yes, 5 numbers should be circled.

b. (Point to the dot for each numeral as you say:) This number should be circled.

- (Then say:) So all 5 numbers should be circled.

c. Here's a harder rule. Listen: **All the numbers but one** of them should be circled. Listen again: All the numbers but one of them should be circled. Raise your hand when you know how many should be circled.

- Everybody, if all the numbers but one should be circled, how many should be circled? (Signal.) *4.*
- It doesn't matter which number we don't circle. Four of them should be circled. Watch.
- (Circle the first four numbers.)
- Did I circle all the numbers? (Signal.) *No.*
- Did I circle all **but one** of them? (Signal.) *Yes.*
- There are 5 numbers. I circled all but one of them. So how many numbers did I circle? (Signal.) *4.*

d. New problem.
(Change number line to show:)

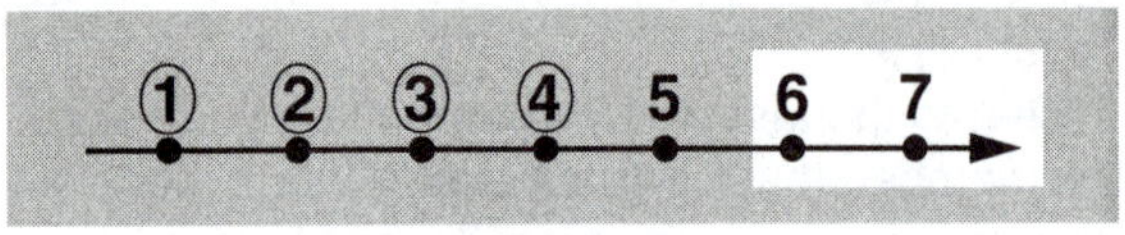

- How many numbers are on this number line? (Signal.) *7.*
- There are **7** numbers on this number line. Listen: All but one of them should be circled. Raise your hand when you know how many numbers should be circled.
- Everybody, how many numbers should be circled? (Signal.) *6.*
- (Circle **5** and **6**.) There are 7 numbers. All but one of them is circled. Everybody, how many are circled? (Signal.) *6.*
- Remember, all but one is just 1 less than all of them.

Workbook Practice

a. Open your workbook to Lesson 94 and find part 1. √

- I'll tell you some problems that tell about all but one. You'll write the answer for each problem.

b. Touch space A. Here's the problem: 5 bugs were on a leaf. All but 1 of the bugs flew home. How many bugs flew home? Remember, there were 5 bugs in all, and all but 1 flew home. That's 1 less than all of them. Everybody, write the answer. Raise your hand when you're finished. √

- Listen: If 5 bugs were on a leaf and all but 1 of the bugs flew home, how many bugs flew home? (Signal.) *4.*
- Raise your hand if you got it right.

c. Touch space B. Here's the problem: 10 boys were at a party. All but 1 of the boys went home. How many boys went home? Everybody, write the answer. Raise your hand when you're finished. √

- Listen: If 10 boys were at a party and all but 1 of the boys went home, how many boys went home? (Signal.) *9.*
- Raise your hand if you got it right.

d. Touch space C. Here's the problem: 6 girls were playing ball. All but 2 of them went home. How many girls went home? Write the answer. Raise your hand when you're finished. √

- Listen: If 6 girls were playing ball and all but 2 of them went home, how many girls went home? (Signal.) *4.*
- Raise your hand if you got it right.

e. Touch space D. Here's a problem of a different type: A bug met 4 other bugs. How many bugs were there in all? Write the answer. Raise your hand when you're finished. √

- Listen: If a bug met 4 other bugs, how many bugs were there in all? (Signal.) *5.*
- Raise your hand if you got it right.

f. Touch space E. Here's the problem: Tom went walking with 8 other boys. How many boys were walking? Write the answer. Raise your hand when you're finished. √

- Listen: If Tom went walking with 8 other boys, how many boys were walking? (Signal.) *9.*
- Raise your hand if you got it right.

Money

Children work a variety of money problems. Most problems present rows of coins. The initial coins are dimes and pennies. This set reinforces what children are learning about place value. Dimes and pennies work just like tens and ones. Other coin problems provide children with practice in fixing up a row so it corresponds to a price tag at the end of the row. Fixing up the row may involve adding pennies or crossing out pennies.

The first coin problems appear in Lesson 74. The introduction treats coin problems as problems involving T's and lines. In this lesson, children write numbers for T's and lines immediately before working the coin problems. Children are then shown that dimes work like T's and the number of dimes is written in the first part of the box. Pennies are like lines. Their number is written in the "leftover" part of the box. Here's the introduction:

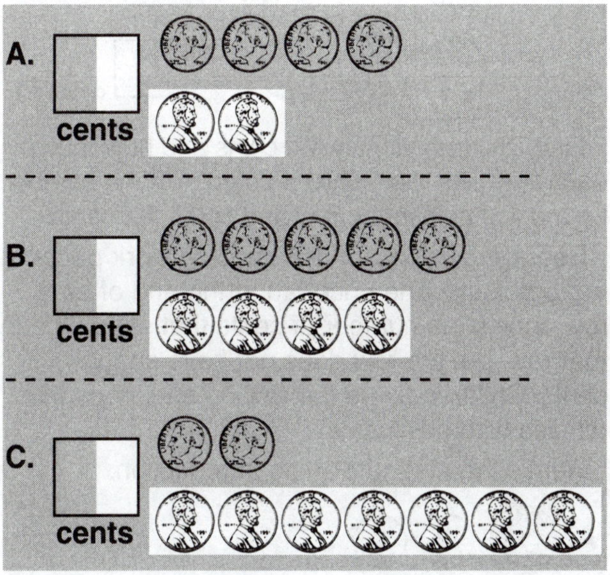

a. You've worked with **T's** and lines. You can do the same thing with dimes and pennies.
b. Listen: A **T** stands for 10. A dime stands for 10. A dime is worth 10 cents.
- Touch the coins in the top row of item A. Those are dimes. What are they? (Signal.) *Dimes.*
- How many cents is each dime worth? (Signal.) *10.*
- That's just like a **T.** It's worth **10.**
- You know that a **line** stands for 1. A **penny** also stands for 1. A penny is worth 1 cent.
- Touch the coins in the bottom row of item A. Those are pennies. What are they? (Signal.) *Pennies.*
- How many cents is a penny worth? (Signal.) *1.*
- That's just like a **line.** It's worth **1.**

c. Everybody, how many cents is a **dime** worth? (Signal.) *10.*
- How many cents is a **penny** worth? (Signal.) *1.*
(Repeat step c until firm.)

d. Each item in part 2 shows dimes and pennies. You're going to write the number of cents for each item.
e. Touch item A. Count the dimes to yourself. Raise your hand when you know how many dimes there are.
- Everybody, how many dimes? (Signal.) *4.*
- That's like 4 **T's.** So what number do you start with? (Signal.) *40.*
- Say **40** and then count the pennies. Get ready. (Signal.) *40, 41, 42.*
- Everybody, what numeral goes in the box? (Signal.) *42.*
- Yes, item A shows 42 cents: 4 dimes and 2 pennies.

f. Touch item B. Count the dimes to yourself. Raise your hand when you know how many dimes there are.
- Everybody, how many dimes? (Signal.) *5.*
- So what number do you start with? (Signal.) *50.*
- Say **50** and then count the pennies. Get ready. (Signal.) *50, 51, 52, 53, 54.*
- Everybody, what numeral goes in the box? (Signal.) *54.*
- Yes, item B shows 54 cents: 5 dimes and 4 pennies.

g. Touch item C. Count the dimes to yourself. Raise your hand when you know how many dimes there are.
- Everybody, how many dimes. (Signal.) *2.*
- So what number do you start with. (Signal.) *20.*
- Say **20** and then count the pennies. Get ready. (Signal.) *20, 21, 22, 23, 24, 25, 26, 27.*
- Everybody, what numeral goes in the box? (Signal.) *27.*
- Yes, item C shows 27 cents: 2 dimes and 7 pennies.

h. Your turn: Count the dimes and pennies in each item. Write the numeral that goes in each box. Raise your hand when you're finished.
(Observe children and give feedback.)

i. Check your work.
- Touch item A. There are 4 dimes and 2 pennies. Everybody, how many cents is that? (Signal.) *42.*
- Touch item B. There are 5 dimes and 4 pennies. Everybody, how many cents is that? (Signal.) *54.*
- Touch item C. There are 2 dimes and 7 pennies. Everybody, how many cents is that? (Signal.) *27.*

j. Raise your hand if you got all these cents problems right.
- That's good smart work!

Beginning with Lesson 80, children work problems involving two groups of dimes.

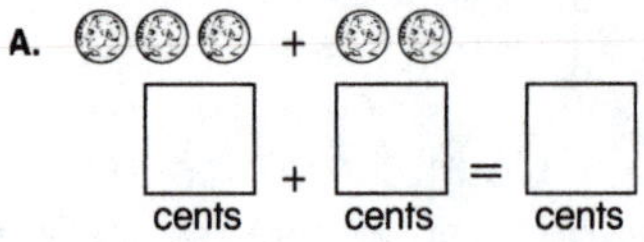

a. Find part 6. Each problem shows dimes. You're going to complete the fact for each problem.

b. Touch problem A. The problem shows 3 dimes plus 2 more dimes. Touch the 3 dimes you start with. √

- There are 3 dimes. How many cents is 3 dimes? (Signal.) *30.*
- So what numeral do you write in the first box? (Signal.) *30.*
- Write **30** in the first box below the dimes. Raise your hand when you're finished.
  (Observe children and give feedback.)
- Listen: Touch the dimes that are after the plus sign. √
- There are 2 dimes. So what numeral do you write? (Signal.) *20.*
- Write **20** in the box after the plus sign. Raise your hand when you're finished.
  (Observe children and give feedback.)
- Now you just figure out the answer and write it in the last box. You have the problem: 30 plus 20 equals what number? What's the answer? (Signal.) *50.*
- Write **50** in the box after the equal sign.
  (Write on the board:)

A. 30 + 20 = 50

- Here's the fact you should have for problem A. That fact shows you that if you have 3 dimes and you plus 2 more dimes, you end up with 50 cents. Raise your hand if you wrote the problem and the answer just the way I did it on the board.

For this problem, the children write the number of cents for the first group of dimes and for the second group. Then children add to find the total. (They have been taught the strategy of looking at the first digit of each value. 3 plus 2 equals 5. So, 30 plus 20 equals 50.)

In Lesson 82, children begin working with sets of coins that are not ordered.

a. You're going to write the numerals for dimes and pennies, but just look at how mixed up the coins are. This is going to be very hard.

b. Touch item A. Listen: Count the dimes to yourself. Just the dimes. Be careful. Raise your hand when you know how many dimes there are.

- Everybody, how many dimes? (Signal.) *3.*
- So what number do you say for the dimes? (Signal.) *30.*
- Say **30.** Then count the pennies to yourself. Be careful. Raise your hand when you know how many cents there are.
- Everybody, how many cents are there? (Signal.) *34.*
- Yes, there are 34 cents.

Children count the dimes and determine the number of dimes. There are three dimes. So, the children say 30 and count the pennies.

In Lesson 92, children work with sets of coins that involve nickels and quarters.

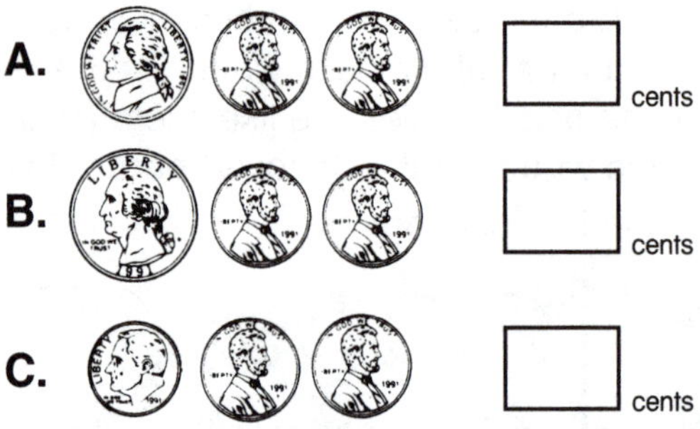

First, children identify the coins and how much each is worth. Next, children start with the number for the first coin in the row and count the cents.

Beginning in Lesson 95, children work price-tag problems. The price tag at the end of each row shows the number of cents that should be in that row, but the row does not have enough cents. Children fix up the row by adding pennies (circles with a P inside).

Here's the first part of the introduction:

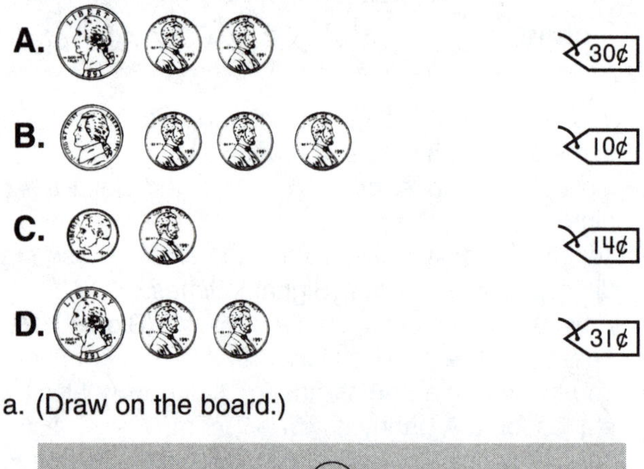

a. (Draw on the board:)

- You're going to draw pennies for the problems we're going to do next. Here's how you do it. You make a circle with a **P** inside. The **P** stands for **penny.**

- (Write on the board:)

¢

- This funny sign stands for cents. You'll see it in the problems you'll work.

Workbook Practice

a. Find part 2. These are coin problems. The price tag at the end of each coin row shows how many cents should be in the row, but the coins are wrong. Pennies are missing.

b. Touch row A. The price tag shows how much a toy costs. Remember, that funny sign stands for cents. How much does the toy cost? (Signal.) *30 cents.*

- Touch the first coin in the row. What coin is that? (Signal.) *A quarter.*
- How many cents is a quarter worth? (Signal.) *25.*

c. Say the number for the quarter and then count for the pennies. Get ready. (Signal.) *25, 26, 27.* (Repeat step c until firm.)

d. What number did you end up with? (Signal.) *27.*

- But the price tag says 30 cents, not 27 cents. Listen: The pennies are missing for 28, 29, and 30. Your turn: Draw in the missing pennies. When you're done, count the cents to yourself and make sure that you have 30 cents in the row. Raise your hand when you're finished. (Observe children and give feedback.)
- Everybody, count all the pennies you drew for price-tag A. Raise your hand when you know how many pennies you drew.
- Everybody, how many did you draw? (Signal.) *3.*
- If you drew 3, you did it the right way.
- Count the 30 cents for price tag A. Start with **25** and then count for the pennies. Get ready. Count. (Signal.) *25, 26, 27, 28, 29, 30.*

e. Touch price-tag B. How many cents does that price tag show? (Signal.) *10 cents.*

- Touch the first coin in row B. What coin is that? (Signal.) *A nickel.*
- How many cents is a nickel worth? (Signal.) *5.*

f. Say the number for the nickel and then count for the pennies. Get ready. Count. (Signal.) *5, 6, 7, 8.* (Repeat step f until firm.)

g. What number did you end up with? (Signal.) *8.*

- But the row should have 10 cents, not 8 cents. Fix up the row so it has 10 cents. Raise your hand when you're finished. (Observe children and give feedback.)
- Everybody, how many pennies did you draw? (Signal.) *2.*
- Raise your hand if you drew 2 pennies.
- Everybody, start with **5** and then count for the pennies. Get ready. Count. (Signal.) *5, 6, 7, 8, 9, 10.*

The final problem type presents price tags that may have too many or too few cents. Children fix up each row either by drawing pennies or by crossing out pennies.

During the later parts of Level A, coin problems make additional connections with what the children are learning about place value, word problems, and other types of problem solving.

Measurement

In Level A, children learn basic relationships and units of length measurement. Children learn to estimate 1 inch and 2 inches, and then use a ruler to measure lines (vertical or horizontal) and the sides of rectangles.

Work with measurement is mechanically difficult for children. The basic idea that the ruler must start where the line starts is difficult for some children to grasp. Measurement activities may take longer than you would expect. Take the time that is necessary to bring the children to a solid level of performance. Their performance on more complicated measurement activities in later levels of the program will benefit greatly if they learn the fundamentals of measuring.

The first exercise begins in Lesson 101. For this and other measurement activities, children need a primary ruler. The simpler the ruler, the better. In Lesson 101, children estimate 1 and 2 inches.

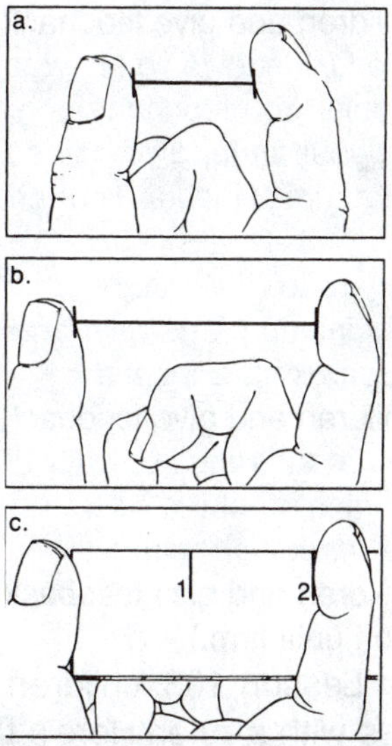

Note: Each child will need a primary ruler for this exercise.

a. Find part 2.

b. Touch picture A. That picture shows how long 1 inch is. The space between the fingers is 1 inch.

c. Your turn: Put your fingers over the fingers in the picture. √

- Now hold up your fingers so that you have a 1-inch space between your fingers.
  (Observe children and give feedback.)
- Everybody, how big is the space you're showing me? (Signal.) *1 inch.*

d. Everybody, clap your hands.
- Now show me 1 inch again. Don't measure. Just show me 1 inch. √
- To see how close you came to 1 inch, keep that space between your fingers and put it over the space in picture A. Raise your hand if you came pretty close.
  (Praise children who raise their hand.)

e. Touch picture B. That picture shows 2 inches. Put your fingers over the fingers in the picture. Then hold them up and show me 2 inches. Everybody, show me 2 inches.
  (Observe children and give feedback.)
- Everybody, how big is the space you're showing me? (Signal.) *2 inches.*

f. Everybody, clap your hands.
- Now show me 2 inches again. √
- To see how close you came to 2 inches, keep that space between your fingers and put your fingers over picture B. Raise your hand if you came pretty close.
  (Praise children who raise their hand.)

g. Listen: Everybody, hold up your fingers to show me **1 inch.** 1 inch. √
- Check it against picture A to see how close you came.
  (Observe children and give feedback.)

h. Touch picture C. It shows you how to measure 2 inches on a ruler. You touch the beginning of the ruler and put your finger on the line for number 2. That's the mark for 2 inches. Your turn: Hold your ruler.

i. Use your fingers to measure off 2 inches.
- Touch the beginning of the ruler and put your finger on the mark for 2 inches.
  (Observe children and give feedback.)
- Listen: Measure off 1 inch on your ruler. 1 inch.
- Touch the beginning of the ruler and put your finger on the mark for 1 inch.
  (Observe children and give feedback.)
  (Repeat step i until firm.)

Beginning in Lesson 103, children measure horizontal lines with a ruler. Here's the demonstration that precedes the workbook exercise and the first line children measure:

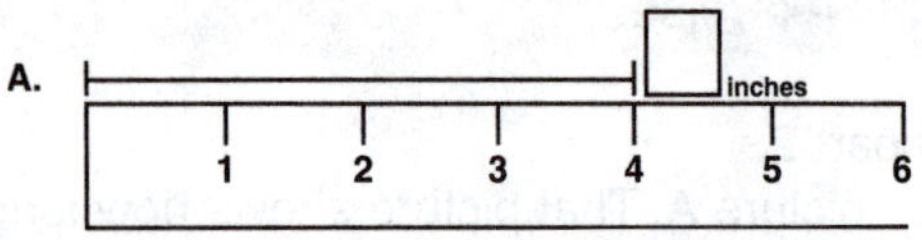

Note: Each child will need a primary ruler.

a. (Hold up your ruler.) There are numbers on your ruler. (Point to the numbers on your ruler as you say:) Here's 1, here's 2, here's 3. The numbers tell about the number of inches from the beginning of the ruler.

b. Listen: Touch the mark at **4** on your ruler. 4. √
- That line marks 4 inches from the beginning of the ruler.
- Listen: Touch the mark at **8** on your ruler. 8. √
- That line marks 8 inches from the beginning of the ruler.

c. (Draw a line **10** inches long on the board:)

- You're going to measure some lines. When you measure a line, you always put the beginning of your ruler at the beginning of the line. I'm going to measure this line, so I'll show you where my ruler goes.
- The ruler is in the right place. Watch.
  (Correctly position your ruler:)

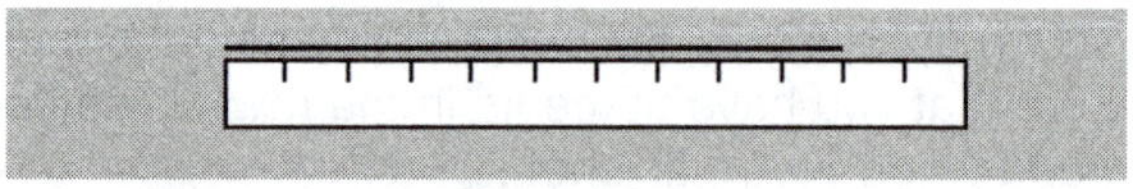

- (Move your ruler to the right:)

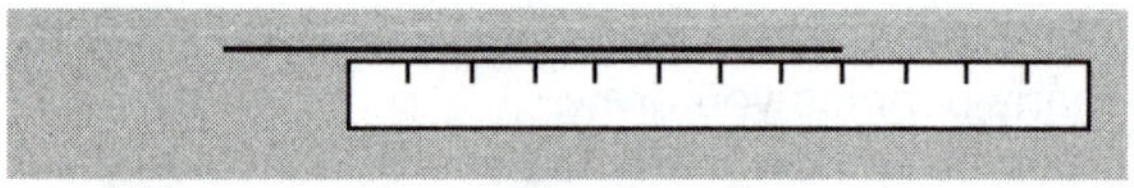

- You can't have your ruler start here.
- (Move your ruler to the left:)

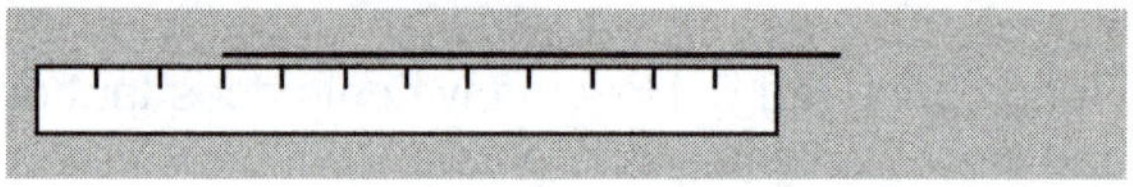

  You can't have your ruler start here.
- (Move your ruler to the correct position.) Your ruler must be right here, so it begins at the same place the line begins. Then you can see how long the line is by finding the end of the line and reading the number on the ruler.
- (Point to the end of the line.) Here's the end of the line. It's right at the mark for **10** on my ruler. So you know how long this line is. How long? (Signal.) *10 inches.*

Workbook Practice

a. Find part 2. Your turn: Everybody, measure 1 inch on your ruler. Use your fingers and measure off 1 inch. Remember, start at the beginning of the ruler and put your finger at the mark for 1 inch. Hold up your fingers to show me 1 inch.
  (Observe children and give feedback.)

- Everybody, how big is the space you're showing me? (Signal.) *1 inch.*

b. Touch item A. It shows you where to put your ruler to measure a line. Everybody, put your ruler right over the ruler in the picture. Start your ruler at the mark that shows where the line begins.
(Observe children and give feedback.)

- Everybody, touch the end of the line you're measuring—the end of the line, not the beginning.
- The end of the line should be right above a number on your ruler. The number tells how many inches long the line is.
- Everybody, how many inches long is line A? (Signal.) *4 inches.*
- Yes, 4 inches. The end of the line is right on the mark for **4** on your ruler.

The three biggest problems that children have with this skill are the following:

1) Children do not keep the ruler still. The ruler may start out being positioned correctly, but it doesn't stay there.

2) Children do not start their ruler where the line starts. They simply put their ruler under the line.

3) Children do not read the appropriate number on their ruler.

Unfortunately, there is no way to provide children feedback without observing what they are doing. If you know what their problems are, you can reduce the time it takes for them to learn how to use a ruler correctly. Praise children who are not making the common mistakes. "Ginger, good job of starting your ruler right where the line starts...." "James, show me the number for the mark at the end of the line.... That's it. Good finding...." "Tina, good holding your ruler steady. That's hard to do, isn't it?"

In subsequent lessons, children measure vertical lines and the length and width of rectangles.

Estimation

The two major types of estimation activities in Level A involve drawing or completing rectangles according to specifications (make the rectangle just as high as the first rectangle) and those in which children estimate the relative size of objects. They do this by expressing how many times longer or higher the object is than a reference object.

The estimation activities begin in Lesson 110 with children practicing a preskill that is assumed by estimation tasks: referring to component dimensions of objects. Children often have trouble with the idea that objects have both height and width. The purpose of the introduction is to make it clear that a rectangle may be higher than another but not as wide, or it may be wider but just as high, and so forth.

These activities are not presented earlier in the program because much of the work done in subjects other than math in the first grade helps prepare children for this work.

Here is the activity from Lesson 110.

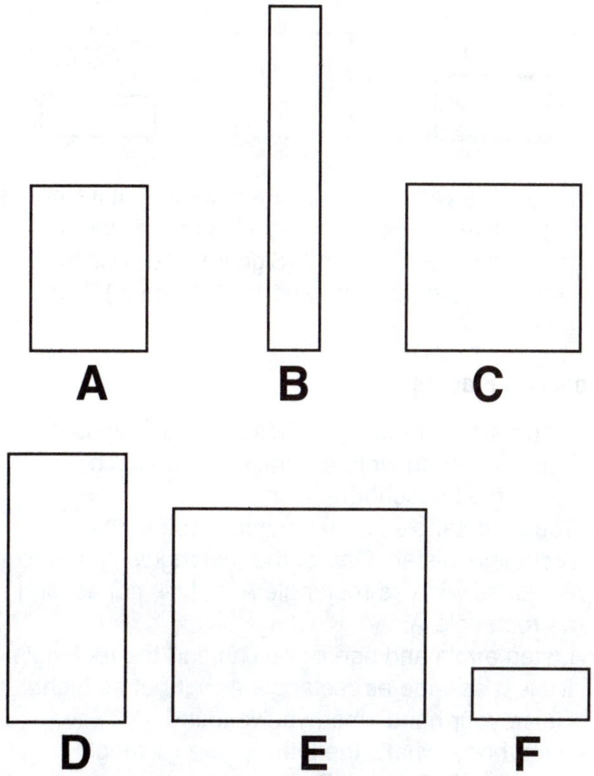

a. (Draw on the board:)

- Here's a shape that's called a rectangle. What's it called? (Signal.) *A rectangle.*

b. I'm going to make another rectangle that's just about as wide as this rectangle.
(Draw a rectangle that's the same width but higher:)

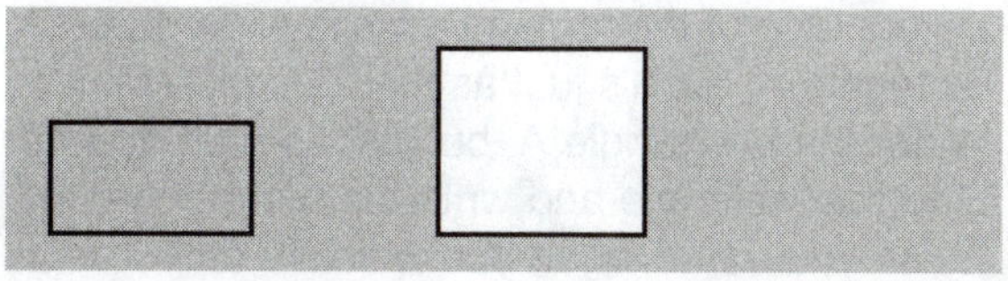

- (Draw a line across the bottom of the first rectangle.)

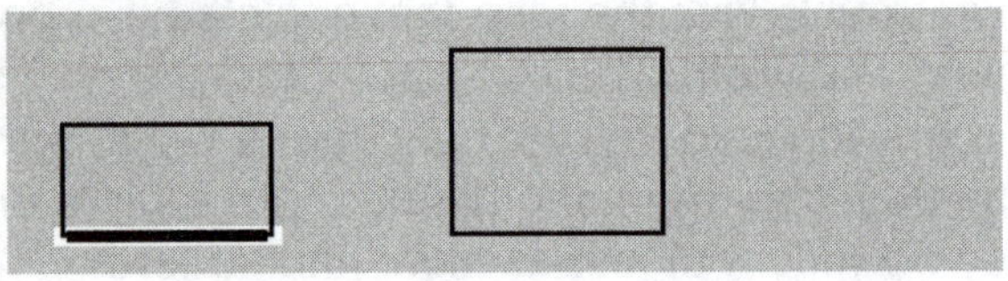

- See how wide this rectangle is? The second rectangle is just about as wide. But the second rectangle is higher.

c. I'm going to make another rectangle that is just about as wide as the first rectangle.
(Draw a third rectangle:)

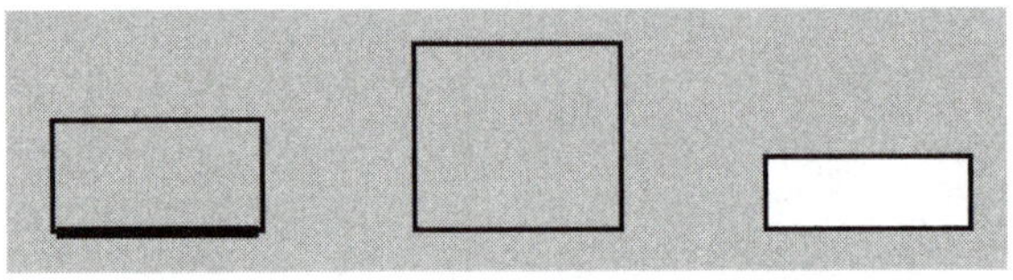

- It's just as wide as the first rectangle, but it's not as high. Listen: Which rectangle is highest, the first, the second or the third? (Signal.) *The second.*
- Which rectangle is the shortest? (Signal.) *The third.*

Workbook Practice

a. Find part 4. I'm going to describe rectangles. You're going to write a number inside each rectangle I describe.

b. Touch rectangle A. Take a good look at that rectangle. Listen: One of the rectangles in that row is just as wide as rectangle A, but it's not as high as rectangle A.
- Listen again and see if you can find the rectangle. It's just as wide as rectangle A, but not as high. Raise your hand when you've found it.
- Everybody, what's the letter of the rectangle I described? (Signal.) *F.*
- Write the number **1** in that rectangle. Raise your hand when you're finished.
(Observe children and give feedback.)

c. Listen: One of these rectangles is just as wide as rectangle A, but it's higher than rectangle A. It's just as wide, but it's higher. Raise your hand when you've found it.
- Write the number **2** in the rectangle that's just as wide as rectangle A but higher. Raise your hand when you're finished. √
- Everybody, what's the letter of the rectangle with the number **2** in it? (Signal.) *D.*

d. Listen: One of these rectangles is wider than rectangle A, but it's just as high. Listen again: Wider than rectangle A, but just as high. Your turn: Find the rectangle and write the number **3** in it. Raise your hand when you're finished. √
- Everybody, what's the letter of the rectangle with the number **3** in it? (Signal.) *C.*

e. Raise your hand if you found all the right rectangles.

If children have trouble, tell them to use their fingers and show you how wide and how high the first rectangle is. Then repeat the description: "Find the rectangle that is just as (wide or high)."

Make sure that children are quite firm at identifying the appropriate rectangles in the activities presented in Lessons 110 and 113.

In Lesson 114, children complete rectangles so they correspond to verbal descriptions. This is a powerful estimation activity because it gives children practice in applying information about units of measurement. The activity in Lesson 114 consists of a board demonstration followed by workbook practice. Here's the activity.

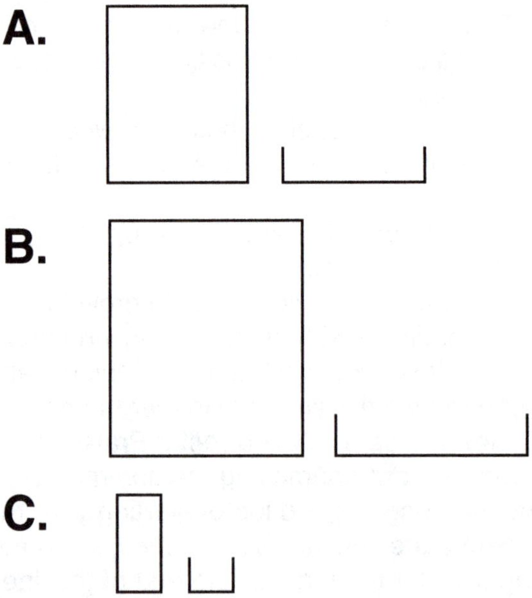

a. (Draw on the board:)

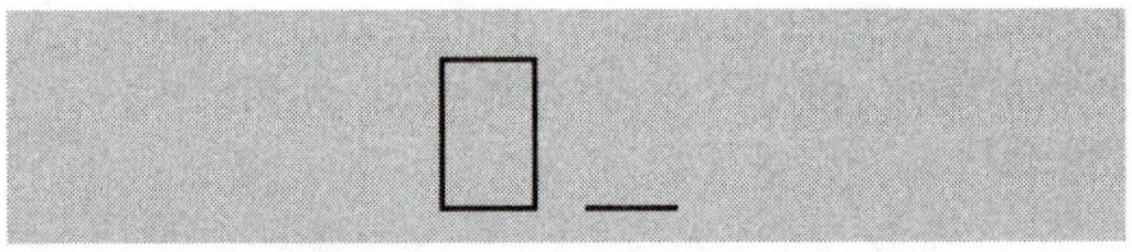

- (Point to the rectangle.) Here's a rectangle. You can see how high it is and how wide it is.
- (Point to the line next to the rectangle.) Here's the start of another rectangle. This is just the bottom part. Is this bottom part shorter, just as wide or wider than the rectangle? (Signal.) *Just as wide.*
- Listen: I'm going to complete this rectangle so it is just about as high as the first rectangle. Watch. (Complete the rectangle:)

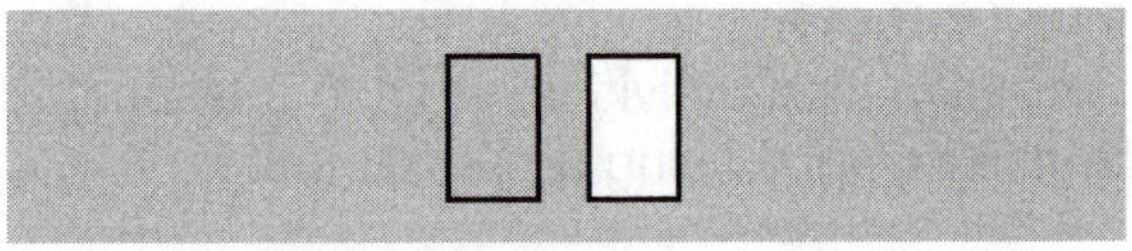

- I did it.

b. (Erase the top part of the second rectangle:)

- New game. This time, I'm going to complete this rectangle so it's higher than the first rectangle. Watch.
  (Complete the rectangle:)

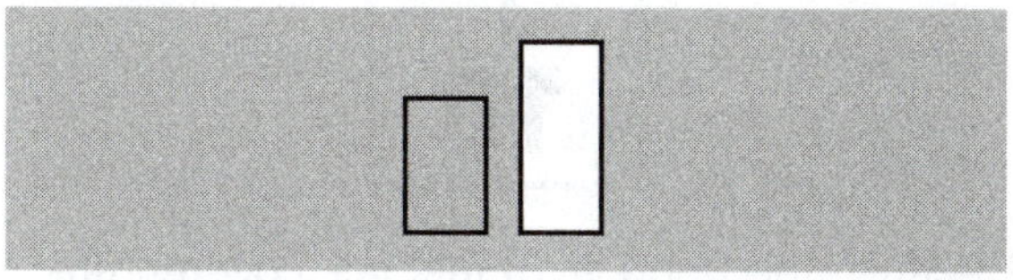

- I did it again. The rectangle I completed is higher than the first rectangle.

c. (Erase the top part of the second rectangle:)

- New game. Who can complete this rectangle so it's not as high as the first rectangle?
- (Call on a child.) Make it shorter.
- (After rectangle is completed:) Is that rectangle shorter than the first one?

Workbook Practice

a. Find part 2.

b. Touch rectangle A. Next to that rectangle, you're going to complete a rectangle that is just as high as rectangle A. Do it. Raise your hand when you're finished.
(Observe children and give feedback.)

c. Touch rectangle B. Next to that rectangle, you're going to complete a rectangle that is not as high as rectangle B. It's shorter. Do it. Raise your hand when you're finished.
(Observe children and give feedback.)

d. Touch rectangle C. Next to that rectangle, you're going to complete a rectangle that is higher than rectangle C. Do it. Raise your hand when you're finished.
(Observe children and give feedback.)

e. We have some pretty good rectangle makers.

In later lessons, children do similar tasks. Some require them to work with rectangles that show only the left side. They complete these rectangles so they are either wider, narrower, or just as wide as the model rectangle.

Overlapping the rectangle construction activities are those that involve estimating the relative height and length of objects. For all these activities, the children first estimate how tall or wide an object is by referring to a reference object. "How many times as tall as the boy is that tree?" Children write their estimation number for each object.

Next, children cut out a strip of reference objects. (For the example involving the boy, children cut out a strip of boys, one on top of the other.) Children use the strip of reference objects to measure each of the objects, and then they write the measurement number (how many times as tall the object actually is).

These activities give children very concrete practice in relating estimation to measurement. The activities are designed to motivate children to become good estimators. They also set the stage for activities that provide measurement numbers for the reference object. Here's the activity from Lesson 111. In this activity, children do not write estimation numbers, simply measurement numbers.

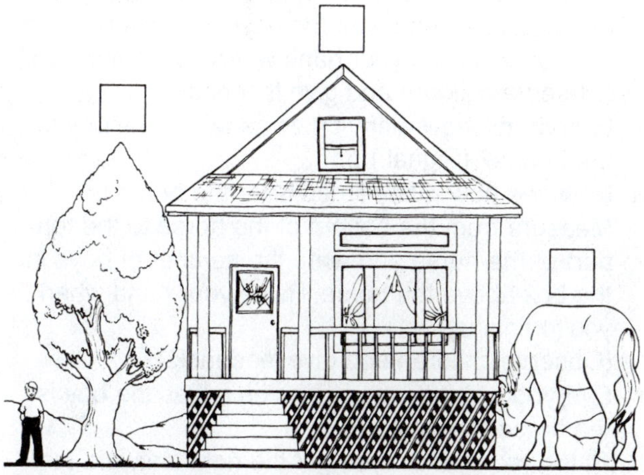

Note: Each child will need a pair of scissors for this exercise.

a. Find part 4. This is a new kind of problem. The boy in the picture wants to tell how many times as tall the tree is, the house is and the horse is.

b. Touch the tree. That tree is taller than the boy. But how many times as tall as the boy is that tree? Is it 2 times as tall as the boy, 3 times as tall, 4 times as tall? (Call on individual children:) What do you think?

c. Touch the house. Look at how high that house is. I wonder if it's 3 times as tall as the boy.
(Call on individual children:) How many times as tall as the boy do you think it is?

d. Turn to the last page of your workbook and find the stack of boys. (Hold up workbook and touch the stack of boys.)

- You're going to cut out the whole stack of boys. Then you can measure the tree, the house, and the horse to see how many times as tall as the boy they are.
- Cut out the stack of boys. Cut along the dotted line. Raise your hand when you're finished.
- Turn back to part 4 of Lesson 111.

e. Everybody, use your stack of boys to measure the tree. Start the bottom of your stack of boys right at the line at the bottom of the tree. Then count the boys to the top of the tree. Raise your hand when you know how many boys it takes to get to the top of the tree.
(Observe children and give feedback.)
- Everybody, how many boys does it take to get to the top of the tree? (Signal.) *4.*
- Write **4** in the box above the tree. √
- The tree is 4 times as tall as the boy.

f. Look at the house.
(Call on individual children:) Do you think that's 4 times as tall as the boy?
- How many times as tall do you think the house is?
- Everybody, use your stack of boys to measure the house. Write the number in the box above the house. Remember, start your stack at the bottom of the house and count the boys to the very top of the house. Raise your hand when you're finished.
(Observe children and give feedback.)
- Everybody, how many times as tall as the boy is the house? (Signal.) *5.*

g. Now see how many times taller the horse is. Measure from the bottom of the horse to the top part of the horse and write the number of boys in the box above the horse. Raise your hand when you're finished.
(Observe children and give feedback.)
- Everybody, how many times as tall as the boy is the horse? (Signal.) *2.*

h. Raise your hand if you got the right answers for everything.

In step E, you provide children with the rule for measurement that parallels the rule used for measuring with a ruler. "Start the bottom of your stack of boys right at the line at the bottom of the tree."

When you observe and give feedback, praise children who have their strip positioned properly. "Good. The bottom of your stack is right on the line at the bottom of the tree."

In lessons 112 through 116, children work on activities similar to that in 111. Starting in 113, children first write estimation numbers, then measurement numbers. The workbook presents two boxes above each object. Children write the number for their estimate in the top box. Then they measure and write their measurement number in the bottom box. Some of the tasks require children to estimate the length (horizontal dimension) of objects.

Lesson 117 introduces a reference object that works just like a T: A basketball hoop 10 feet high. It is drawn so that it looks like a T:

Because the hoop is 10 feet tall, children are able to express the height of objects, both when estimating and when measuring. To estimate the height, children estimate how many times as tall as the hoop the object is. If it's 3 times as tall as the hoop, they estimate 3 T's. That's 30. Similarly, when they measure, they measure the number of hoops and write the number for that number of T's. The practice is quite similar to what the children have done when writing numbers from T's.

Here's the first part of the activity from Lesson 117.

> ***Note:*** Each child will need a pair of scissors for this exercise.

a. Find part 2. This is the hardest estimation problem you could imagine. You're going to estimate how tall things are, but you're going to estimate the number of **feet** tall they are, not how many times as tall they are.

b. Touch the basketball hoop in the little box. A basketball hoop is 10 feet tall. The **10** under the hoop shows it's 10 feet tall. You're going to write estimation numbers for the other objects. Here's how you do it. That basketball hoop looks like a **T** and it's just like a **T** because it's 10 feet tall.

So you just estimate how many **T's** each of the other objects is. If you think an object is 3 **T's**, that's 30 feet.

c. If you think it's 6 **T's**, how many feet is that? (Signal.) *60.*
- If you think it's 4 **T's**, how many feet is that? (Signal.) *40.*
- And if you think it's 2 **T's**, how many feet is that? (Signal.) *20.*
(Repeat step c until firm.)

d. Your turn: Touch the top box above the tree. Estimate how many **T's** the tree is. Write the number for that many **T's** in the top box. Raise your hand when you're finished.
(Observe children and give feedback.)
- Raise your hand if you thought the tree is 4 **T's.** What number did you write for 4 **T's?** (Signal.) *40.*
- Raise your hand if you thought the tree is 5 **T's.** What number did you write for 5 **T's**? (Signal.) *50.*
- I hope nobody wrote a silly number like 4 or 5. Remember, that **T** is 10 feet tall. So it would be **very** silly to estimate the tree to be 4 feet tall.

e. Touch the building. Estimate how many **T's** the building is and write **the number** for that many **T's** in the top box. Raise your hand when you're finished.
(Observe children and give feedback.)
- Who thought the building is 5 **T's**? What number did you write for 5 **T's**? (Signal.) *50.*
- Who thought the building is 6 **T's**? What number did you write for 6 **T's**? (Signal.) *60.*
- I hope nobody wrote a silly number like 5 or 6. Remember, that **T** is 10 feet tall. So that building can't be 5 or 6 feet tall.

f. Touch the telephone pole. Estimate how many **T's** the telephone pole is and write **the number** for that many **T's** in the top box. Raise your hand when you're finished.
(Observe children and give feedback.)
- Who thought the telephone pole is 4 **T's**? What number did you write for 4 **T's**? (Signal.) *40.*
- Who thought the telephone pole is 5 **T's**? What number did you write for 5 **T's**? (Signal.) *50.*

g. Now you're going to measure the objects and write the measurement numbers. First, turn to the last page of your workbook and cut out your stack of basketball hoops. Raise your hand when you're finished.

h. Turn back to your workbook page and measure the tree. Remember, you have to count **10** for each hoop. It works just like **T's.** Write your measurement number for the tree in the bottom box. Don't write anything silly like 4 or 5. Raise your hand when you're finished.
(Observe children and give feedback.)
- Everybody, how many feet tall is the tree? (Signal.) *50.*
- Yes, it's 50 feet tall. That's 5 **T's.** Raise your hand if you wrote **50** in the measurement box for the tree.

The later lessons of Level A are heavy in measurement and estimation. These activities reinforce much of what children have learned throughout the program, and the children develop skills with measuring, estimating, and observing that will help them in later levels of *Connecting Math Concepts.*

Conceptual-Manipulative Activities

Each lesson includes extension activities that you may choose to present. These activities may be useful to strengthen some of the concepts and operations taught in the program. Note, however, that these are additional activities. They are not to replace the activities specified for the various lessons, and they should not be presented if their presentation means that the children will move too slowly through the program. The 120 lessons should be completed during the school year. Some of the children may need additional work on the activities presented in the main program. Other children may have very few problems. A possible arrangement is to work with the lower performers at a time when the higher performers can engage in the conceptual and manipulative activities. If children are not firm on the program content, however, work on program skills, not on extensions.

Also, the activities recommended merely show how to relate what has been taught to different types of problem or conceptual formats. If particular activities work well in terms of your class structure, while others tend to be more difficult to manage, use the activities that work well. Substitute them for suggested activities that are less manageable.

Here are the main types of extension activities:

Summary of Level A Activities

COUNTING:

PLACE VALUE:

MORE/LESS:

EQUALITY:

NUMBER PATTERNS:

ADDITION:

SUBTRACTION:

ADDITION AND SUBTRACTION:

MONEY:

PROBLEM SOLVING:

ESTIMATION:

LESSONS WITH MANIPULATIVE ACTIVITIES:

1–5, 7–9, 11, 15–18, 21–26, 28–35, 37–74, 77, 81–90, 96–103, 105–114, 116, 118, 120

LESSONS WITH COOPERATIVE LEARNING:

1–19, 21–70, 75, 76, 78–92, 95–100, 102, 103, 106–109, 112–114, 116, 118, 120

Appendix A

Connecting Math Concepts
Level A Cumulative Test 1 (Lessons 1–30)

EXERCISE 1 COUNTING NUMBERS THAT ARE MORE

a. Find part 1. You're going to write numbers that are more.
b. Touch the tree. √
- Listen: On the spaces after the tree, write the numbers that are more than 12. More than 12.
- Raise your hand when you're finished.

c. Touch the spider. √
- Listen: On the spaces after the spider, write the numbers that are more than 9. More than 9.
- Raise your hand when you're finished.

EXERCISE 2 NUMERALS FOR OBJECTS

a. Find part 2.
b. Touch the group of pennies. √
- Touch the group of fish. √
- Touch the group of skunks. √

c. Here's what you are going to do. Count the objects. Write the numeral that shows how many are in the group. Write the numeral in the box above the group.
- Raise your hand when you're finished.

EXERCISE 3 MAKING LINES FOR NUMERALS

a. Find part 3.
b. You're going to make the right number of lines below each numeral. Do it.
c. Read each numeral to yourself and make the right number of lines.
- Raise your hand when you've written lines for both numerals. (Observe children.)

EXERCISE 4 MORE/LESS

a. Find part 4.
b. Some of the groups in part 4 have 3. Some of the groups have more than 3. Here's the rule: All the groups that have more than 3 should be crossed out. Once more: All the groups that have more than 3 should be crossed out.
- Listen: Count how many are in each group. If a group has more than 3, cross it out. Don't do anything to groups that have 3.
- Raise your hand when you're finished.

EXERCISE 5 PLUSSING 1

a. Everybody, find part 5. These are plus-1 questions.
b. Touch the question for the star. √ Everybody, read the question for the star. Get ready. (Signal.) *9 plus 1 equals what number?*
- Touch the question for the moon. Get ready. (Signal.) *4 plus 1 equals what number?*
- Touch the question for the tree. √ Everybody, read the question for the tree.
- Get ready. (Signal.) *6 plus 1 equals what number?*
- Touch the question for the dog. Everybody, read the question for the dog.
- Get ready. (Signal.) *3 plus 1 equals what number?*

c. Your turn: Write answers to all the plus-1 questions.
- Raise your hand when you're finished.

EXERCISE 6 PLUSSING 1

a. Everybody, find part 6. These are more plus-1 questions.
b. Your turn: Write answers to all the questions in part 6.
- Pencils down when you're finished.

EXERCISE 7 MAKING LINES FOR EVENTS

a. Find part 7.
- Touch the white box next to the dog. √

b. You're going to make lines in that box. Get your pencils ready.
- Each time I clap, you make a line. Here I go. (Clap 5 times at 1-second intervals.)

c. New game: Touch the white box next to the moon. Get ready to make your lines. Here I go. (Clap 7 times.)
d. Last game: Touch the white box next to the star. √ Get ready to make your lines. Here I go. (Clap 4 times.)
e. Now you're going to count the lines in each box and write the numeral in the shaded part of the box.
- Raise your hand when you're finished.

EXERCISE 8 ORDINAL NUMBERS

a. Find part 8. There's a column of things. I'll tell you rules about those things. You'll mark them.
b. Listen: The third thing should have a circle around it. Listen again: The third thing should have a circle around it. What should the third thing have around it? (Signal.) *A circle.*
c. Find the third thing and make a circle around it.
- Raise your hand when you're finished.

d. The fifth thing should have a box around it. Find the fifth thing and make a box around it.
- Raise your hand when you're finished.

EXERCISE 9 COUNTING NUMBERS THAT ARE MORE

a. Find part 9.
b. These are number lines that show only the first number. You'll write the missing numbers for each number line.
- Raise your hand when you're finished.

EXERCISE 10 PLUSSING 2

a. Find part 10. You're going to write answers to plus-2 questions.

b. Touch question A. √ Read question A. Get ready. (Signal.) *5 plus 2 equals what number?*
c. Touch question B. √ Read question B. Get ready. (Signal.) *9 plus 2 equals what number?*
d. Touch question C. √ Read question C. Get ready. (Signal.) *3 plus 2 equals what number?*
e. Touch question D. √ Read question D. Get ready. (Signal.) *7 plus 2 equals what number?*
f. Your turn: Write answers to all the plus-2 questions.
- Raise your hand when you're finished.

EXERCISE 11 GROUPS THAT HAVE LESS

a. Find part 11. Some of the groups in part 11 have less than 4. Here's the rule: All the groups that have less than 4 should be crossed out. Once more: All the groups that have less than 4 should be crossed out.
b. Listen: Remember, only the groups that have less than 4 should be crossed out.
- Raise your hand when you're finished with part 11.

Cumulative Test 1 PERCENT SUMMARY

Score	%	Score	%
72	100	61	85
71	99	60	83
70	97	59	82
69	96	58	81
68	94	57	79
67	93	56	78
66	92	55	76
65	90	54	75
64	89	53	74
63	88	52	72
62	86	51	71

CUMULATIVE TEST 1 SCORING CHART

PART	SCORE	POSSIBLE SCORE	PASSING SCORE
1	1 for each number	6	5
2, 3	2 for each item	Parts 2, 3 combined 10	8
4	1 for each group of lines	5	5
5, 6	2 for each item	Parts 5, 6 combined 16	14
7	EACH ITEM: Number of Lines 2; Number written 1; Total 3	9	8
8	1 for each object	5	5
9	1 for each number	8	8
10	2 for each item	8	6
11	1 for each group of items	5	5
	Total	**72**	

Cumulative Test 1 REMEDIES

Test Part	Lesson and (Exercise)
1	17 (3), 18 (7), 19 (8)
2	4 (5), 5 (4), 6 (5), 7 (5), 8 (4), 9 (3), 10 (4)
3	3 (3), 4 (3), 5 (5), 6 (6), 7 (6), 9 (4)
4	18 (2), 19 (9), 20 (4
5	17 (3), 18 (3), 19 (6), 20 (5), 21 (4), 22 (4), 23 (6)
6	15 (2), 16 (3), 24 (3), 25 (2), 26 (4), 27 (5), 28 (6), 29 (7)
7	2 (1), 5 (3), 6 (4), 7 (4), 8 (3), 9 (2), 12 (5), 13 (4), 14 (4)
8	11 (3), 12 (2), 13 (2), 14 (2), 17 (2), 18 (6), 19 (7)
9	17 (7), 18 (7), 19 (8), 25 (3), 26 (2), 27 (2), 28 (3), 29 (2)
10	24 (4), 25 (1), 26 (1), 27 (4), 28 (5), 29 (4), 30 (5), 31 (2)
11	28 (2), 29 (6), 30 (4), 31 (5)

Connecting Math Concepts Level A Cumulative Test 2 (Lessons 1–60)

EXERCISE 1 COUNTING NUMBERS THAT ARE MORE

To test students who are new to CMC, present only the parts that do not have a gray screen.

a. Find part 1. These are number lines that show only the first number.
b. Your turn: Write the missing numbers for each number line.
- Raise your hand when you're finished.

EXERCISE 2 PLACE VALUE

a. Find part 2. The first item has already been worked. The numeral 42 is written in the box.
b. Touch the T's below the numeral. The T's tell about the first digit of the numeral. There are four T's, so the first digit is 4.
- Touch the 4. √
- Now touch the lines after the T's. √ The lines tell about the second digit of the numeral. There are two lines, so the second digit is two.
- Touch the second digit of the numeral. √ Remember, the number of T's tell how to write the first digit. The number of lines tell how to write the second digit.

c. Your turn: Write the numeral for item A and item B.
- Raise your hand when you're finished.

EXERCISE 3 SUBTRACTION/ADDITION

a. Find part 3.
b. Your turn: Write the answers.
- Raise your hand when you're finished.

EXERCISE 4 MISSING MIDDLE TERM

a. Find part 4. You're going to work these hard problems that tell what you do to get from one number to another number on the number line.
b. Your turn: You're going to fill in the box for each problem. You'll write a sign and a number.

Remember, the first number in each problem tells where you start. The other number tells where you end up. When you write the sign and number in the box, you should have a fact you know.

- Raise your hand when you're finished with part 4.

EXERCISE 5 NUMBER LINE TENS

a. Find part 5.
b. Your turn: Write all the missing numerals.
- Raise your hand when you're finished.

EXERCISE 6 GROUPS THAT HAVE LESS

a. Find part 6. Some of the groups in part 6 have less than 5. Here's the rule: All the groups that have less than 5 should be crossed out. Once more: All the groups that have less than 5 should be crossed out.
b. Listen: Remember, only the groups that have less than 5 should be crossed out.
- Raise your hand when you're finished with part 6.

EXERCISE 7 PROBLEM SOLVING
Word Problems

a. Find part 7. You're going to write number problems the fast way. I'll read each story problem twice. Then you'll write the whole number problem.
b. Touch line A. √ Here's the problem. Listen carefully: A bug starts at 7 on the number line. Then the bug plusses 2 places. The bug ends up at what number?
- Listen again: A bug starts at 7. Then the bug plusses 2. The bug ends up at what number?
- Your turn: Write the number problem. Then write the answer. Raise your hand when you're finished.

c. Touch line B. √ Here's the problem. Listen carefully: A bug starts at 6 on the number line. Then the bug minuses 1 place. The bug ends up at what number?
- Listen again: A bug starts at 6. Then the bug minuses 1 place. The bug ends up at what number?
- Your turn: Write the number problem. Then write the answer.
- Raise your hand when you're finished.

EXERCISE 8 PLACE VALUE ALIGNMENT

a. Find part 8.
b. Your turn: Write the numerals in columns.
- Raise your hand when you're finished.

EXERCISE 9 PROBLEM SOLVING
Word Problems

a. Find part 9. You're going to write number problems the fast way. I'll read each story problem twice. Then you'll write the whole number problem.
b. Touch line A. √ Here's the problem. Listen carefully: A bug starts at 8 on the number line. Then the bug plusses some places. The bug ends up at 10 on the number line.
- Listen again: A bug starts at 8. Then the bug plusses some places. The bug ends up at 10.
- Your turn: Write the problem. Then write the answer.
- Raise your hand when you're finished.

c. Touch line B. √ Here's the problem. Listen carefully: A bug starts at 6 on the number line. Then the bug minuses some places. The bug ends up at 5 on the number line.
- Listen again: A bug starts at 6. Then the bug minuses some places. The bug ends up at 5.
- Your turn: Write the problem. Then write the answer.
- Raise your hand when you're finished.

EXERCISE 10 ORDINAL NUMBERS

a. Find part 10. There's a column of things. The first thing is an equals sign.
b. I'll tell you rules about those things. You'll mark them.
- Listen: The fourth thing should have a circle around it. Listen again: The fourth thing should have a circle around it. Find the fourth thing and make a circle around it.
- What are you going to make around the fourth thing? (Signal.) *A circle.*
- Raise your hand when you're finished.

c. Listen: The second thing should be crossed out. Listen again: The second thing should be crossed out.
- What are you going to do to the second thing? (Signal.) *Cross it out.*
- Find the second thing and cross it out.
- Raise your hand when you're finished.

d. Listen: The fifth thing should have a box around it. Listen again: The fifth thing should have a box around it.
- What are you going to make around the fifth thing? (Signal.) *A box.*
- Raise your hand when you're finished.

Cumulative Test 2 PERCENT SUMMARY			
Score	%	Score	%
89	100	76	85
88	99	75	84
87	98	74	83
86	96	73	82
85	95	72	81
84	94	71	80
83	93	70	79
82	92	69	78
81	91	68	76
80	89	67	75
79	88	66	74
78	88	65	73
77	87	64	72

CUMULATIVE TEST 2 SCORING CHART

PART	SCORE	POSSIBLE SCORE	PASSING SCORE
1	1 for each number	12	11
2	EACH ITEM: 1 for each digit; Total 2	4	4
3	2 for each item	24	20
4	EACH ITEM: Sign 2; Number 2; Total 4	16	14
5	1 for each number	7	7
6	1 for each group	5	5
7, 9	EACH ITEM: Problem 2; Answer 1; Total 3	Parts 7, 9 combined: 12	10
8	1 for each number	4	4
10	1 for each object	5	5
	Total	**89**	

Cumulative Test 2 REMEDIES	
Test Part	**Lesson and (Exercise)**
1	Remedies for Mastery Test 4 (1), Mastery Test 5 (1)
2	41 (2), 42 (3), 43 (3)
3A–F	36 (4), 37 (2), 38 (3), 39 (3), 52 (4), 53 (4)
3L	40 (6)
3H, I	42 (2), 43 (4), 44 (4), 45 (4), 46 (4), 47 (3), 48 (4), 49 (4), 50 (3), 51 (6)
4	48 (3), 49 (3), 50 (5), 51 (7), 52 (6), 54 (7), 56 (5)
5	54 (5), 55 (6), 56 (3), 57 (3), 58 (4), 59 (3), 60 (3)
6	28 (2), 29 (6), 30 (4), 31 (5)
7	47 (5), 48 (2), 49 (2), 50 (2), 51 (5), 52 (5), 53 (5)
8	58 (3), 59 (6), 60 (7), 61 (5)
9	53 (6), 54 (6), 55 (4), 56 (7), 57 (5), 58 (6)
10	11 (3), 12 (2), 13 (2), 14 (2), 17 (2), 18 (6), 19 (7)

Connecting Math Concepts
Level A Cumulative Test 3 (Lessons 1–90)

EXERCISE 1 PROBLEM SOLVING
Word Problems

To test students who are new to CMC, present only the parts that do not have a gray screen.

a. Find part 1. You're going to write number problems the fast way. I'll read each story problem twice. Then you'll write the whole number problem.

b. Problem A: A bug is at 7 on the number line. Then the bug minuses one place. The bug ends up at what number?
- Listen again: A bug is at 7 on the number line. Then the bug minuses one place. The bug ends up at what number?
- Write the problem and the answer for problem A.
- Pencils down when you're finished.

c. Problem B: A bug starts at 10 on the number line. Then the bug goes to a number that is 2 more. The bug ends up at what number?
- Listen again: A bug starts at 10 on the number line. Then the bug goes to a number that is 2 more. The bug ends up at what number?
- Write problem B and work it.
- Pencils down when you're finished.

d. Problem C: Jeff has 9. Cheryl has 2 more than Jeff. How many does Cheryl have?
- Listen again: Jeff has 9. Cheryl has 2 more than Jeff. How many does Cheryl have?
- Write problem C and work it.
- Pencils down when you're finished.

EXERCISE 2 PLUSSING 1

a. Find part 2. I'll say some problems. You'll write the answers.
b. Touch the space for problem A.
- Here's the problem: 1 plus 47 equals what number? Listen again: 1 plus 47 equals what number?
- Write the answer.
- Pencils down when you're finished.

c. Touch the space for problem B. √
- Here's the problem: 76 plus 1 equals what number? Listen again: 76 plus 1 equals what number?
- Write the answer.
- Pencils down when you're finished.

EXERCISE 3 PROBLEM SOLVING
Word Problems

a. Find part 3.
b. Write both facts for the problem.
- Pencils down when you're finished.

EXERCISE 4 MORE/LESS

a. Find part 4.
- The numbers for item A are 7 and 5.

b Circle the bigger number for item A.
c. Then circle the bigger number for items B and C.
- Pencils down when you're finished.

EXERCISE 5 PLACE VALUE

a. Find part 5. You're going to write T's and lines for these two-digit numerals.
- You'll write T's to show the first digit, and lines to show the second digit.
- The first item has already been worked. The numeral is 26. The first digit is 2. So there are two T's below the first digit. Touch those T's. √
- The second digit of 26 is 6. So there are six lines below the second digit. Touch those lines. √ Remember, make T's to show the number for the first digit and lines to show the number for the second digit.

b. Make the T's and lines in the box below item A and item B.
- Pencils down when you're finished.

EXERCISE 6 PLACE VALUE

- Find part 6. You're going to write numerals for T's and lines.
- Pencils down when you're finished.

EXERCISE 7 MONEY

a. Find part 7. Write the number of cents in each item.
- Pencils down when you're finished.

EXERCISE 8 TEST COMPLETION

a. You'll finish the rest of the test on your own.
b. Find part 8. You'll write each problem in a column and work it.
- You'll finish the rest of the test on your own.

c. Find part 10. You'll write a sign and a number to complete each equation.
- You'll finish the rest of the test on your own.

d. Find part 13. You'll complete the number lines.
e. Your turn: Go back to part 8. Finish the rest of the test on your own. Pencils down when you're finished.

Cumulative Test 3
PERCENT SUMMARY

Score	%	Score	%
117	100	99	84.5
116	99	98	84
115	98	97	83
114	97	96	82
113	96.5	95	81
112	96	94	80
111	95	93	79
110	94	92	78.5
109	93	91	78
108	92	90	77
107	91	89	76
106	90.5	88	75
105	90	87	74
104	89	86	73.5
103	88	85	73
102	87	84	72
101	86	83	71
100	85	82	70

CUMULATIVE TEST 3 SCORING CHART					
PART	SCORE			POSSIBLE SCORE	PASSING SCORE
1	EACH ITEM			12	10
	Problem 2	Answer 2	Total 4		
2	2 for each item			4	4
3	2 for each item			4	4
4	1 for each item			3	3
5,6	1 for each item			Parts 5, 6 combined 6	6
7	3 for each item			6	6
8	2 for each item			4	4
9	3 for each item			6	6
10	EACH ITEM			12	10
	Sign 2	Number 2	Total 4		
11	2 for each number			6	6
12	EACH ITEM			6	5
	Answer 2	Digits in correct columns 1	Total 3		
13	1 for each number			8	8
14	2 for each item			8	8
15	2 for each item			8	6
16	2 for each item			24	20
	Total			**117**	

Cumulative Test 3 REMEDIES	
Test Part	**Lesson and (Exercise)**
1A	47 (5), 48 (2), 49 (2), 50 (2), 51 (5), 52 (5), 53 (5)
1B, C	84 (2), 85 (3), 86 (2), 87 (3), 88 (6), 89 (5), 90 (5)
2	80 (2), 82 (5), 84 (1)
3	64 (4), 65 (4), 66 (4), 67 (6), 68 (7), 69 (7), 70 (5)
4	88 (3, 4), 89 (3, 4), 90 (4)
5	70 (4), 71 (3), 72 (5), 73 (5), 74 (2)
6	41 (2), 42 (3), 43 (3)
7	74 (3), 75 (4), 76 (3), 80 (6), 81 (4), 82 (1), 83 (3)
8	79 (1), 80 (1), 81 (2), 82 (4), 83 (4), 84 (4), 87 (5), 90 (3)
9	85 (2), 86 (1), 87 (4), 88 (2)
10	48 (3), 49 (3), 50 (5), 51 (7), 52 (6), 54 (7), 56 (5)
11A	64 (6), 65 (6), 68 (5), 69 (5), 70 (6), 71 (5), 72 (6), 73 (6), 74 (7), 80 (2)
11B, C	73 (3), 78 (2), 79 (1), 80 (1), 81 (2), 82 (4), 83 (4), 84 (4), 87 (5), 90 (3)
12	77 (3), 78 (2), 79 (1), 80 (1), 81 (2), 82 (4), 83 (4), 84 (4), 87 (5), 90 (3)
13	Remedies for Mastery Test 4 (1), Mastery Test 5 (1)
14	77 (6), 78 (5), 79 (2), 80 (5), 81 (1), 82 (2), 83 (2), 84 (3), 85 (1), 86 (3), 87 (6), 88 (5)
15	67 (3), 68 (3), 69 (2), 70 (3), 71 (4), 75 (1), 76 (4)
16	36 (4), 37 (2), 38 (3), 39 (3), 40 (6), 42 (2), 43 (4), 44 (4), 45 (4), 46 (4), 47 (3), 48 (4), 49 (4), 50 (3), 51 (6), 52 (4), 53 (4)

Connecting Math Concepts Level A Cumulative Post Test (Lessons 1–120)

Materials: Ruler and a sharpened pencil.

> ***Note:*** Students should not use a ruler for part 9.

EXERCISE 1

a. Find part 1. Measure how high and how wide the rectangle is.

- Write the number of inches for the width in the box next to the rectangle. Write the number of inches for the height in the box on top of the rectangle. Raise your hand when you're finished.

b. Put your rulers away.

EXERCISE 2

- Find part 2. √
- Work the problems.
- Raise your hand when you're finished.

EXERCISE 3

a. Find part 3. I'm going to say some tough problems. You'll write the answers.
b. Problem A. Listen: You have 43 and you subtract 1. Everybody, Write the number you end up with.
- (Repeat problem once, if necessary.) √

c. Problem B. Listen: You have 46 and you add 2. Write the number you end up with.
- (Repeat problem once, if necessary.) √

d. Problem C. Listen: You have 40 and you subtract 10. Write the number you end up with.
- (Repeat problem once, if necessary.) √

e. Problem D. Listen: You have 47 and you subtract 46. Write the number you end up with.
- (Repeat problem once, if necessary.) √

f. Problem E. Listen: You have 40 and you add 30. Write the number you end up with.
- (Repeat problem once, if necessary.) √

EXERCISE 4

a. Find part 4. Below each number, you'll make a T for each 10 and a line for each 1.
b. Item A is 57. Ask yourself, how many tens are in 57? Make that many T's in the box below 57. Then ask yourself, how many ones are in 57? Make that many lines in the box below 57.
- Make T's and lines for problems a, b, and c in part 4.
- Raise your hand when you're finished.

EXERCISE 5

- Find part 5. Each item shows a row of coins. For each item, write the number of cents in the box at the end of the row.
- Raise your hand when you're finished.

EXERCISE 6

- Find part 6. For each item, circle the number that is bigger. If the numbers are the same, don't circle either number. Then complete the sign to show whether the numbers are equal **or** one number is more than the other. Each sign should look like one of the signs at the top of part 6.
- Raise your hand when you're finished.

EXERCISE 7

a. Find part 7. Touch the signs shown at the top of part 7.
b. For each item, complete the bottom statement. Then show whether the sides are equal or whether one side is more than the other.
- Raise your hand when you're finished.

EXERCISE 8

a. Find part 8. You're going to write answers to problems.
b. Problem A: There were 8 bugs on a branch. 1 bug flew away. Then 1 more bug flew away.
- Listen again: A branch had 8 bugs, 1 flew away. 1 more flew away. Write the number of bugs that ended up on the branch. √

c. Problem B: Jane met 3 girls. Then 1 more girl joined them.
- Listen again: Jane met 3 girls. Then 1 more joined them. Write the number of girls there were. √

d. Problem C: Joan had 8 dollars. She spent 7 dollars. Then she spent 1 dollar.
- Listen again: Joan had 8. She spent 7. Then she spent 1 more. Write the number of dollars Joan ended up with. √

EXERCISES 9–13

a. You're going to work the rest of the test on your own.
b. Find part 9. You'll write a sign and a number to complete each question.
c. Find part 13. You'll complete the number lines.
- Your turn: Work the problems in parts 9 through 13 on your own.
- Raise your hand when you're finished.

Final Cumulative Test
PERCENT SUMMARY

Score	%	Score	%
84	100	71	85
83	99	70	83
82	98	69	82
81	96	68	81
80	95	67	80
79	94	66	79
78	93	65	77
77	92	64	76
76	90	63	75
75	89	62	74
74	88	61	73
73	87	60	71
72	86	59	70

FINAL CUMULATIVE TEST SCORING CHART			
PART	SCORE	POSSIBLE SCORE	PASSING SCORE
1	2 for each number	4	4
2	1 for each item	12	10
3	2 for each item	10	8
4	EACH ITEM Number of T's 1 / Number of lines 1 / Total 2	6	5
5	2 for each item	6	6
6	1 for each item	3	3
7	EACH ITEM Answer 1 / Sign 1 / Total 2	4	4
8	2 for each item	6	4
9	EACH ITEM Sign 2 / Number 1 / Total 3	9	9
10	2 for each number	4	4
11, 12	3 for each item	Parts 11, 12 combined 12	9
13	1 for each number	8	8
	Total	**84**	

Final Cumulative Test REMEDIES	
Test Part	**Lesson and (Exercise)**
1	103 (3), 104 (6), 105 (7), 106 (4), 107 (3), 108 (4), 109 (3), 110 (1), 115 (6)
2A, I	77 (6), 78 (5), 79 (2), 80 (5)
2B	64 (6), 65 (6), 68 (5), 69 (5), 70 (6), 71 (5), 72 (6), 73 (6), 74 (7), 75 (6), 80 (2)
2C	73 (3), 74 (4), 75 (3), 76 (6), 77 (4), 78 (6)
2D	52 (2), 53 (2), 54 (2), 55 (2), 56 (2), 57 (2), 58 (2), 59 (2), 60 (2), 61 (2), 62 (1)
2E	37 (3), 38 (5), 39 (4), 40 (4), 41 (6)
2F, J	100 (3), 101 (6), 102 (4), 103 (2), 104 (5), 105 (4), 106 (2), 107 (4), 108 (3)
2G, K	64 (2), 65 (3), 66 (3), 67 (3), 68 (3), 69 (2), 70 (3), 71 (4)
2H, I	32 (6), 33 (4), 34 (4), 35 (2), 36 (3)
3	116 (4), 117 (4), 118 (1), 119 (1), 120 (1)
4	70 (4), 71 (3), 72 (5), 73 (5), 74 (2)
5	92 (5), 93 (4), 94 (5)
6	91 (2), 92 (2), 93 (3), 94 (3), 95 (5)
7	109 (1), 110 (2), 111 (4), 112 (3), 113 (3), 114 (6), 115 (2)
8	103 (4), 104 (4), 105 (5), 106 (6), 107 (5), 108 (2), 109 (5)
9	48 (3), 49 (3), 50 (5), 51 (7), 52 (6), 54 (7), 56 (5)
10	85 (2), 86 (1), 87 (4), 88 (2)
11	106 (7), 107 (7), 108 (5)
12	101 (2), 102 (7), 103 (5), 104 (7), 105 (6)
13	Remedy for Mastery Test 4 (1), Mastery Test 5 (1)

NAME ____________________

DATE ____________________

Part 1

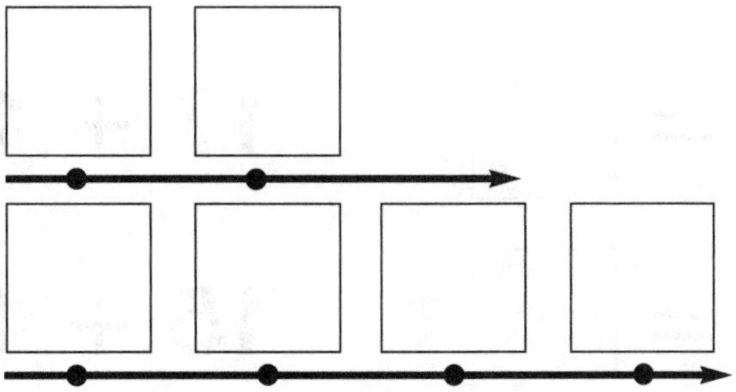

Part 2

Part 3

4 6

________ ________

Part 4

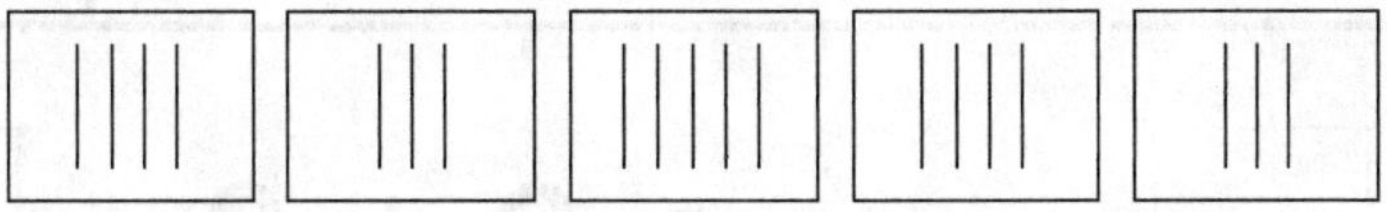

Part 5

 9 + 1 = ☐

 6 + 1 = ☐

 4 + 1 = ☐

 3 + 1 = ☐

NAME ______________________

DATE ______________________

Part 6

$13 + 1 = \square$ $17 + 1 = \square$

$14 + 1 = \square$ $15 + 1 = \square$

Part 7

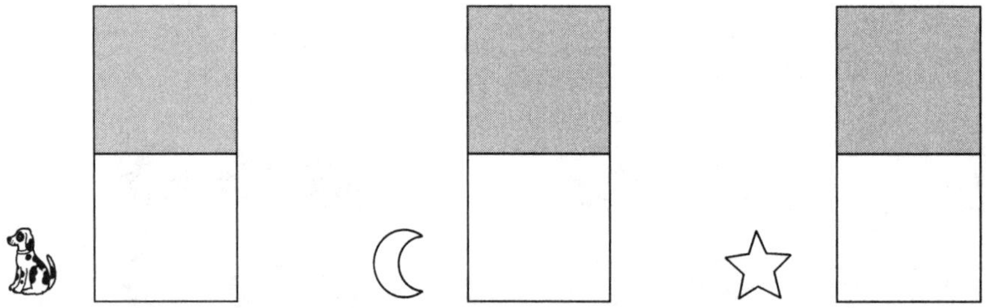

Part 8

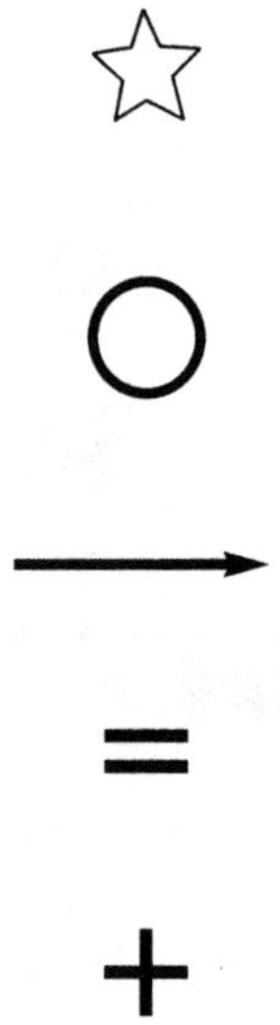

Part 9

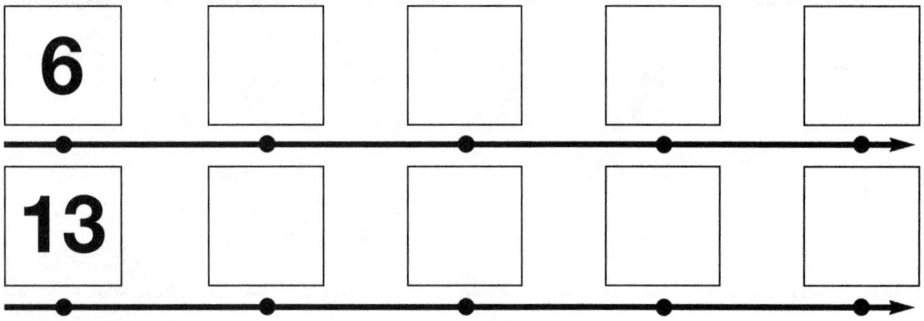

Part 10

A. $5 + 2 = \square$ C. $3 + 2 = \square$

B. $9 + 2 = \square$ D. $7 + 2 = \square$

Part 11

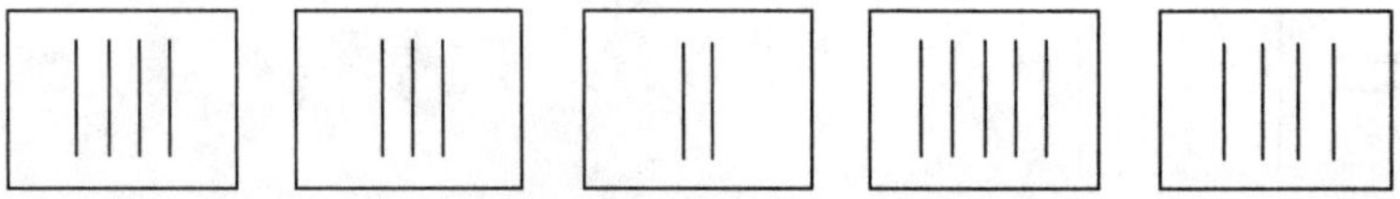

NAME ____________________

DATE ____________________

Part 1

A. | 35 | ☐ | ☐ | ☐ | ☐ |

B. | 26 | ☐ | ☐ | ☐ | ☐ |

C. | 17 | ☐ | ☐ | ☐ | ☐ |

Part 2

4	2		
T T T T	||		

A.

T T	||||

B.

T T	|||

Part 3

A. 8 − 0 = ☐

B. 6 − 1 = ☐

C. 9 − 0 = ☐

D. 7 − 1 = ☐

E. 10 − 0 = ☐

F. 4 − 1 = ☐

G. 5 + 5 = ☐

H. 0 + 3 = ☐

I. 0 + 9 = ☐

J. 4 + 2 = ☐

K. 9 + 2 = ☐

L. 8 + 1 = ☐

Part 4

4 ☐ = 3

8 ☐ = 10

6 ☐ = 7

NAME ______________________

DATE ______________________

Part 5

1	0
2	0
7	0

Part 6

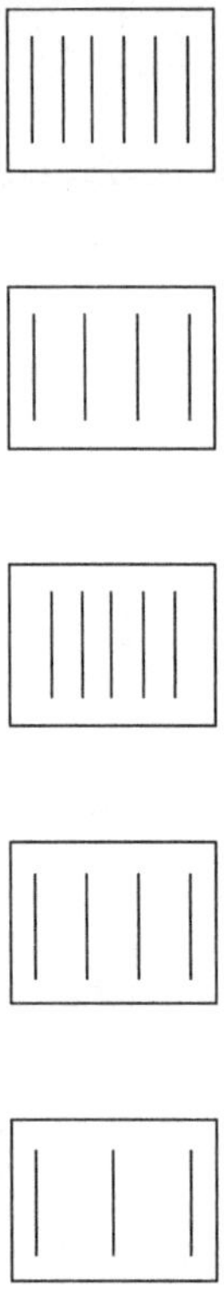

Part 7

A. ______________________

B. ______________________

Part 8

A.	B.	C.	D.
32	7	13	2

A.		
B.		
C.		
D.		

Part 9

A. ______________________

B. ______________________

Part10

=

+

☾

☆

→

NAME ______________________

DATE ______________________

Part 1

A. ______________________

B. ______________________

C. ______________________

Part 2

A. ______________________

B. ______________________

Part 3

______________________ →

______________________ ←

Part 4

A. 7 5

B. 1 4

C. 9 3

Part 5

26

T T	||| |||

A. 35

B. 42

Part 6

T T T T |||

Part 7

A.

B.

NAME ____________________

DATE ____________________

Part 8

A. $9 + 1 = 10$ | | |

B. $11 - 2 = 9$ | | |

Part 9

A.
```
  7
  1
+ 2
```

B.
```
  7
  4
+ 1
```

Part 10

7 ☐ = 9

14 ☐ = 12

8 ☐ = 7

Part 11

A. $60 + 10 =$ ☐

B. $60 - 10 =$ ☐

C. $80 - 20 =$ ☐

Part 12

A.

	9
+	2

B.

2	0
+3	0

Part 13

37				

18				

NAME ____________________

DATE ____________________

Part 14

A. $5 + 2 =$ ☐

B. $5 + 3 =$ ☐

C. $5 + 5 =$ ☐

D. $2 + 2 =$ ☐

Part 15

A. $12 + 1 =$ ☐

B. $12 - 2 =$ ☐

C. $8 - 1 =$ ☐

D. $8 - 2 =$ ☐

Part 16

$9 - 1 =$ ☐　$10 - 1 =$ ☐　$9 + 0 =$ ☐

$4 - 0 =$ ☐　$5 - 1 =$ ☐　$2 + 6 =$ ☐

$7 - 1 =$ ☐　$0 + 5 =$ ☐　$1 + 4 =$ ☐

$8 - 0 =$ ☐　$1 + 8 =$ ☐　$7 + 2 =$ ☐

NAME ______________________

DATE ______________________

Part 1

☐ inches

☐ inches

Part 2

a. 3 + 6 = ☐

b. 50 + 20 = ☐

c. 40 − 10 = ☐

d. 1 + 56 = ☐

e. 0 + 5 = ☐

f. 8 − 8 = ☐

g. 7 − 2 = ☐

h. 4 + 2 = ☐

i. 5 + 3 = ☐

j. 10 − 9 = ☐

k. 5 − 2 = ☐

l. 7 + 2 = ☐

Part 3

a. ______ b. ______ c. ______ d. ______ e. ______

Part 4

a. 57

☐

b. 30

☐

c. 15

☐

Part 5

☐ cents

☐ cents

☐ cents

Part 6

< = >

a. 4 ___ 3   b. 11 ___ 14   c. 2 ___ 2

NAME ______________________

DATE ______________________

Part 7

< = >

a. $3 + 6 = 9$

$3 + 6$ __ 10

b. $9 - 2 = 7$

$9 - 2$ __ 5

Part 8

a. ______ **b.** ______ **c.** ______

Part 9

a. 4 ☐ = 3

b. 11 ☐ = 13

c. 17 ☐ = 9

Part 10

a.

$$\begin{array}{r} 1 \\ 2 \\ +\ 6 \\ \hline \end{array}$$

b.

$$\begin{array}{r} 3 \\ 2 \\ +\ 2 \\ \hline \end{array}$$

Part 11

a.

$$\begin{array}{r} 56 \\ -\ 40 \\ \hline \end{array}$$

b.

$$\begin{array}{r} 75 \\ -\ 51 \\ \hline \end{array}$$

Part 12

a.

$$\begin{array}{r} 47 \\ +\ 42 \\ \hline \end{array}$$

b.

$$\begin{array}{r} 63 \\ +\ 33 \\ \hline \end{array}$$

Part 13

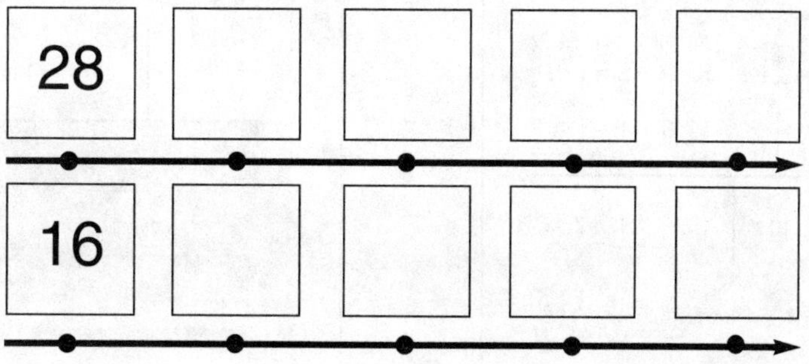

CONNECTING MATH CONCEPTS
LEVEL A CUMULATIVE TEST 1
LESSONS 1–30

NAME ______
DATE ______

Part 1

13 14

10 11 12 13

Part 2

6 4 6

Part 3

4 6

Part 4

Part 5

☆ 9 + 1 = 10

6 + 1 = 7

☾ 4 + 1 = 5

3 + 1 = 4

CONNECTING MATH CONCEPTS
LEVEL A CUMULATIVE TEST 1 (CONT'D)
LESSONS 1–30

NAME ______
DATE ______

Part 6

13 + 1 = 14

17 + 1 = 18

14 + 1 = 15

15 + 1 = 16

Part 7

5 7 4

Part 8

☆ ○ → = +

Part 9

6 7 8 9 10

13 14 15 16 17

Part 10

A. 5 + 2 = 7

C. 3 + 2 = 5

B. 9 + 2 = 11

D. 7 + 2 = 9

Part 11

CONNECTING MATH CONCEPTS
LEVEL A CUMULATIVE TEST 2
LESSONS 1–60

NAME ______
DATE ______

Part 1

A. 35 36 37 38 39

B. 26 27 28 29 30

C. 17 18 19 20 21

Part 2

4	2
TT TT	II

A.

2	4
TT	IIII

B.

2	3
TT	III

Part 3

A. 8 − 0 = 8

B. 6 − 1 = 5

C. 9 − 0 = 9

D. 7 − 1 = 6

E. 10 − 0 = 10

F. 4 − 1 = 3

G. 5 + 5 = 10

H. 0 + 3 = 3

I. 0 + 9 = 9

J. 4 + 2 = 6

K. 9 + 2 = 11

L. 8 + 1 = 9

Part 4

4 −1 = 3

8 +2 = 10

6 +1 = 7

CONNECTING MATH CONCEPTS
LEVEL A CUMULATIVE TEST 2 (CONT'D)
LESSONS 1–60

NAME ______
DATE ______

Part 5

1	0
2	0
3	0
4	0
5	0
6	0
7	0
8	0
9	0
10	0

Part 6

Part 7

A. 7 + 2 = 9

B. 6 − 1 = 5

Part 8

A.	B.	C.	D.
32	7	13	2

A.	3	2
B.		7
C.	1	3
D.		2

Part 9

A. 8 + 2 = 10

B. 6 − 1 = 5

Part 10

= ✱ ☾ ☆ →

CONNECTING MATH CONCEPTS
LEVEL A CUMULATIVE TEST 3
LESSONS 1–90

NAME ______________
DATE ______________

Part 1

A. 7 − 1 = [6]

B. 10 + 2 = [12]

C. 9 + 2 = [11]

Part 2

A. 48

B. 77

Part 3

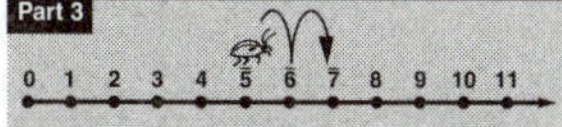

6 + 1 = 7 [→]

7 − 1 = 6 [←]

Part 4

A. (7) 5

B. 1 (4)

C. (9) 3

Part 5

26: TT |||
A. 35: TT T |||
B. 42: TT TT ||

Part 6

[4] [3]
TTTT |||

Part 7

A. [4] [5]

B. [6] [2]

CONNECTING MATH CONCEPTS
LEVEL A CUMULATIVE TEST 3 (CONT'D)
LESSONS 1–90

NAME ______________
DATE ______________

Part 8

A. 9 + 1 = 10 — 9 + 1 = 10

B. 11 − 2 = 9 — 11 − 2 = 9

Part 9

A. 7 + 1 + 2 = 10

B. 7 + 4 + 1 = 9

Part 10

7 [+ 2] = 9

14 [− 2] = 12

8 [− 1] = 7

Part 11

A. 60 + 10 = [70]

B. 60 − 10 = [50]

C. 80 − 20 = [60]

Part 12

A. 9 + 2 = 11

B. 20 + 30 = 50

Part 13

37	38	39	40	41
18	19	20	21	22

CONNECTING MATH CONCEPTS
LEVEL A CUMULATIVE TEST 3 (CONT'D)
LESSONS 1–90

NAME ______________
DATE ______________

Part 14

A. 5 + 2 = [7] C. 5 + 5 = [10]

B. 5 + 3 = [8] D. 2 + 2 = [4]

Part 15

A. 12 + 1 = [11] C. 8 − 1 = [7]

B. 12 − 2 = [10] D. 8 − 2 = [6]

Part 16

9 − 1 = [8] 10 − 1 = [9] 9 + 0 = [9]

4 − 0 = [4] 5 − 1 = [4] 2 + 6 = [8]

7 − 1 = [6] 0 + 5 = [5] 1 + 4 = [5]

8 − 0 = [8] 1 + 8 = [9] 7 + 2 = [9]

CONNECTING MATH CONCEPTS
LEVEL A CUMULATIVE POST TEST
LESSONS 1–120

NAME ______________
DATE ______________

Part 1

[3] inches

[2] inches

Part 2

a. 3 + 6 = [9] g. 7 − 2 = [5]

b. 50 + 20 = [70] h. 4 + 2 = [6]

c. 40 − 10 = [30] i. 5 + 3 = [8]

d. 1 + 56 = [57] j. 10 − 9 = [1]

e. 0 + 5 = [5] k. 5 − 2 = [3]

f. 8 − 8 = [0] l. 7 + 2 = [9]

Part 3

a. 42 b. 48 c. 30 d. 1 e. 70

Part 4

a. 57: TTTTT |||||||

b. 30: TTT

c. 15: T |||||

Part 5

[13] cents

[8] cents

[28] cents

Part 6

< = >

a. (4) > 3 b. 11 < (14) c. 2 = 2

CONNECTING MATH CONCEPTS
LEVEL A CUMULATIVE POST TEST (CONT'D)
LESSONS 1–120

NAME ______________
DATE ______________

Part 7

< = >

a. 3 + 6 = 9
3 + 6 < 10

b. 9 − 2 = 7
9 − 2 > 5

Part 8

a. 6 b. 4 c. 0

Part 9

a. 4 [−1] = 3

b. 11 [+2] = 13

c. 17 [−8] = 9

Part 10

a. 1 + 2 + 6 = 9

b. 3 + 2 + 2 = 7

Part 11

a. 56 − 40 = 16

b. 75 − 51 = 24

Part 12

a. 47 + 42 = 89

b. 63 + 33 = 96

Part 13

28	29	30	31	32

16	17	18	19	20

CCUMULATIVE TEST PERFORMANCE
GROUP SUMMARY

Note: Scoring and Remedies follow the teacher presentation for each test.

		Cumulative Test 1											Cumulative Test 2									
		Check parts not passed											Check parts not passed									
	Name	1	2	3	4	5	6	7	8	9	10	11	1	2	3	4	5	6	7	8	9	10
1.																						
2.																						
3.																						
4.																						
5.																						
6.																						
7.																						
8.																						
9.																						
10.																						
11.																						
12.																						
13.																						
14.																						
15.																						
16.																						
17.																						
18.																						
19.																						
20.																						
21.																						
22.																						
23.																						
24.																						
25.																						
26.																						
27.																						
28.																						
29.																						
30.																						

CUMULATIVE TEST PERFORMANCE
GROUP SUMMARY

Note: Scoring and Remedies follow the teacher presentation for each test.

		Cumulative Test 3 Check parts not passed															
	Name	1	2	3	4	5	6	7	8	9	10	11	12	13	14	15	16
1.																	
2.																	
3.																	
4.																	
5.																	
6.																	
7.																	
8.																	
9.																	
10.																	
11.																	
12.																	
13.																	
14.																	
15.																	
16.																	
17.																	
18.																	
19.																	
20.																	
21.																	
22.																	
23.																	
24.																	
25.																	
26.																	
27.																	
28.																	
29.																	
30.																	

CUMULATIVE TEST PERFORMANCE
GROUP SUMMARY

Note: Scoring and Remedies follow the teacher presentation for each test.

	Name	Final Cumulative Test — Check parts not passed												
		1	2	3	4	5	6	7	8	9	10	11	12	13
1.														
2.														
3.														
4.														
5.														
6.														
7.														
8.														
9.														
10.														
11.														
12.														
13.														
14.														
15.														
16.														
17.														
18.														
19.														
20.														
21.														
22.														
23.														
24.														
25.														
26.														
27.														
28.														
29.														
30.														

Appendix B

	Objectives	Lessons
FOLLOWING INSTRUCTIONS		
	Cross out specified pictures	1,2
COUNTING		
Rote Counting	Say the next number	1-8
	Count to a specified number	4-7, 17
	Count from a number to a number	12-15, 20-22, 28-61, 68, 96-98, 100, 102, 104-108, 111
Rational Counting	Count events	2, 3, 5-9, 12-14
Ordinal Numbers	Follow instructions with ordinal numbers	11-14
	Answer questions involving ordinal numbers	17-19
Counting Backward	Count backward to a specified number	18-27, 29, 31-33, 61-60
Counting by 10	Complete a tens number line	54-60
SYMBOLS		
Symbol Writing	Trace and copy symbols	1-17, 19
	Write number series	11-20
	Write symbols and groups of symbols from dictation	21-26
Symbol Identification	Cross out backward digits	2-15
	Say the name	2, 4-9, 11, 12, 14, 16, 19
Numerals and Counters	Draw lines for numerals	3-7, 9
	Write numerals for counters	4-10
	Match numerals and counters	10, 11, 14-19

MORE/LESS/ EQUAL	Objectives	Lessons
More	Say (mark) numbers that are more	6-8, 10, 23, 24, 30
	Say numbers that are 1 more	9, 10, 16
	Write numbers that are more	17-19, 25-29
	Mark groups that are more than a given number	18-20
	Say (write) numbers that are 2 more	19-23
	Say (write) numbers that are 3 more	70-76
	Identify numbers on a number line that are more than a specified number	88, 89
	Identify the greater number	88-90, 92
Equality	Make both sides of equations have the same number	15, 16
Less	Say (write) the number just before a specified number	23-26
	Say numbers that are less	27
	Indicate groups that are less than a specified number	28-31
	Say (write) numbers that are 1 less	32-35
	Say numbers that are 2 less	62, 63
More/Less Discriminatin	Discriminate values that are more, less or equal	34, 35
	Make the greater-than or less-than sign between numbers	91, 93-95

ADDITION/SUBTRACTION

Addition	Say (mark) answers to + 1 questions	11-14
	Write answers to + 1 questions	15-29
	Say (write) answers to + 2 questions	24-31
	Write problems from dictation or from a number line	25, 27-29, 43, 44

Objectives	Lessons
Write answers to orally presented + 1 problems	29, 30, 40-42
Write answers to + 1 and + 2 problems	32-36
Write answers to zero + problems	37-41, 47
Write (say) answers to orally presented problems with a 2-digit value and an addend of 0, 1 or 2	40-42, 51-62, 72, 75, 80, 82, 84-90
Write answers to "turned around" + 1 and + 2 addition problems	42-51
Write and solve addition problems with tens numbers	57-63
Write answers to orally presented problems that start with) +, 1 + or 2 +	50, 64-67
Write (say) answers to problems that add 10 and 20	64, 65, 68-75, 80
Write answers to orally presented problems that begin with a tens number and add a 1-digit number	67-69, 86, 112
Write answers to problems that + 3	77-80
Use fact derivation to solve + 3 problems	81-85
Write answers to problems with 3 addends	85-88
Write answers to + 2 and + 3 problems	86-88
Represent "doubles" facts on the number line	89, 90
Say "doubles" facts	91-97
Write answers to orally presented problems with 2 tens numbers	95-100
Write answers to "turned around" + 3 facts	96-99, 101, 102
Respond to "add" rather than "plus"	101, 102
Write answers to 2-digit column addition problems	101-105

Subtraction

Write answers to −1 problems	36-40
Write answers to problems that − 1 or − 0	52, 53
Write answers to −2 problems	64-66
Write answers to problems that − 0, − 1 or − 2	67-71

	Objectives	Lessons
	Write answers to problems that begin with 2-digit numbers, and − 1 or − 2	72-76, 91, 92, 99, 103, 104
	Write answers to problems that − 10 or − 20	73-78
	Write subtraction problems with an answer of zero	100-102
	Write subtraction pfoblems with an answer of 1	103-108
	Write answers to column subtraction problems	106-108
	Work subtraction problems with an answer of 0 or 1	109-111
Addition/ Subtraction Discrimination	Write addition and subtraction facts from number lines	45-47, 63
	Write addition and subtraction facts based on number-family relationships	64-72, 86
	Write answers to problems with tens	85-87
	Respond to mental arithmetic questions	49, 55, 93, 94, 106-108, 110, 112-120
	Respond to the words "add" and "subtract"	104, 105
	Write answers to column-addition and column-subtraction problems	109, 110
	Read "box" as "how many"	118-120

PLACE VALUE

Objectives	Lessons
Write teen numbers from dictation	16-20, 23, 24
Write teen numbers from models	30-33
Write 2-digit numbers (beyond 20) from dictation	31-44, 46, 51, 54, 56
Write 2-digit numbers from models	41-43, 62-65, 74, 77, 78
Count to identify digits	51
Work with facts or numbers in columns	52-61, 69, 70, 77-84, 87, 90, 93, 96

Objectives	Lessons
Write Ts for tens, then write the 2-digit numeral	66-69
Represent 2-digit numerals with Ts and lines	70-73

PROBLEM SOLVING

Objectives	Lessons
Find missing addend or subtrahend for number problems	45-47
Find missing addend for orally presented number problems	55, 56, 59, 60
Write problems and answers for bug-on-a-number-line stories	47-53
Find missing middle term (number and sign) in number problems	48-52, 54, 56
Solve bug-on-a-number-line problems with missing addend or subtrahend	53-58
Solve bug-on-a-number-line problems with the unknown as the middle or last term	59-63, 67, 69, 72
Write facts for more/less story problems on the number line	73-77
Indicate whether an action story calls for addition or subtraction	76-80, 83
Solve action problems	78-83
Solve comparison problems	84-87
Solve problems involving "joining"	91, 92
Solve various problems of previously-taught types	88-90, 93, 109-120
Solve problems with the phrase "all but"	94-96, 99, 100
Solve 3-addend problems	97-102
Figure out whether to add or subtract	104-107
Solve problems that start with a number and add 2 numbers or subtract 2 numbers	105-108
Solve problems that require =, $<$, or $>$ sign	109-111
Solve 2 problems, then write the sign that compares the answers	112-115
Solve problems with multiple solutions	116-119

APPLICATION	Objectives	Lessons
Money	Write the cents for a row of eimes and pennies	74-76
	Write the cents for two groups of dimes	80, 81
	Write the cents for dimes and pennies mixed in a row	82, 83
	Identify coins and their value	91
	Write the cents for a nickel, a dime or a quarter followed by pennies	92-94
	Add pennies to a row of coins to obtain a price-tag value	95-97
	Add or cross our pennies in a row of coins to obtain a price-tag value	98-100
Measurement	Show 1 and 2 inches with fingers	101, 102
	Measure horizontal and vertical lines to the nearest whole inch	103-107
	Measure rectangles	108-110, 115
Estimation	Estimate to identify particular rectangles	110-113
	Extimate relative height, then measure height using non-standard units	111-116
	Estimate to complete rectangles that approximate descriptions	114-120
	Estimate height in multiples of 10 feet	117-120

Skills Profile

Student's name ______________________ Grade or year in school __________

Teacher's name ______________________

Starting lesson ______________________ Date __________

Last lesson completed __________ Date __________ Number of days absent ______

Summary of In-program Test Performance

	Part 1	Part 2	Part 3	Part 4	Part 5	Part 6	Part 7	Part 8	Part 9
Test 1	+ −	+ −	+ −						
Test 2	+ −	+ −	+ −	+ −	+ −				
Test 3	+ −	+ −	+ −	+ −	+ −				
Test 4	+ −	+ −	+ −	+ −	+ −				
Test 5	+ −	+ −	+ −	+ −	+ −				
Test 6	+ −	+ −	+ −	+ −	+ −	+ −			
Test 7	+ −	+ −	+ −	+ −	+ −	+ −			
Test 8	+ −	+ −	+ −	+ −	+ −	+ −	+ −	+ −	
Test 9	+ −	+ −	+ −	+ −	+ −	+ −	+ −		
Test 10	+ −	+ −	+ −	+ −	+ −	+ −	+ −	+ −	
Test 11	+ −	+ −	+ −	+ −	+ −	+ −	+ −	+ −	+ −
Test 12	+ −	+ −	+ −	+ −	+ −				

The charts on pages 119 to 122 may be reproduced to make a skills profile for each student. The charts summarize the skills presented in *Connecting Math Concepts A* and provide space for indicating the date on which the student completes the lessons in which the skills are taught.

Name ______________________

Skills	Taught in these Lessons	Date Lessons Completed
FOLLOWING INSTRUCTIONS		
Crosses out specified pictures	1, 2	
COUNTING		
Rote Counting		
Says the next number	1-8	
Counts to a specified number	4-7	
Counts from a number to a number	12-111	
Rational Counting		
Counts events	2-14	
Ordinal Numbers		
Follows insturctions with ordinal numbers	11-16	
Answers questions involving ordinal numbers	17-19	
Counting Backward		
Counts backward to a specified number	18-70	
Counting by 10		
Completes a tens number line	54-60	
SYMBOLS		
Symbol Writing		
Copies symbols	1-19	
Writes number series	11-20	
Writes symbols and groups of symbols from dictation	21-26	
Symbol Identification		
Crosses our backward digits	2-15	
Says the name	2-19	
Numerals and Counters		
Draws lines for numerals	3-9	
Writes numerals for counters	4-10	
Matches numerals and counters	10-19	

Skills	Taught in these Lessons	Date Lessons Completed
MORE/LESS/EQUAL		
More		
Says (marks) numbers that are more	6-30	
Writes numbers that are more	17-29	
Marks groups that are more than a given number	18-20	
Says (writes) numbers that are 2 more	19-23	
Says (writes) numbers that are 3 more	70-76	
Circles numbers on a number line that are more than a specified number	88, 89	
Circles the larger number	88-92	
Equality		
Makes both sides of equations have the same number	15, 16	
Less		
Says (writes) the number just before a specified number	23-26	
Indicates groups that are less than a specified number	27-31	
Says (writes) numbers that are 1 less	34, 35	
Says numbers that are 2 less	91-95	
More/Less Discrimination		
Discriminatesvalues that are more, less or equal	34, 35	
Makes the greater-than or less-than sign between numbers	91-95	

Name ______________________________

Skills	Taught in these Lessons	Date Lessons Completed
ADDITION/SUBTRACTION		
Addition		
Says (marks) answers to + 1 questions	11-14	
Writes answers to + 1 questions	15-29	
Says (writes) answers to +2 questions	24-31	
Writes problems from dictation or from a number line	25-44	
Writes answers to orally presented + 1 problems	29-42	
Writes answers to + 1 and + 2 problems	32-36	
Writes answers to zero + problems	37-47	
Writes (says) answers to orally presented problems with a 2-digit value and an addend of 0, 1 or 2	40-90	
Writes answers to "turned around" + 1 and +2 addition problems	42-51	
Writes answers to orally presented problems that start with 0 +, 1 + or 2 +	50-67	
Writes and solves addition problems with tens numbers	57-63	
Writes (says) answers to problems that add 10 and 20	64-80	
Writes answers to orally presented problems that begin with a tens number	67-112	
Writes answers to problems that + 3	77-80	
Uses fact dervation to solve + 3 problems	81-85	
Writes answers to problems with 3 addeneds	85-88	
Writes answers to + 2 and + 3 problems	86-88	
Represents "doubles" facts on the number line	89, 90	
Says "doubles" facts	91-97	

Skills	Taught in these Lessons	Date Lessons Completed
Writes answers to orally presented problems with 2 tens numbers	95-100	
Writes answers to "turned around" + 3 facts	96-102	
Respond to "add" rather than "plus"	101, 102	
Writes answers to column addition problems	101-105	
Subtraction		
Writes answers to − 1 problems	36-40	
Writes answers to problems that − 1 or − 0	52, 53	
Writes answers to 2 2 problems	64-66	
Writes answers to problems that − 0, − 1 or − 2	67-71	
Writes answers to problems that begin with 2-digit numbers and − 1 or − 2	72-104	
Writes answers to problems that − 10 or − 20	73-78	
Writes subtraction problems with an answer of zero	100-102	
Writes subtraction problems with an answer of 1	103-108	
Writes answers to column subtraction problems	106-108	
Works subtraction problems with an answer of 0 or 1	109-111	
Addition/Subtraction Discrimination		
Writes addition and subtraction facts from number lines	45-63	
Writes addition and subtraction facts based on number-family relationships	64-86	
Writes answers to problems with tens numbers	85-87	
Responds to mental arithmetic questions	49-120	

Name ______________________

Skills	Taught in these Lessons	Date Lessons Completed
Responds to the words "add" and "subtract"	104, 105	
Writes answers to column-addition and column-subtraction problems	109, 110	
Reads "box" as "how many"	118-120	
PLACE VALUE		
Writes teen numbers from dictation	16-24	
Writes teen numbers	30-33	
Writes 2-digit numbers (beyond 20) from dictation	31-56	
Writes tens and twenties numbers from representations	41-74	
Counts to identify digits	51, 52	
Works with facts to numbers in columns	52-96	
Writes Ts for tens, then write the 2-digit numeral	70-78	
Represents 2-digit numerals with Ts and lines	70-78	
PROBLEM SOLVING		
Finds missing addend or subtrahend for number problems	45-47	
Writes problems and answers for stories about a bug-on-a-number-line	47-53	
Finds missing middle term (number and sign) in number problems	48-60	
Solves bug-on-a-number-line problems with a missing addend or subtrahend	53-58	
Solves bug-on-a-number-line problems with the unknow as the middle or last term	59-72	
Writes facts for more/less story problems on the number line	73-77	

Skills	Taught in these Lessons	Date Lessons Completed
Indicates whether an action story calls for addition subtraction	76-83	
Solves action problems	78-83	
Solves comparison problems	84-90	
Solves problems involving "joining"	91, 92	
Solves various problem of previously-taught types	92-120	
Solves problems with the phrase "all but"	94-100	
Solves 3-addend problems	97-102	
Figures out whether to add or subtract	104-107	
Solves prblems that start with a number and add 2 numbers or subtract 2 numbers	105-108	
Solves problems that require 5, ,, or . sign	109-111	
Solves 2 problems, then writes the sign that compares the answers	112-115	
Solves problems with multiple solutions	116-119	
APPLICATION **Money**		
Writes the cents for a row of dimes and pennies	74-76	
Writes the cents for 2 groups of dimes	80, 81	
Writes the cents for dimes and pennies mixed in a row	82, 83	
Identifies coins and their value	91	
Writes the cents for anickel, a dime or a quarter followed by pennies	92-94	
Adds pennies to a row of coins to obtain a price-tag value	95-97	
Adds or crosses out pennies in a row of coins to obtain a price-tab value	98-100	

Name ______________________

Skills	Taught in these Lessons	Date Lessons Completed
MEASUREMENT		
Shows 1 and 2 inches with fingers	101, 102	
Measures horizontally and vertically oriented lines to the nearest whole inch	103-107	
Measures rectangles	108-115	

Skills	Taught in these Lessons	Date Lessons Completed
ESTIMATION		
Estimates to identify particular rectangles	110-113	
Estimates relative height, then measures height using non-standard units	111-116	
Estimates to complete rectangles that approximate descriptions	114-120	
Estimates height in multiples of 10 feet	117-120	

10-LESSON TEST PERFORMANCE GROUP SUMMARY

Note: Test remedies are specified in the *Presentation Book.* Percent Summary is specified in the *Answer Key.*

		Test 1				Test 2						Test 3					
		Check parts not passed			Total %	Check parts not passed					Total %	Check parts not passed					Total %
	Name	**1**	**2**	**3**		**1**	**2**	**3**	**4**	**5**		**1**	**2**	**3**	**4**	**5**	
1.																	
2.																	
3.																	
4.																	
5.																	
6.																	
7.																	
8.																	
9.																	
10.																	
11.																	
12.																	
13.																	
14.																	
15.																	
16.																	
17.																	
18.																	
19.																	
20.																	
21.																	
22.																	
23.																	
24.																	
25.																	
26.																	
27.																	
28.																	
29.																	
30.																	
	Number of Students Not Passed = NP																
	Total number of students = T																
	Remedy needed if NP/T = 25% or more																

10-LESSON TEST PERFORMANCE
GROUP SUMMARY

Note: Test remedies are specified in the *Presentation Book*. Percent Summary is specified in the *Answer Key*.

		Test 4						Test 5					
		Check parts not passed					Total %	Check parts not passed					Total %
	Name	**1**	**2**	**3**	**4**	**5**		**1**	**2**	**3**	**4**	**5**	
1.													
2.													
3.													
4.													
5.													
6.													
7.													
8.													
9.													
10.													
11.													
12.													
13.													
14.													
15.													
16.													
17.													
18.													
19.													
20.													
21.													
22.													
23.													
24.													
25.													
26.													
27.													
28.													
29.													
30.													
	Number of Students Not Passed = NP												
	Total number of students = T												
	Remedy needed if NP/T = 25% or more												

10-LESSON TEST PERFORMANCE
GROUP SUMMARY

Note: Test remedies are specified in the *Presentation Book.* Percent Summary is specified in the An*swer Key.*

	Name	Test 6							Test 7						
		Check parts not passed						Total %	Check parts not passed						Total %
		1	**2**	**3**	**4**	**5**	**6**		**1**	**2**	**3**	**4**	**5**	**6**	
1.															
2.															
3.															
4.															
5.															
6.															
7.															
8.															
9.															
10.															
11.															
12.															
13.															
14.															
15.															
16.															
17.															
18.															
19.															
20.															
21.															
22.															
23.															
24.															
25.															
26.															
27.															
28.															
29.															
30.															
	Number of Students Not Passed = NP														
	Total number of students = T														
	Remedy needed if NP/T = 25% or more														

10-LESSON TEST PERFORMANCE GROUP SUMMARY

Note: Test remedies are specified in the *Presentation Book.* Percent Summary is specified in the *Answer Key.*

	Name	Test 8									Test 9							
		Check parts not passed								Total %	Check parts not passed							Total %
		1	2	3	4	5	6	7	8		1	2	3	4	5	6	7	
1.																		
2.																		
3.																		
4.																		
5.																		
6.																		
7.																		
8.																		
9.																		
10.																		
11.																		
12.																		
13.																		
14.																		
15.																		
16.																		
17.																		
18.																		
19.																		
20.																		
21.																		
22.																		
23.																		
24.																		
25.																		
26.																		
27.																		
28.																		
29.																		
30.																		
	Number of Students Not Passed = NP																	
	Total number of students = T																	
	Remedy needed if NP/T = 25% or more																	

10-LESSON TEST PERFORMANCE
GROUP SUMMARY

Note: Test remedies are specified in the *Teacher Presentation Book.* Percent Summary is specified in the *Answer Key*.

		Test 10									Test 11									
		Check parts not passed								Total %	Check parts not passed									Total %
	Name	1	2	3	4	5	6	7	8		1	2	3	4	5	6	7	8	9	
1.																				
2.																				
3.																				
4.																				
5.																				
6.																				
7.																				
8.																				
9.																				
10.																				
11.																				
12.																				
13.																				
14.																				
15.																				
16.																				
17.																				
18.																				
19.																				
20.																				
21.																				
22.																				
23.																				
24.																				
25.																				
26.																				
27.																				
28.																				
29.																				
30.																				
	Number of Students Not Passed = NP																			
	Total number of students = T																			
	Remedy needed if NP/T = 25% or more																			

10-LESSON TEST PERFORMANCE
GROUP SUMMARY

Note: Test remedies are specified in the *Presentation Book.* Percent Summary is specified in the *Answer Key.*

	Name	Test 12					
		Check parts not passed					Total %
		1	**2**	**3**	**4**	**5**	
1.							
2.							
3.							
4.							
5.							
6.							
7.							
8.							
9.							
10.							
11.							
12.							
13.							
14.							
15.							
16.							
17.							
18.							
19.							
20.							
21.							
22.							
23.							
24.							
25.							
26.							
27.							
28.							
29.							
30.							
	Number of Students Not Passed = NP						
	Total number of students = T						
	Remedy needed if NP/T = 25% or more						